Innocent Merriment

INNOCENT MERRIMENT

An Anthology of Light Verse

SELECTED BY

Franklin P. Adams

("F. P. A.")

Whittlesey House

McGRAW-HILL BOOK COMPANY, INC.

NEW YORK · LONDON

INNOCENT MERRIMENT

PUBLISHED BY WHITTLESEY HOUSE
A division of the McGraw-Hill Book Company, Inc.

Printed in the United States of America by The Maple Press Co., York, Pa.

Introduction

IT WAS the condescending, patronizing attitude of book reviewers and critics toward light verse that caused me to write innumerable newspaper paragraphs, from time to time, assailing the patronizers. Their loftiness is based on fear—fear that the critic's readers will think that he is a light-minded fellow; a man who feels that it is creditable to praise Robinson Jeffers; but to come right out and say that Dorothy Parker is a better poet is anarchy. I am opposed to the ranking system in art or literature. Yet the Pulitzer Award for Poetry has never been given to a writer of Light Verse. Of course, Edwin Arlington Robinson, Edna St. Vincent Millay, Stephen Vincent Bénét, Archibald MacLeish, and Leonard Bacon have written light verse; but it is a small fraction of their work; and most of the other so-called serious poets are ashamed of their lightness.

Not that most poets wouldn't prefer to write a great serious poem to the best light verse ever written. If I could write either the best "serious" poem or the best piece of light verse, I would vote for lightness, nor is my wine from these grapes sour. I am unashamed. I am unapologetic. Much have I traveled in the realms of verse. Most of mine was mediocre; and almost all of it was written to catch newspaper deadlines. Bad light verse is more to be condemned, it sets the teeth more on edge, than bad serious poetry. Light verse should be flawless in execution; it should have something to say, and say it well. It needs little critical ability to tell whether light verse is good or bad; the difference between good and bad "serious" poetry is far less obvious. They speak of light verse, the critics. They never say that anybody is a heavy-verse writer.

There is another deterrent to the reading of much first-rate serious poetry; it is too long. And when it is short, it is a sonnet, or a sonnet sequence. I, for one, find it hard to keep my mind on a sonnet sequence, as I do upon a newspaper comic strip. It requires concentration that I dislike, I, who become absorbed in a cross-word puzzle and whose concentration on scholastic matters—*cf.* records of Armour Institute, Chicago—was—nor have I lost the habit—good.

The first verse that I remember was light, for my first reading was *Davy and the Goblin*, and my seven-year-old delight in "A capital ship for an ocean trip was The Walloping Window-Blind" and "The night was thick and hazy when the Piccadilly Daisy" was boundless. And though, as I learned later, the late Charles Edward Carryl wrote *Davy* for his son Guy, and the subtitle was *What Followed Reading "Alice's Adventures in Wonderland,"* I always thought—and I always shall think—that Charles Edward Carryl was superior to Lewis Carroll. A minority opinion, but I was well along in years before I read *Alice* with enjoyment. Lewis Carroll still seems to me chiefly a writer for adults.

This anthology might have been called *Light Verse I Like.* I have objected to the title of Clifton Fadiman's compendium of predilections—*Reading I've Liked*—solely on the ground of tense, for it implies that, although once he may have liked those pieces, he does so no longer. And the reading Mr. Fadiman has liked includes not one poem.

The verses in this anthology are the light verses I like, and only those. Many of them I have liked—not to say adored—for many years. Nor is anything included that I don't like, regardless of its appearances, and countless reappearances, in other treasuries and anthologies of light verse. Certain writers have bored me, for example, Mr. Richard Barham of the Ingoldsby Legends. I just don't like them. This may seem sacrilege, as the inclusion of other bards of mirth may be. Do I think, for example, that I have a right to put in my own stuff, and omit "The Jackdaw of Rheims"? Yes, because I like a few things of mine better than I do Ingoldsby. The Estate of Richard Barham, decd., is at liberty to consult my attorneys.

Yet, in the course of putting these verses on the assembly line, my courage has failed. For the temptation has been strong to make an anthology composed of Calverley's *Verses and Fly Leaves*, *The Bab Ballads*, and almost all of Dorothy Parker. I am sure that everything that these poets have written was put together with that extreme care and patience that light verse deserving the adjective requires.

I realize that if I had to give, in an examination paper, my definition of light verse, I should probably fail. Nonponderous is the best that I could do.

I realize also that the subdivisions I have used, for convenience, are inadequate. Many of the verses under "Burlesque—Parody" might have gone into "Satire" or "Love." The best parody is high criticism; generally satirical. I know that if readers are anything like me, they won't read the Introduction. But this is by way of warning them not to object that this or that poem has been placed, or misplaced, in this or that category.

I have been guided in my choices by many things—by memory, by my rejoicing to have remembered these things. The first anthology I ever saw, as well as the first book of verse I recall, was Bryant's *Library of Poetry and Song*, and it was the section labeled "Humorous and Satirical" that delighted my youthful heart and soft waxy mind.

Herein are poems that are found in other anthologies; and many others that make their anthologistic debut. I do not feel that because a poem may seem hackneyed through having appeared in every anthology—like "The Yarn of the 'Nancy Bell'" or "Casey at the Bat"—it should be excluded. Nor do I feel that I should exclude some verses that were contributed to The Conning Tower pseudonymously, the identities of whose authors are unknown, and unknowable.

All anthology compilers are assailed—and always with justice—for their sins of omission. In 1920, when the late

Carolyn Wells's *The Book of Humorous Verse* first was published, I took her to versified task for having omitted any poem of T. A. Daly's. In the next edition Daly appeared. But when I assembled a book of some verse that had been contributed to The Conning Tower, I received a ballade from Miss Wells whose Envoy was:

> Your judgment is flawless, sir, I'll say;
> You skimmed the cream of the lot, no doubt;
> I'll ballyhoo strong for the book—but say—
> Why the hell did you leave me out?

That was an obvious and unforgivable dereliction, and it may be that this book has omissions even more conspicuous. Some of them are attributable to the faulty judgment—oh, yes, it is—of the compiler; some have been made because the difficulties of getting permission from the owners of the copyrights were all but insurmountable. This alone accounts for the omission of some of your—and my—favorites. And some verses, such as "Don Juan," I have left out because their inclusion would have made the book unwieldy. I have omitted those Ogden Nash verses that carry what is known as the Ogden Nash trade-mark. You will find his predecessors, Thomas Hood (1799–1845) with "Our Village," and W. S. Gilbert (1836–1911) with "Lost Mr. Blake." I sincerely doubt whether Mr. Nash got the urge to write his irregularly metered rhymes from either of these poems; or indeed whether he ever had heard of them.

As the swift seasons rolled, I fought against the pretentious condescension of the reviewers. I objected when, for instance, Mr. Albert Jay Nock, then editor of the *Freeman*, wrote, "like the Caucasian in the jingle, the native American was played out." The jingle referred to by Mr. Nock is Bret Harte's "Further Language from Truthful James." Its prosodic scheme is precisely that of Swinburne's "Hertha":

> Do I sleep? Do I dream?
> Do I wonder and doubt?
> Are things what they seem?

Or are visions about?
Is our civilization a failure?
Or is the Caucasian played out?

"Clearly," I wrote, in the *New York World*, now as dead as Mr. Nock's *Freeman*, "calling anything that isn't a ponderous piece of poetry a jingle is as typical of the reviewer's attitude as it is revelatory. Humorous verse, light verse, must be referred to as jingles, or amusing of its kind, or good for that sort of thing."

On the occasion of the 1939 Pulitzer Award to John Gould Fletcher's *Collected Poems*, with which I had no quarrel, I said that my vote would have been cast for Ogden Nash's *I'm a Stranger Here Myself*. "Satire and comedy, apparently," I wrote, "are all right on the stage; but those qualities in verse, although highly readable and usually short, get no public laurels." And, if I may again quote, The Conning Tower of May 14, 1930, said, in part: "'But who were the judges,' asked Mr. Lewis Gannett of the *Herald Tribune*, 'and why on earth did they give the poetry award to the cold intellectual chiseling of Conrad Aiken's *Selected Poems* when they had Elinor Wylie's *Angels and Earthly Creatures* in their field of choice?' The judges, as Mr. Gannett might easily have found out, were Dr. Wilbur L. Cross, Dr. Bliss Perry, and Mr. Brian Hooker. We have no violent conviction about their choice. To paraphrase Montague Glass, if they don't feel it, they don't feel it. If they don't feel that Elinor Wylie's poetry is worthier of award than Conrad Aiken's, that is all there is to it. We question the linesman's decision that says 'Out!' to any ball hit by Dorothy Parker or Samuel Hoffenstein; we question the decision, but we can't do anything about it; if the ball is 'out' to the committee, what care they how 'in' it be, to our—in their opinion—cock-eyed vision?"

There is much to be said about anthologies, and about light verse. But *Haec gemmae sunt*. Not *my* jewels, but those of my stringing. Take them or leave them, in, I hope, the order named.

Much of what I have said has been better said by Arthur Guiterman, thus:

ANTHOLOGISTICS

Since one anthologist put in his book
Sweet things by Morse, Bone, Potter, Bliss, and Brook,
All subsequent anthologists, of course
Have quoted Bliss, Brook, Potter, Bone, and Morse.
For, should some rash anthologist make free
To print selections, say, from you and me,
Omitting with a judgment all his own
The classic Brook, Morse, Potter, Bliss, and Bone,
Contemptuous reviewers, passing by
Our verses, would unanimously cry,
"What manner of anthology is this
That leaves out Bone, Brook, Potter, Morse, and Bliss!"

And here, with its virtues of inclusion and its sins of exclusion, is *Innocent Merriment*. The great and irksome labor incident to permissions and indexing, as well as patience with my impatience, was achieved by my assistant, Miss Martha E. Clave.

FRANKLIN P. ADAMS.

Acknowledgments

IN THE course of compiling this anthology, the following publishers and authors kindly granted permission to reprint the poems included here. If any have inadvertently been omitted, suitable acknowledgment will be made in the next printing.

Reginald Arkell: "When the War Will End," by Reginald Arkell, from "War Rumours."

Spencer Bentley: "My Angeline," and "The Tattooed Man," by Harry B. Smith.

The Bobbs-Merrill Company: "The Man in the Moon," by James Whitcomb Riley, from "Rhymes of Childhood," copyright 1890, 1918.

Bowes & Bowes (Cambridge) Ltd.: "On a Rhine Steamer" and "On a Parisian Boulevard," under the heading "England and America," "Imitation of Robert Browning," and "Sincere Flattery" by James Kenneth Stephen, from "Lapsus Calami and Other Verses."

Brandt & Brandt: "Aaron Burr" and "Andrew Jackson," by Stephen Vincent Benét, from "A Book of Americans," published by Farrar & Rinehart, Inc., copyright 1933, by Rosemary and Stephen Vincent Benét; "She Is Overheard Singing," and "Thursday," by Edna St. Vincent Millay, from "A Few Figs from Thistles," published by Harper & Brothers, copyright 1918, 1919, 1922, by Edna St. Vincent Millay; "Travel," by Edna St. Vincent Millay, from "Second April," published by Harper & Brothers, copyright 1921, by Edna St. Vincent Millay.

Burns Oates & Washbourne, Ltd.: "A Ballade of Suicide," by G. K. Chesterton, from "The Collected Poems of G. K. Chesterton."

Chicago Tribune: "Reflection," by Kurt M. Stein.

Constable & Company, Ltd.: "Sir Christopher Wren," by E. C. Bentley, from "Baseless Biographies."

Dodd, Mead & Company, Inc.: "A Ballade of Suicide" and "Wine and Water," by G. K. Chesterton, from "The Collected Poems of G. K. Chesterton," copyright 1911; "The Conversational Reformer," by Harry Graham, from "Familiar Faces"; "Barney McGee," by Richard Hovey; "The Poster Girl," by Carolyn Wells, from "Idle Idyls."

Doubleday, Doran & Company, Inc.: "Wasted Ammunition," by Stoddard King, from "The Raspberry Tree," copyright 1930; "Study of an Elevation, in Indian Ink," by Rudyard Kipling, from "Departmental Ditties and Barrack-Room Ballads," copyright 1892, 1893, 1899; "certain maxims of archy," and "mehitabel sings a song," by Don Marquis, from "archy and mehitabel," copyright 1927, 1930; "King Cophetua and the Beggar Maid," by Don Marquis, from "Sonnets to a Red-Haired Lady and Famous Love Affairs," copyright 1922.

Estate of William Henry Drummond: "The Wreck of the 'Julie Plante' " by William Henry Drummond.

Gerald Duckworth, Ltd.: "The Frog" and "The Yak," by Hilaire Belloc, from "Bad Child's Book of Beasts."

E. P. Dutton & Company, Inc.: "Poem for Mother's Day," by Margaret Fishback, from "I Feel Better Now"; "Anthologistics," "Constitution for a League of Nations," "Elegy," "Experts on Woman," and "Mavrone," by Arthur Guiterman, from "Lyric Laughter and Other Poems by Arthur Guiterman"; "Song to My Love," by Laurence McKinney, from "Garden Clubs and Spades"; "From a Full Heart," by A. A. Milne, from "The Sunny Side."

Forbes & Company: "If I Should Die To-Night" and "The Pessimist," by Ben King, from "Ben King's Verse."

Harcourt, Brace & Company, Inc.: "Mia Carlotta" and "The Tides of Love," by T. A. Daly, from "Selected Poems of T. A. Daly"; "Biography" and "R. I. P.," by Jan Struther, from "The Glass-Blower and Other Poems," copyright 1941, by Jan Struther; "Frustrate," by Louis Untermeyer, from "———and Other Poets."

Harper & Brothers: "The Sycophantic Fox and the Gullible Raven," by Guy Wetmore Carryl, from "Fables for the Frivolous"; "Apostrophe to a Pram Rider," by E. B. White, from "The Fox of Peapack"; "Affidavit in Platitudes" and "The Circus," by E. B. White, from "The Lady Is Cold."

Henry Holt and Company, Inc.: "The Golf Links," by Sarah N. Cleghorn, from "Portraits and Protests"; "What Literature Needs:" by John A. Holmes, from "Fair Warning."

Houghton Mifflin Company: "On an Intaglio Head of Minerva" and "Thalia," by Thomas Bailey Aldrich; "Robinson Crusoe's Story" and "The Walloping Window-Blind," by Charles Edward Carryl, from "Davy and the Goblin"; "How the Helpmate of Blue-Beard Made Free with a Door," by Guy Wetmore Carryl, from "Grimm Tales Made Gay"; "Boston Nursery Rhymes," by Rev. Joseph Cook; "Fable," by Ralph Waldo Emerson; the poems by Francis Bret Harte; "Good and Bad Luck," by John Hay; the poems by Oliver Wendell Holmes; "The Courtin'" and "What Mr. Robinson Thinks," by James Russell Lowell; "Early Rising" and "Rhyme of the Rail," by John G. Saxe; "Mary and the Lamb," by Frank Dempster Sherman; "Darius Green and His Flying-Machine," by John Townsend Trowbridge; "Skipper Ireson's Ride," by John Greenleaf Whittier.

Alfred A. Knopf: "The Frog" and "The Yak," by Hilaire Belloc, from "Bad Child's Book of Beasts"; "Might and Right," by Clarence Day, from "After All"; "Thais" and "Tristan and Isolda," by Newman Levy, from "Opera Guyed."

John Lane, The Bodley Head, Ltd.: "Here Is the Tale," "Rural Bliss," and "A Rustic Song," by Anthony C. Deane, from "New Rhymes for Old."

Life Publishing Co. (Austrian & Lance): "The Old Hokum Buncombe," by Robert E. Sherwood, from "Poems from Life."

J. B. Lippincott Company: "Stairs," by Oliver Herford, from "Excuse It Please."

Little, Brown & Company: "Admiral Byrd" and "The Japanese," by Ogden Nash, from "The Face Is Familiar," and "Traveler's Rest" from "I'm a Stranger Here Myself."

Liveright Publishing Corporation: "Poems in Praise of Practically Nothing" and "Poems of Passion, Carefully Restrained So as to Offend Nobody," by Samuel Hoffenstein, from "Poems in Praise of Practically Nothing."

Lothrop, Lee & Shepard Company: "The Ideal Husband to His Wife," by Sam Walter Foss.

The Macmillan Company: "For My Father" and "Spring Signs," by Rachel Field; "Villon's Straight Tip to All Cross Coves," by William Ernest Henley; "Blow Me Eyes!" and "Song for a Cracked Voice," by Wallace Irwin, from "Random Rhymes"; "Simon Legree—a Negro Sermon," by Vachel Lindsay, from "The Chinese Nightingale and Other Poems," and from "Collected Poems"; "The Old Hokum Buncombe," by Robert E. Sherwood, from "Poems from Life."

The Macmillan Company of Canada, Ltd.: "Study of an Elevation, in Indian Ink," by Rudyard Kipling, from "Departmental Ditties and Barrack-Room Ballads."

Methuen & Co., Ltd.: "Wine and Water," by G. K. Chesterton, from "The Collected Poems of G. K. Chesterton"; "Ballade of Sporific Absorption," by J. C. Squire, from "The Nonsensibus"; Finale to "Perseverance; or Half a Coronet," by A. P. Herbert, from "Mild and Bitter."

The New Yorker: "The Anatomy of Humor" and "We Have Been Here Before," by Morris Bishop; "Historical Incidents," by Clarence Day; "Obit on Parnassus," by F. Scott Fitzgerald; "Artist," by Ernestine Mercer.

Oxford University Press: "The Famous Ballad of the Jubilee Cup," by Arthur T. Quiller-Couch, from "Green Bays," New and enlarged edition, 1930; "Lady Jane," by Arthur T. Quiller-Couch, from "Green Bays"; "Biography" and "R. I. P.," by Jan Struther, from "The Glass-Blower and Other Poems."

Penn State Froth: "This Smoking World," by Graham Lee Hemminger.

A. D. Peters: "Tripe," by J. B. Morton.

Punch: "In Winter," by C. H. Bretherton; "The Contented Bachelor" and "Ode to the Nightingale," by Major John Kendall; "In Praise of Commonplace," "The Old Songs," and "The Seamy Side of Motley," by Sir Owen Seaman.

G. P. Putnam's Sons: "A Winter Madrigal," "Public Aid for Niagara Falls," and "We Have Been Here Before," by Morris Bishop, from "Spilt Milk."

Random House, Inc.: "America, I Love You," by Bert Kalmar and Harry Ruby, from "The Kalmar and Ruby Song Book."

Charles Scribner's Sons: The poems by H. C. Bunner, from "Poems of H. C. Bunner"; the poems by Eugene Field, from "The Poems of Eugene Field"; "At the Ball Game," by Roswell Martin Field; "The Lacquer Liquor Locker" and "Lessons in Limericks," by David McCord, from "Bay Window Ballads"; "Miniver Cheevy," by Edwin Arlington Robinson, from "Town Down the River"; "Prosit Neujahr," by George Santayana.

Martin Secker: " 'How They Do It:' Mr. W. H. Davies and Sir Henry Newbolt," by J. C. Squire, from "Tricks of the Trade."

The Viking Press: The poems by Dorothy Parker, from "Not So Deep as a Well," copyright 1926, 1928, 1931, 1936; "Ballade of Big Plans," by Dorothy Parker, from "Enough Rope," copyright 1926.

ACKNOWLEDGMENTS XV

A. P. Watt & Son: "Sir Christopher Wren," by E. C. Bentley, from "Baseless Biographies"; "A Ballade of Suicide," and "Wine and Water," by G. K. Chesterton, from "The Collected Poems of G. K. Chesterton"; "To an Ungentle Critic," by Robert Graves, from "Fairies and Fusiliers"; Finale to "Perseverance; or Half a Coronet," by A. P. Herbert, from "Mild and Bitter"; "Study of an Elevation, in Indian Ink," by Rudyard Kipling, from "Departmental Ditties and Barrack-Room Ballads"; " 'How They Do It:' *Mr. W. H. Davies* and *Sir Henry Newbolt*," by J. C. Squire, from "Tricks of the Trade."

Yale University Press: "Exit God," by Gamaliel Bradford, from "Shadow Verses."

Gratitude for permission to reprint verses included in this volume hereby is expressed to the following, as well as to those contributors to The Conning Tower whose names and initials are unidentifiable:

Georgine M. Adams, Samuel Hopkins Adams, Maxwell Anderson, Ed Anthony.

Ruth Fitch Bartlett, Rosemary Benét, Stephen Vincent Benét, William Rose Benét, Morris Bishop, Milton Bracker, Mrs. H. C. Bunner, Gelett Burgess.

Frank Chase, Junius Cooper.

Mrs. Clarence Day, Fairfax Downey, for the "Rise and Fall of Valentines" originally published under the title of "The Origin of Valentines" by the Sprague-Coleman Company as a chorus song with music by Arthur Hall.

Irwin Edman.

Edna Ferber, Margaret Fishback, James Montgomery Flagg, Corey Ford.

Al Graham, Arthur Guiterman.

Clayton Hamilton, Sara Henderson Hay, Samuel Hoffenstein, John A. Holmes, Brian Hooker.

Wallace Irwin.

Orrick Johns.

Bert Kalmar, George S. Kaufman, John Kieran, Arthur Kober, Arthur Kramer.

Harold A. Larrabee, Newman Levy.

George Macy, David McCord, Phyllis McGinley, Laurence McKinney, Hughes Mearns, Ernestine Mercer, Edna St. Vincent Millay, Albert G. Miller, Christopher Morley.

Ogden Nash.

Oliver Opdyke.

Dorothy Parker, David Fisher Parry, Louis Paul, Arthur Pederson.

Edwin Meade Robinson, Henry Morton Robinson, Selma Robinson, Harry Ruby.

Fred Saidy, Nate Salsbury, Robert E. Sherwood, Kurt M. Stein, Albert Stillman, Julian Street.

Mrs. Bert Leston Taylor, Deems Taylor, Rufus Terral.

Charles A. Wagner, George Frisbie Whicher, E. B. White, William Allen White, Charles D. Woodberry.

Thomas R. Ybarra.

Contents

Burlesque · Parody

THE BITER BIT

The sun is in the sky, mother, the flowers are springing fair
And the melody of woodland birds is stirring in the air;
The river, smiling to the sky, glides onward to the sea,
And happiness is everywhere, oh, mother, but with me!

They are going to the church, mother—I hear the marriage
    bell
It booms along the upland—oh! it haunts me like a knell;
He leads her on his arm, mother, he cheers her faltering step,
And closely to his side she clings—she does, the demirep!

They are crossing by the stile, mother, where we so oft have
    stood,
The stile beside the shady thorn, at the corner of the wood;
And the boughs, that wont to murmur back the words that
    won my ear,
Wave their silver branches o'er him, as he leads his bridal
    fere.

He will pass beside the stream, mother, where first my hand
    he pressed,
By the meadow where, with quivering lip, his passion he
    confessed;
And down the hedgerows where we've strayed again and yet
    again;
But he will not think of me, mother, his broken-hearted
    Jane!

He said that I was proud, mother, that I looked for rank
    and gold,
He said I did not love him—he said my words were cold;
He said I kept him off and on, in hopes of higher game—
And it may be that I did, mother; but who hasn't done the
    same.

I did not know my heart, mother—I know it now too late;
I thought that I without a pang could wed some nobler
    mate;

3

But no nobler suitor sought me—and he has taken wing,
And my heart is gone, and I am left a lone and blighted
    thing.

You may lay me in my bed, mother—my head is throbbing
    sore;
And, mother, prithee, let the sheets be duly aired before;
And, if you'd please, my mother dear, your poor desponding
    child,
Draw me a pot of beer, mother, and, mother, draw it mild!
                             WILLIAM E. AYTOUN

COMFORT IN AFFLICTION

"Wherefore starts my bosom's lord?
    Why this anguish in thine eye?
Oh, it seems as thy heart's chord
    Had broken with that sigh!

"Rest thee, my dear lord, I pray,
    Rest thee on my bosom now!
And let me wipe the dews away,
    Are gathering on thy brow.

"There, again! that fevered start
    What, love! husband! is thy pain?
There is a sorrow in thy heart,
    A weight upon thy brain!

"Nay, nay, that sickly smile can ne'er
    Deceive affection's searching eye;
'Tis a wife's duty, love, to share
    Her husband's agony.

"Since the dawn began to peep,
    Have I lain with stifled breath;
Heard thee moaning in thy sleep,
    As thou wert at grips with death.

"Oh, what joy it was to see
    My gentle lord once more awake!

Tell me, what is amiss with thee?
   Speak, or my heart will break!"

"Mary, thou angel of my life,
   Thou ever good and kind;
'Tis not, believe me, my dear wife,
   The anguish of the mind!

"It is not in my bosom, dear,
   No, nor in my brain, in sooth;
But, Mary, oh, I feel it here,
   Here in my wisdom tooth!

"Then give,—oh, first, best antidote,—
   Sweet partner of my bed!
Give me thy flannel petticoat
   To wrap around my head!"

            WILLIAM E. AYTOUN

IN WINTER

Boreas blows on his high wood whistle,
   Over the coppice and down the lane
Where the goldfinch chirps from the haulm of the thistle
   And mangolds gleam in the farmer's wain.
Last year's dead and the new year's sleeping
   Under its mantle of leaves and snow;
Earth holds beauty fast in her keeping
   But Life invincible stirs below.

Runs the sap in each root and rhizome,
   Primrose yellow and snowdrop cold,
Windyflowers when the chiffchaff flies home,
   Lenten lilies with crowns of gold.
Soon the woods will be blithe with bracken,
   April whisper of lambs at play;
Spring with triumph—and our old black hen
   (Thank the Lord!) will begin to lay.

            C. H. BRETHERTON

BEHOLD THE DEEDS!

CHANT ROYAL

(Being the Plaint of Adolphe Culpepper Ferguson, Salesman of Fancy Notions, held in durance of his Landlady for a failure to connect on Saturday night)

I

I would that all men my hard case might know;
    How grievously I suffer for no sin:
I, Adolphe Culpepper Ferguson, for lo!
    I, of my landlady am lockèd in.
For being short on this sad Saturday,
Nor having shekels of silver wherewith to pay,
She has turned and is departed with my key;
Wherefore, not even as other boarders free,
    I sing (as prisoners to their dungeon stones
When for ten days they expiate a spree):
    Behold the deeds that are done of Mrs. Jones!

II

One night and one day have I wept my woe;
    Nor wot I when the morrow doth begin,
If I shall have to write to Briggs & Co.,
    To pray them to advance the requisite tin
For ransom of their salesman, that he may
Go forth as other boarders go alway—
As those I hear now flocking from their tea,
Led by the daughter of my landlady
    Pianoward. This day for all my moans,
Dry bread and water have been servèd me.
    Behold the deeds that are done of Mrs. Jones!

III

Miss Amabel Jones is musical, and so
    The heart of the young he-boarder doth win,
Playing "The Maiden's Prayer," adagio—
    That fetcheth him, as fetcheth the banco skin
The innocent rustic. For my part, I pray:

That Badarjewska maid may wait for aye
Ere sits she with a lover, as did we
Once sit together, Amabel! Can it be
   That all of that arduous wooing not atones
For Saturday shortness of trade dollars three?
   Behold the deeds that are done of Mrs. Jones!

IV

Yea! she forgets the arm was wont to go
   Around her waist. She wears a buckle whose pin
Galleth the crook of the young man's elbow;
   I forget not, for I that youth have been.
Smith was aforetime the Lothario gay.
Yet once, I mind me, Smith was forced to stay
Close in his room. Not calm, as I, was he;
But his noise brought no pleasaunce, verily.
   Small ease he gat of playing on the bones,
Or hammering on his stove-pipe, that I see.
   Behold the deeds that are done of Mrs. Jones!

V

Thou, for whose fear the figurative crow
   I eat, accursed be thou and all thy kin!
Thee will I show up—yea, up will I show
   Thy too thick buckwheats, and thy tea too thin.
Ay! here I dare thee, ready for the fray!
Thou dost not keep a first-class house, I say!
It does not with the advertisements agree.
Thou lodgest a Briton with a pugaree,
   And thou hast harbored Jacobses and Cohns,
Also a Mulligan. Thus denounce I thee!
   Behold the deeds that are done of Mrs. Jones!

ENVOY

Boarders! the worst I have not told to ye:
She hath stole my trousers, that I may not flee
   Privily by the window. Hence these groans,

There is no fleeing in a *robe de nuit*.
Behold the deeds that are done of Mrs. Jones!

H. C. BUNNER

HOME, SWEET HOME WITH VARIATIONS

BEING SUGGESTIONS OF THE VARIOUS STYLES IN WHICH AN OLD THEME
MIGHT HAVE BEEN TREATED BY CERTAIN METRICAL COMPOSERS

FANTASIA

I

THE ORIGINAL THEME AS JOHN HOWARD PAYNE WROTE IT:

'Mid pleasures and palaces though we may roam,
Be it ever so humble, there's no place like home!
A charm from the skies seems to hallow it there,
Which, seek through the world, is not met with elsewhere.

Home, home! Sweet, Sweet Home!
There's no place like Home!

An exile from home, splendor dazzles in vain!
Oh, give me my lowly thatched cottage again!
The birds singing gaily that came at my call!
Give me them! and the peace of mind, dearer than all.

Home, home! Sweet, Sweet Home!
There's no place like Home!

II

(As ALGERNON CHARLES SWINBURNE MIGHT HAVE WRAPPED
IT UP IN VARIATIONS)

[*'Mid pleasures and palaces—*]

As sea-foam blown of the winds, as blossom of brine that is
    drifted
  Hither and yon on the barren breast of the breeze,
Though we wander on gusts of a god's breath shaken and
    shifted,
  The salt of us stings and is sore for the sobbing seas.
For home's sake hungry at heart, we sicken in pillared
  porches

Of bliss made sick for a life that is barren of bliss,
For the place whereon is a light out of heaven that sears not
    nor scorches,
  Nor elsewhere than this.

[*An exile from home, splendor dazzles in vain!*]

For here we know shall no gold thing glisten,
  No bright thing burn, and no sweet thing shine;
Nor Love lower never an ear to listen
  To words that work in the heart like wine.
    What time we are set from our land apart,
    For pain of passion and hunger of heart,
Though we walk with exiles fame faints to christen,
  Or sing at the Cytherean's shrine.

[VARIATION: *An exile from home*—]

Whether with him whose head
Of gods is honorèd,
  With song made splendent in the sight of men—
    Whose heart most sweetly stout,
    From ravishing France cast out,
  Being firstly hers, was hers most wholly then—
    Or where on shining seas like wine
    The dove's wings draw the drooping Erycine.

[*Give me my lowly thatched cottage*—]

For Joy finds Love grow bitter,
And spreads his wings to quit her,
At thought of birds that twitter
  Beneath the roof-tree's straw—
  Of birds that come for calling,
  No fear or fright appalling,
  When dews of dusk are falling,
Or daylight's draperies draw.

[*Give me them! and the peace of mind*—]

Give me these things then back, though the giving
  Be at cost of earth's garner of gold;

There is no life without these worth living,
   No treasure where these are not told.
For the heart give the hope that it knows not,
   Give the balm for the burn of the breast—
For the soul and the mind that repose not,
   O, give us a rest!

III

(As Mr. Francis Bret Harte Might Have Woven It
into a Touching Tale of a Western Gentleman in a
Red Shirt)

   Brown o' San Juan,
      Stranger, I'm Brown.
   Come up this mornin' from 'Frisco—
      Be'n a-saltin' my specie-stacks down.

   Be'n a-knockin' around,
      Fer a man from San Juan,
   Putty consid'able frequent—
      Jes' catch onter that streak o' the dawn!

   Right thar lies my home—
      Right thar in the red—
   I could slop over, stranger, in po'try—
      Would spread out old Shakspoke cold dead.

Stranger, you freeze to this: there ain't no kinder gin-palace,
Nor no variety-show lays over a man's own rancho.
Maybe it hain't no style, but the Queen in the Tower o'
      London,
Ain't got naathin' I'd swop for that house over thar on the
      hill-side.

Thar is my ole gal, 'n' the kids, 'n' the rest o' my live-stock;
Thar my Remington hangs, and thar there's a griddle-cake
      br'ilin'—
For the two of us, pard—and thar, I allow, the heavens
Smile more friendly-like than on any other locality.

Stranger, nowhere else I don't take no satisfaction.
Gimme my ranch, 'n' them friendly old Shanghai chickens—
I brung the original pair f'm the States in eighteen-'n'-
fifty—
Gimme me them and the feelin' of solid domestic comfort.

Yer parding, young man—
  But this landscape a kind
Er flickers—I 'low 'twuz the po'try—
  I thought that my eyes hed gone blind.

* * *

Take that pop from my belt!
  Hi, thar!—gimme yer han'—
Or I'll kill myself—Lizzie—she's left me—
  Gone off with a purtier man!

Thar, I'll quit—the ole gal
  An' the kids—run away!
I be derned! Howsomever, come in, pard—
  The griddle-cake's thar, anyway.

IV

(As Austin Dobson Might Have Translated It from
Horace, if It Had Ever Occurred to Horace
to Write It)

RONDEAU

Calatiis in remotis voluptates
Si quaeris . . .
    —Flaccus, Q. Horatius, *Carmina, Lib. V, 1.*

At home alone, O Nomades,
Although Maecenas' marble frieze
  Stand not between you and the sky,
  Nor Persian luxury supply
Its rosy surfeit, find ye ease.

Tempt not the far Aegean breeze;
With home-made wine and books that please,
  To duns and bores the door deny,
    At home, alone.

Strange joys may lure. Your deities
Smile here alone. Oh, give me these:
  Low eaves, where birds familiar fly,
  And peace of mind, and, fluttering by,
My Lydia's graceful draperies,
    At home, *alone*.

v

(As It Might Have Been Constructed in 1744, Oliver
  Goldsmith, at 19, Writing the First Stanza,
    and Alexander Pope, at 52, the Second)

Home! at the word, what blissful visions rise,
Lift us from earth, and draw toward the skies;
'Mid mirag'd towers, or meretricious joys,
Although we roam, one thought the mind employs:
Or lowly hut, good friend, or loftiest dome,
Earth knows no spot so holy as our Home.
There, where affection warms the father's breast,
There is the spot of heav'n most surely blest.
Howe'er we search, though wandering with the wind
Through frigid Zembla, or the heats of Ind,
Not elsewhere may we seek, nor elsewhere know,
The light of heaven upon our dark below.

When from our dearest hope and haven reft,
Delight nor dazzles, nor is luxury left,
We long, obedient to our nature's law,
To see again our hovel thatched with straw:
See birds that know our avenaceous store
Stoop to our hand, and thence repleted soar:
But, of all hopes the wanderer's soul that share,
His pristine peace of mind's his final prayer.

VI

(As Walt Whitman Might Have Written All Around It)

1

You over there, young man with the guide-book, red-bound,
    covered flexibly with red linen,
Come here, I want to talk with you; I, Walt, the Manhat-
    tanese, citizen of these States, call you.
Yes, and the courier, too, smirking, smug-mouthed, with
    oil'd hair; a garlicky look about him generally; him,
    too, I take in, just as I would a coyote or a king, or a
    toad-stool, or a ham-sandwich, or anything, or anybody
    else in the world.
Where are you going?
You want to see Paris, to eat truffles, to have a good time;
    in Vienna, London, Florence, Monaco, to have a good
    time; you want to see Venice.
Come with me. I will give you a good time; I will give you
    all the Venice you want, and most of the Paris.
I, Walt, I call to you. I am all on deck! Come and loafe with
    me! Let me tote you around by your elbow and show
    you things.
You listen to my ophicleide!
Home!
Home, I celebrate. I elevate my fog-whistle, inspir'd by the
    thought of home.
Come in!—take a front seat; the jostle of the crowd not
    minding; there is room enough for all of you.
This is my exhibition—it is the greatest show on earth—
    there is no charge for admission.
All you have to pay me is to take in my romanza.

2

1. The brown-stone house; the father coming home worried
    from a bad day's business; the wife meets him in the
    marble pav'd vestibule; she throws her arms about him;
    she presses him close to her; she looks him full in the

face with affectionate eyes; the frown from his brow disappearing.

Darling, she says, *Johnny has fallen down and cut his head; the cook is going away, and the boiler leaks.*

2. The mechanic's dark little third-story room, seen in a flash from the Elevated Railway train; the sewing-machine in a corner; the small cook-stove; the whole family eating cabbage around a kerosene lamp; of the clatter and roar and groaning wail of the Elevated train unconscious; of the smell of the cabbage unconscious.

Me, passant, in the train, of the cabbage not quite so unconscious.

3. The French Flat; the small rooms, all right-angles, un-individual; the narrow halls; the gaudy, cheap decorations everywhere.

The janitor and the cook exchanging compliments up and down the elevator-shaft; the refusal to send up more coal, the solid splash of the water upon his head, the language he sends up the shaft, the triumphant laughter of the cook, to her kitchen retiring.

4. The widow's small house in the suburbs of the city; the widow's boy coming home from his first day down town; he is flushed with happiness and pride; he is no longer a school-boy, he is earning money; he takes on the airs of a man and talks learnedly of business.

5. The room in the third-class boarding-house; the mean little hard-coal fire, the slovenly Irish servant-girl making it, the ashes on the hearth, the faded furniture, the private provender hid away in the closet, the dreary backyard out the window; the young girl at the glass, with her mouth full of hairpins, doing up her hair to go downstairs and flirt with the young fellows in the parlor.

6. The kitchen of the old farm-house; the young convict just return'd from prison—it was his first offense, and the judges were lenient to him.

He is taking his first meal out of prison; he has been receiv'd back, kiss'd, encourag'd to start again; his lungs, his nostrils expand with the big breaths of free air; with shame, with wonderment, with a trembling joy, his heart too, expanding.

The old mother busies herself about the table; she has ready for him the dishes he us'd to like; the father sits with his back to them, reading the newspaper, the newspaper shaking and rustling much; the children hang wondering around the prodigal—they have been caution'd: *Do not ask where our Jim has been; only say you are glad to see him.*

The elder daughter is there, palefac'd, quiet; her young man went back on her four years ago; his folks would not let him marry a convict's sister. She sits by the window, sewing on the children's clothes, the clothes not only patching up; her hunger for children of her own invisibly patching up.

The brother looks up; he catches her eye, he fearful, apologetic; she smiles back at him, not reproachfully smiling, with loving pretence of hope smiling—it is too much for him; he buries his face in the folds of the mother's black gown.

7. The best room of the house, on the Sabbath only open'd; the smell of horse-hair furniture and mahogany varnish; the ornaments on the what-not in the corner; the wax fruit, dusty, sunken, sagged in, consumptive-looking, under a glass globe, the sealing-wax imitation of coral; the cigar boxes with shells plastered over, the perforated card-board motto.

The kitchen; the housewife sprinkling the clothes for the fine ironing to-morrow—it is Third-day night, and the plain things are ready iron'd, now in cupboards, in drawers stowed away.

The wife waiting for the husband—he is at the tavern, jovial, carousing; she, alone in the kitchen sprinkling clothes —the little red wood clock with peaked top, with pendulum wagging behind a pane of gayly painted glass, strikes twelve.

The sound of the husband's voice on the still night air—he is singing: *We won't go home until morning!*—the wife

arising, toward the wood-shed hastily going, stealthily
    entering, the voice all the time coming nearer, inebriate,
    chantant.
The wood-shed; the club behind the door of the wood-shed;
    the wife annexing the club; the husband approaching,
    always inebriate, chantant.
The husband passing the door of the wood-shed; the club
    over his head, now with his head in contact; the sudden
    cessation of the song; the temperance pledge signed the
    next morning; the benediction of peace over the
    domestic foyer temporarily resting.

3

I sing the soothing influences of home.
You, young man, thoughtlessly wandering, with courier, with
    guide-book wandering,
You hearken to the melody of my steam-calliope
Yawp!

H. C. Bunner

BALLAD

The auld wife sat at her ivied door,
    (*Butter and eggs and a pound of cheese*)
A thing she had frequently done before;
    And her spectacles lay on her apron'd knees.

The piper he piped on the hilltop high,
    (*Butter and eggs and a pound of cheese*)
Till the cow said "I die," and the goose asked "Why?"
    And the dog said nothing, but search'd for fleas.

The farmer he strode through the square farmyard;
    (*Butter and eggs and a pound of cheese*)
His last brew of ale was a trifle hard—
    The connection of which the plot one sees.

The farmer's daughter hath frank blue eyes;
    (*Butter and eggs and a pound of cheese*)

She hears the rooks caw in the windy skies,
   As she sits at her lattice and shells her peas.

The farmer's daughter hath ripe red lips;
   (*Butter and eggs and a pound of cheese*)
If you try to approach her, away she skips
   Over tables and chairs with apparent ease.

The farmer's daughter hath soft brown hair;
   (*Butter and eggs and a pound of cheese*)
And I met with a ballad, I can't say where,
   Which wholly consisted of lines like these.

She sat with her hands 'neath her dimpled cheeks,
   (*Butter and eggs and a pound of cheese*)
And spake not a word. While a lady speaks
   There is hope, but she didn't even sneeze.

She sat, with her hands 'neath her crimson cheeks;
   (*Butter and eggs and a pound of cheese*)
She gave up mending her father's breeks,
   And let the cat roll in her new chemise.

She sat with her hands 'neath her burning cheeks,
   (*Butter and eggs and a pound of cheese*)
And gazed at the piper for thirteen weeks;
   Then she follow'd him o'er the misty leas.

Her sheep follow'd her, as their tails did them,
   (*Butter and eggs and a pound of cheese*)
And this song is consider'd a perfect gem,
   And as to the meaning, it's what you please.
                CHARLES STUART CALVERLEY

THE COCK AND THE BULL

You see this pebble-stone? It's a thing I bought
Of a bit of a chit of a boy i' the mid o' the day—
I like to dock the smaller parts-o'-speech,

As we curtail the already cur-tailed cur
(You catch the paronomasia, play 'po' words?)
Did, rather, i' the pre-Landseerian days.
Well, to my muttons. I purchased the concern,
And clapt it i' my poke, having given for same
By way o' chop, swop, barter or exchange—
"Chop" was my snickering dandiprat's own term—
One shilling and fourpence, current coin o' the realm.
O-n-e one and f-o-u-r four
Pence, one and fourpence—you are with me, sir?—
What hour it skills not: ten or eleven o' the clock,
One day (and what a roaring day it was
Go shop or sight-see—bar a spit o' rain!)
In February, eighteen sixty nine,
Alexandrina Victoria, Fidei,
Hm—hm—how runs the jargon? being on throne.

Such, sir, are all the facts, succinctly put,
The basis or substratum—what you will—
Of the impending eighty thousand lines.
"Not much in 'em either," quoth perhaps simple Hodge.
But there's a superstructure. Wait a bit.

Mark first the rationale of the thing:
Hear logic rivel and levigate the deed.
That shilling—and for matter o' that, the pence—
I had o' course upo' me—wi' me say—
(*Mecum's* the Latin, make a note o' that)
When I popp'd pen i' stand, scratched ear, wiped snout,
(Let everybody wipe his own himself)
Sniff'd—tch!—at snuffbox; tumbled up, he-heed,
Haw-haw'd (not he-haw'd, that's another guess thing.)
Then fumbled at, and stumbled out of, door,
I shoved the timber ope wi' my omoplat;
And *in vestibulo*, i' the lobby to-wit,
(Iacobi Facciolati's rendering, sir,)
Donned galligaskins, antigropeloes,
And so forth; and, complete with hat and gloves,

One on and one a-dangle i' my hand,
And ombrifuge (Lord love you!) case o' rain,
I flopp'd forth, 'sbuddikins! on my own ten toes,
(I do assure you there be ten of them)
And went clump-clumping up hill and down dale
To find myself o' the sudden i' front o' the boy.
Put case I hadn't 'em on me, could I ha' bought
This sort-o'-kind-o'-what-you-might-call-toy,
This pebble-thing, o' the boy-thing? Q. E. D.
That's proven without aid for mumping Pope,
Sleek porporate or bloated Cardinal.
(Isn't it, old Fatchaps? You're in Euclid now.)
So, having the shilling—having i' fact a lot—
And pence and halfpence, ever so many o' them,
I purchased, as I think I said before,
The pebble (*lapis, lapidis,-di,-dem,-de*—
What nouns 'crease short i' the genitive, Fatchaps, eh?)
O, the boy, a bare-legg'd beggarly son of a gun,
For one-and-fourpence. Here we are again.

Now Law steps in, bewigged, voluminous-jaw'd;
Investigates and re-investigates.
Was the transaction illegal? Law shakes head.
Perpend, sir, all the bearings of the case.

At first the coin was mine, the chattel his.
But now (by virtue of the said exchange
And barter) *vice versa* all the coin,
Rer juris operationem, vests
I' the boy and his assigns till ding o' doom;
In saecula saeculo-o-o-orum;
(I think I hear the Abate mouth out that.)
To have and hold the same to him and them . . .
Confer some idiot on Conveyancing.
Whereas the pebble and every part thereof,
And all that appertaineth thereunto,
Quodcunque pertinet ad em rem,
(I fancy, sir, my Latin's rather pat)

Or shall, will, may, might, can, could, would, or should,
Subaudi cætera—clap we to the close—
For what's the good of law in a case o' the kind
Is mine to all intents and purposes.
This settled, I resume the thread o' the tale.

Now for a touch o' the vendor's quality.
He says a gen'lman bought a pebble of him,
(This pebble i' sooth, sir, which I hold i' my hand)—
And paid for 't, *like* a gen'lman, on the nail.
"Did I o'ercharge him a ha'penny? Devil a bit.
Fiddlepin's end! Get out, you blazing ass!
Gabble o' the goose. Don't bugaboo-baby *me!*
Go double or quits? Yah! tittup! what's the odds?"
—There's the transaction viewed in the vendor's light.

Next ask that dumpled hag, stood snuffling by,
With her three frowsy blowsy brats o' babes,
The scum o' the kennel, cream o' the filth-heap—Faugh!
Aie, aie, aie, aie! ὀτοτοτοτοτοî,
('Stead which we blurt out Hoighty toighty now)—
And the baker and candlestick maker, and Jack and Gill,
Blear'd Goody this and queasy Gaffer that,
Ask the schoolmaster. Take schoolmaster first.
He saw a gentleman purchase of a lad
A stone, and pay for it *rite*, on the square,
And carry it off *per saltum*, jauntily
Propria quae maribus, gentleman's property now
(Agreeably to the law explain'd above).
In proprium usum, for his private ends,
The boy he chuck'd a brown i' the air, and bit
I' the face the shilling: heaved a thumping stone
At a lean hen that ran cluck clucking by,
(And hit her, dead as nail i' post o' door,)
Then *abiit*—What's the Ciceronian phrase?—
Excessit, evasit, erupit—off slogs boy;
Off like bird, *avi similis*—(you observed
The dative? Pretty i' the Mantuan!)—*Anglice*

Off in three flea skips. *Hactenus*, so far,
So good, *tam bene. Bene, satis, male*,—
Where was I with my trope 'bout one in a quag?
I did once hitch the syntax into verse
Verbum personale, a verb personal,
Concordat—ay, "agrees," old Fatchaps—*cum*
Nominativo, with its nominative,
Genere, i' point of gender, *numero*,
O' number, *et persona*, and person. *Ut*,
Instance: *Sol ruit*, down flops sun, *et* and,
Montes umbrantur, out flounce mountains. Pah!
Excuse me, sir, I think I'm going mad.
You see the trick on't though, and can yourself
Continue the discourse *ad libitum*.
It takes up about eighty thousand lines,
A thing imagination boggles at;
And might, odds-bobs, sir! in judicious hands
Extend from here to Mesopotamy.

CHARLES STUART CALVERLEY

IN THE GLOAMING

In the Gloaming to be roaming, where the crested waves are
.foaming,
And the shy mermaidens combing locks that ripple to their
feet;
When the Gloaming is, I never made the ghost of an endeavour
To discover—but whatever were the hour, it would be
sweet.

"To their feet," I say, for Leech's sketch indisputably teaches
That the mermaids of our beaches do not end in ugly tails,
Nor have homes among the corals; but are shod with neat
balmorals,
An arrangement no one quarrels with, as many might with
scales.

Sweet to roam beneath a shady cliff, of course with some
young lady,

Lalage, Neaera, Haidee, or Elaine, or Mary Ann:
Love, you dear delusive dream, you! Very sweet your victims
    deem you,
    When, heard only by the seamew, they talk all the stuff
    one can.

Sweet to haste, a licensed lover, to Miss Pinkerton, the
    glover;
    Having managed to discover what is dear Neaera's "size":
P'raps to touch that wrist so slender, as your tiny gift you
    tender,
    And to read you're no offender, in those laughing hazel
    eyes.

Then to hear her call you "Harry," when she makes you
    fetch and carry—
    O young men about to marry, what a blessed thing it is!
To be photograph'd—together—cased in pretty Russia
    leather—
    Hear her gravely doubting, whether they have spoilt your
    honest phiz!

Then to bring your plighted fair one first a ring—a rich and
    rare one—
    Next a bracelet, if she'll wear one, and a heap of things
    beside;
And serenely bending o'er her, to inquire if it would bore her
    To say when her own adorer may aspire to call her bride!

Then, the days of courtship over, with your wife to start for
    Dover
    Or Dieppe—and live in clover evermore, whate'er befalls;
For I've read in many a novel that, unless they've souls that
    grovel,
    Folks *prefer* in fact a hovel to your dreary marble halls.

To sit, happy married lovers; Phillis trifling with a plover's
    Egg, while Corydon uncovers with a grace the Sally Lunn,

Or dissects the lucky pheasant—that, I think, were passing
    pleasant,
    As I sit alone at present, dreaming darkly of a Dun.
                   CHARLES STUART CALVERLEY

FATHER WILLIAM

"You are old, Father William," the young man said,
    "And your hair has become very white;
And yet you incessantly stand on your head—
    Do you think, at your age, it is right?"

"In my youth," father William replied to his son,
    "I feared it might injure the brain;
But now that I'm perfectly sure I have none,
    Why, I do it again and again."

"You are old," said the youth, "as I mentioned before,
    And have grown most uncommonly fat;
Yet you turned a back-somersault in at the door—
    Pray, what is the reason of that?"

"In my youth," said the sage, as he shook his grey locks,
    "I kept all my limbs very supple
By the use of this ointment—one shilling the box—
    Allow me to sell you a couple."

"You are old," said the youth, "and your jaws are too weak
    For anything tougher than suet;
Yet you finished the goose, with the bones and the beak—
    Pray, how did you manage to do it?"

"In my youth," said his father, "I took to the law,
    And argued each case with my wife;
And the muscular strength which it gave to my jaw,
    Has lasted the rest of my life."

"You are old," said the youth; "one would hardly suppose
    That your eye was as steady as ever;

Yet you balanced an eel on the end of your nose—
    What made you so awfully clever?"

"I have answered three questions, and that is enough,"
    Said his father; "don't give yourself airs!
Do you think I can listen all day to such stuff?
    Be off, or I'll kick you down-stairs!"

LEWIS CARROLL

TURTLE SOUP

Beautiful soup, so rich and green,
Waiting in a hot tureen!
Who for such dainties would not stoop?
Soup of the evening, beautiful Soup?
Soup of the evening, beautiful Soup?
    Beau—ootiful Soo—oop!
    Beau—ootiful Soo—oop!
Soo—oop of the e—e—evening,
    Beautiful, beautiful Soup!

"Beautiful Soup! Who cares for fish,
Game, or any other dish?
Who would not give all else for two p
Ennyworth only of beautiful Soup?
Pennyworth only of beautiful soup?
    Beau—ootiful Soo—oop!
    Beau—ootiful Soo—oop!
Soo—oop of the e—e—evening,
    Beautiful, beauti—FUL SOUP!"

LEWIS CARROLL

A BALLAD

In the Manner of R - dy - rd K - pl - ng

As I was walkin' the jungle round, a-killin' of tigers an' time;
I seed a kind of an author man a-writin' a rousin' rhyme;
'E was writin' a mile a minute an' more, an' I sez to 'im,
    "'Oo are you?"

Sez 'e, "I'm a poet—'er majesty's poet—soldier an' sailor, too!"
An 'is poem began in Ispahan an' ended in Kalamazoo,
It 'ad army in it, an' navy in it, an' jungle sprinkled through,
For 'e was a poet—'er majesty's poet—soldier an' sailor, too!

An' after, I met 'im all over the world, a doin' of things a host;
'E 'ad one foot planted in Burmah, an' one on the Gloucester coast;
'E's 'alf a sailor an' 'alf a whaler, 'e's captain, cook, and crew,
But most a poet—'er majesty's poet—soldier an' sailor too!
'E's often Scot an' 'e's often not, but 'is work is never through
For 'e laughs at blame, an' 'e writes for fame, an' a bit for revenoo,—
Bein' a poet—'er majesty's poet—soldier an' sailor too!

'E'll take you up to the Ar'tic zone, 'e'll take you down to the Nile,
'E'll give you a barrack ballad in the Tommy Atkins style,
Or 'e'll sing you a Dipsy Chantey, as the bloomin' bo'suns do,
For 'e is a poet—'er majesty's poet—soldier an' sailor too.
An' there isn't no room for others, an' there's nothin' left to do;
'E 'as sailed the main from the 'Orn to Spain, 'e 'as tramped the jungle through,
An' written up all there is to write—soldier an' sailor, too!

There are manners an' manners of writin', but 'is is the *proper* way,
An' it ain't so hard to be a bard if you'll imitate Rudyard K.;
But sea an' shore an' peace an' war, an' everything else in view—
'E 'as gobbled the lot!—'er majesty's poet—soldier an' sailor, too.
'E's not content with 'is Indian 'ome, 'e's looking for regions new,
In another year 'e'll 'ave swept 'em clear, an' what'll the rest of us do?

'E's crowdin' us out!—'er majesty's poet—soldier an' sailor
  too!

GUY WETMORE CARRYL

JACOB

He dwelt among "Apartments let,"
  About five stories high;
A man, I thought, that none would get,
  And very few would try.

A boulder, by a larger stone
  Half hidden in the mud,
Fair as a man when only one
  Is in the neighborhood.

He lived unknown, and few could tell
  When Jacob was not free;
But he has got a wife—and O!
  The difference to me!

PHOEBE CARY

JABBERWOCKY

(As the author of "The Faerie Queene" might have written it)

I

The dewy Dawn from old Tithonus' bed
In orient splendor, rosy-fingered, rose,
And shaking off her dreamy drowsy-hed
Flashed in the east her brillig furbelows.
The slithy toves, as customary, chose
To gyre and gimble in the wabe of light.
The borogoves in bunches did dispose
Their mimsy forms uncouth to left and right,
While the mome raths outgrabe with all their greedy might.

II

The Redcrosse Knight, on curious quest ybent,
Was pricking haste-posthaste across a plain.

Close at his side sage counsel Una lent
Concerning dangers rife in that domain.
"The Jabberwock," quoth she, "to claw is fain
And eke to bite. The Jubjub bird beware.
The frumious Bandersnatch is mortal's bane."
"Ill would it me beseem such not to dare,"
The elfin knight replied, "for love of lady faire."

III

His vorpal sword in hand he fiercely hent,
And far and wide the manxome foe he sought.
At length he rested utterly forspent
Under a Tumtum tree in uffish thought:
When all attonce with fiery fury fraught
The Jabberwock, with eyes that jetted flame
And beastly senses all with rage distraught,
Came whiffling, hideous as the devil's dame,
Thorough the tulgey woods and burbled as he came.

IV

Up sprang the Redcrosse Knight, and round and round,
One, two! One, two! he swung his snickasnee.
The griding blade through scaly armor ground
And half shared through the dragon's gorge, pardee!
Una yswooned such gory sight to see
Of derring-do. The knight renewed attack,
And ere the Jabberwock could turn and flee
Into an hundred pieces him did hack.
Then with his grisly head they went galumphing back.

V

Queene Gloriana greeted them with joy.
And amorously her arms she did entwine
About the beamish, somedele bashful boy.
Una thereat, yblent with jealous tine,
Full furiously flashed her tremulous eyne.
The courtiers chortled, and the bright array
Of faerie knights and ladies pledged with wine

The champion stout and cheered that frabjous day
Till all the woods re-echoed loud, "Callooh! Callay!"

JUNIUS COOPER

HERE IS THE TALE
After Rudyard Kipling

Here is the tale—and you must make the most of it!
Here is the rhyme—ah, listen and attend!
Backwards—forwards—read it all and boast of it
If you are anything the wiser at the end!

Now Jack looked up—it was time to sup, and the bucket
was yet to fill,
And Jack looked round for a space and frowned, then beckoned his sister Jill,
And twice he pulled his sister's hair, and thrice he smote her
side;
"Ha' done, ha' done with your impudent fun—ha' done with
your games!" she cried;
"You have made mud-pies of a marvellous size—finger and
face are black,
You have trodden the Way of the Mire and Clay—now up
and wash you, Jack!
Or else, or ever we reach our home, there waiteth an angry
dame—
Well you know the weight of her blow—the supperless open
shame!
Wash, if you will, on yonder hill—wash, if you will, at the
spring,—
Or keep your dirt, to your certain hurt, and an imminent
walloping!"

"You must wash—you must scrub—you must scrape!"
growled Jack, "you must traffic with cans and pails,
Nor keep the spoil of the good brown soil in the rim of your
finger-nails!
The morning path you must tread to your bath—you must
wash ere the night descends,

And all for the cause of conventional laws and the soap-
makers' dividends!
But if 't is sooth that our meal in truth depends on our
washing, Jill,
By the sacred right of our appetite—haste—haste to the top
of the hill!"

They have trodden the Way of the Mire and Clay, they have
toiled and travelled far,
They have climbed to the brow of the hill-top now, where
the bubbling fountains are,
They have taken the bucket and filled it up—yea, filled it up
to the brim;
But Jack he sneered at his sister Jill, and Jill she jeered at
him:
"What, blown already!" Jack cried out (and his was a biting
mirth!)
"You boast indeed of your wonderful speed—but what is
the boasting worth?
Now, if you can run as the antelope runs, and if you can turn
like a hare,
Come, race me, Jill, to the foot of the hill—and prove your
boasting fair!"

"Race? What is a race" (and a mocking face had Jill as she
spake the word)
"Unless for a prize the runner tries? The truth indeed ye
heard,
For I can run as the antelope runs, and I can turn like a
hare:—
The first one down wins half-a-crown—and I will race you
there!"
"Yea, if for the lesson that you will learn (the lesson of
humbled pride)
The price you fix at two-and-six, it shall not be denied;
Come, take your stand at my right hand, for here is the mark
we toe:
Now, are you ready, and are you steady? Gird up your
petticoats! Go!"

And Jill she ran like a winging bolt, a bolt from the bow
    released,
But Jack like a stream of the lightning gleam, with its path-
    way duly greased:
He ran down hill in front of Jill like a summer-lightning
    flash—
Till he suddenly tripped on a stone, or slipped, and fell to
    the earth with a crash.
Then straight did rise on his wondering eyes the constel-
    lations fair,
Arcturus and the Pleiades, the Greater and Lesser Bear,
The swirling rain of a comet's train he saw, as he swiftly
    fell—
And Jill came tumbling after him with a loud triumphant
    yell:
"You have won, you have won, the race is done! And as for
    the wager laid—
You have fallen down with a broken crown—the half-crown
    debt is paid!"

They have taken Jack to the room at the back where the
    family medicines are,
And he lies in bed with a broken head in a halo of vinegar;
While, in that Jill had laughed her fill as her brother fell to
    earth,
She had felt the sting of a walloping—she hath paid the price
    of her mirth!

Here is the tale—and now you have the whole of it,
Here is the story—well and wisely planned,
Beauty—Duty—these make up the soul of it—
But, ah, my little readers, will you mark and understand?
                            ANTHONY C. DEANE

A RUSTIC SONG

    Oh, I be vun of the useful troibe
      O' rustic volk, I be;

And writin' gennelmen dü descroibe
    The doin's o' such as we;
I don't knaw mooch o' corliflower plants,
    I can't tell 'oes from trowels,
But 'ear me mix ma consonants,
    An' moodle oop all ma vowels!

I talks in a wunnerful dialect
    That vew can hunderstand,
'Tis Yorkshire-Zummerzet, I expect,
    With a dash o' the Oirish brand;
Sometimes a bloomin' flower of speech
    I picks from Cockney spots,
And when releegious truths I teach,
    Obsairve ma richt gude Scots!

In most of the bukes, 'twas once the case
    I 'adn't got much to do,
I blessed the 'eroine's purty face,
    An' I seed the 'ero through;
But now, I'm juist a pairsonage!
    A power o' bukes there be
Which from the start to the very last page
    Entoirely deal with me!

The wit or the point o' what I spakes
    Ye've got to find if ye can,
A wunnerful difference spellin' makes
    In the 'ands of a competent man!
I mayn't knaw mooch o' corliflower plants,
    I mayn't knaw 'oes from trowels,
But I does ma wark, if ma consonants
    Be properly mixed with ma vowels!
                                ANTHONY C. DEANE

OSCULATION

Sarah kissed me when we met,
    So did Kate and Belle and Dora,

So did Jane and Violet,
Dolly, Claribel, and Flora.
They all liked me pretty well—
And—dear girls!—they never hid it.
I don't like to kiss and tell—
Still they did it.

Later in the day I met
(And saluted!) Maude and Daisy,
And I also kissed Cozette,
Clara, Julia, Ruth, and Maisie.
Oh! I'm sorry for Leigh Hunt,
I who've had so many, many,
While poor Leigh's one vaunted stunt
Was with Jenny.

HENRY SYDNOR HARRISON

PLAIN LANGUAGE FROM TRUTHFUL JAMES

TABLE MOUNTAIN, 1870

Which I wish to remark—
  And my language is plain—
That for ways that are dark,
  And for tricks that are vain,
The heathen Chinee is peculiar,
  Which the same I would rise to explain.

Ah Sin was his name;
  And I will not deny
In regard to the same
  What that name might imply;
But his smile it was pensive and childlike,
  As I frequent remarked to Bill Nye.

It was August the third;
  And quite soft was the skies:
Which it might be inferred
  That Ah Sin was likewise;

Yet he played it that day upon William
   And me in a way I despise.

Which we had a small game,
   And Ah Sin took a hand.
It was Euchre. The same
   He did not understand;
But he smiled as he sat by the table,
   With a smile that was childlike and bland.

Yet the cards they were stocked
   In a way that I grieve,
And my feelings were shocked
   At the state of Nye's sleeve:
Which was stuffed full of aces and bowers,
   And the same with intent to deceive.

But the hands that were played
   By that heathen Chinee,
And the points that he made,
   Were quite frightful to see—
Till at last he put down a right bower,
   Which the same Nye had dealt unto me.

Then I looked up at Nye,
   And he gazed upon me;
And he rose with a sigh,
   And said, "Can this be?
We are ruined by Chinese cheap labor—"
   And he went for that heathen Chinee.

In the scene that ensued
   I did not take a hand;
But the floor it was strewed
   Like the leaves on the strand
With the cards that Ah Sin had been hiding,
   In the game "he did not understand."

In his sleeves, which were long,
  He had twenty-four. packs—
Which was coming it strong,
  Yet I state but the facts;
And we found on his nails, which were taper,
  What is frequent in tapers—that's wax.

Which is why I remark,
  And my language is plain,
That for ways that are dark,
  And for tricks that are vain,
The heathen Chinee is peculiar—
  Which the same I am free to maintain.

FRANCIS BRET HARTE

THE WILLOWS

The skies they were ashen and sober,
  The streets they were dirty and drear;
It was night in the month of October,
  Of my most immemorial year;
Like the skies I was perfectly sober,
  As I stopped at the mansion of Shear,—
At the "Nightingale,"—perfectly sober,
  And the willowy woodland, down here.

Here once in an alley Titanic
  Of Ten-pins,—I roamed with my soul,—
  Of Ten-pins,—with Mary, my soul;
They were days when my heart was volcanic,
  And impelled me to frequently roll,
  And made me resistlessly roll,
Till my ten-strikes created a panic
  In the realms of the Boreal pole,
Till my ten-strikes created a panic
  With the monkey atop of his pole.

I repeat, I was perfectly sober,
  But my thoughts they were palsied and sear,—

My thoughts were decidedly queer;
 For I knew not the month was October,
  And I marked not the night of the year;
I forgot that sweet *morçeau* of Auber
  That the band oft performèd down here;
And I mixed the sweet music of Auber
  With the Nightingale's music by Shear.

And now as the night was senescent,
  And star-dials pointed to morn,
  And car-drivers hinted of morn,
At the end of the path a liquescent
  And bibulous lustre was born:
'Twas made by the bar-keeper present,
  Who mixèd a duplicate horn,—
His two hands describing a crescent
  Distinct with a duplicate horn.

And I said: "This looks perfectly regal;
  For it's warm, and I know I feel dry,—
  I am confident that I feel dry.
We have come past the emeu and eagle,
  And watched the gay monkey on high;
Let us drink to the emeu and eagle,—
  To the swan and the monkey on high—
  To the eagle and monkey on high;
For this bar-keeper will not inveigle,—
  Bully boy with the vitreous eye;
He surely would never inveigle,—
  Sweet youth with the crystalline eye."

But Mary, uplifting her finger,
  Said, "Sadly this bar I mistrust,—
  I fear that this bar does not trust.
Oh, hasten! oh, let us not linger!
  Oh, fly!—let us fly—ere we must!"
In terror she cried, letting sink her
  Parasol till it trailed in the dust,—

In agony sobbed, letting sink her
   Parasol till it trailed in the dust,—
   Till it sorrowfully trailed in the dust.

Then I pacified Mary, and kissed her,
   And tempted her into the room,
   And conquer'd her scruples and gloom;
And we passed to the end of the vista,
   But were stopped by the warning of doom—
   By some words that were warning of doom.
And I said, "What is written, sweet sister,
   At the opposite end of the room?"
She sobbed, as she answered, "All liquors
   Must be paid for ere leaving the room."

Then my heart it grew ashen and sober,
   As the streets were deserted and drear—
   For my pockets were empty and drear;
And I cried, "It was surely October,
   On this very night of last year,
   That I journeyed—I journeyed down here—
   That I brought a fair maiden down here,
   On this night of all nights in the year.
   Ah! to me that inscription is clear:
   Well I know now I'm perfectly sober,
Why no longer they credit me here,—
   Well I know now that music of Auber,
And this Nightingale, kept by one Shear."

                         FRANCIS BRET HARTE

ANOTHER CYNICAL VARIATION

Gerald kissed me[1] when he left,
   Just before I put the cat out;[2]
Time, you thief, who are so deft
   In culling sweet things, please leave *that* out!

[1] On the hand!
[2] Indicating late hour in the evening.

Say I'm happy, never bored,[3]
   Say that pain and toil have missed me,[4]
Say I'm young and strong,[5] but Lord
   Gerald kissed me[1]!

HELEN

[3] Never?—well—hardly ever.
[4] Untrue.
[5] Not as young and strong as I used to be.

CULTURE IN THE SLUMS

Inscribed to an Intense Poet

I. RONDEAU

"O crikey, Bill!" she ses to me, she ses.
   "Look sharp," ses she, "with them there sossiges.
Yea! sharp with them there bags of mysteree!
For lo!" she ses, "for lo! old pal," ses she,
   "I'm blooming peckish, neither more nor less."

Was it not prime—I leave you all to guess
How prime!—to have a Jude in love's distress
   Come spooning round, and murmuring balmilee,
"O crikey, Bill!"

For in such rorty wise doth Love express
His blooming views, and asks for your address,
   And makes it right, and does the gay and free
   I kissed her—I did so! And her and me
Was pals. And if that ain't good business,
"O crikey, Bill!"

II. VILLANELLE

Now ain't they utterly too-too
   (She ses, my Missus mine, ses she),
Them flymy little bits of Blue.

Joe, just you kool 'em—nice and skew
   Upon our old meogginee,
Now ain't they utterly too-too?

They're better than a pot'n' a screw,
    They're equal to a Sunday spree,
Them flymy little bits of Blue!

Suppose I put 'em up the flue,
    And booze the profits, Joe? Not me.
Now ain't they utterly too-too?

I do the 'Igh Art fake, I do.
    Joe, I'm consummate; and I *see*
Them flymy little bits of Blue.

Which Joe, is why I ses ter you—
    Aesthetic-like, and limp, and free—
Now *ain't* they utterly too-too,
Them flymy little bits of Blue?

III. BALLADE

I often does a quiet read
    At Booty Shelly's poetry;
I thinks that Swinburne at a screed
    Is really almost too too fly;
    At Signor Vagna's harmony
I likes a merry little flutter;
    I've had at Pater many a shy;
In fact, my form's the Bloomin' Utter.

My mark's a tidy little feed,
    And 'Enery Irving's gallery,
To see old 'Amlick do a bleed,
    And Ellen Terry on the die,
    Or Frankey's ghostes at hi-spy,
And parties carried on a shutter.
    Them vulgar Coupeaus is my eye!
In fact, my form's the Bloomin' Utter.

The Grosvenor's nuts—it is, indeed!
    I goes for 'Olman 'Unt like pie.

It's equal to a friendly lead
    To see B. Jones's judes go by.
    Stanhope he make me fit to cry.
Whistler he makes me melt like butter.
    Strudwick he makes me flash my cly—
In fact, mv form's the Bloomin' Utter.

ENVOY

    I'm on for any Art that's 'Igh;
I talks as quiet as I can splutter;
    I keeps a Dado on the sly;
In fact, my form's the Bloomin' Utter.
                    WILLIAM ERNEST HENLEY

VILLON'S STRAIGHT TIP TO ALL CROSS COVES

"Tout aux tavernes et aux fiells"

Suppose you screeve? or go cheap-jack?
    Or fake the broads? or fig a nag?
Or thimble-rig? or knap a yack?
    Or pitch a snide? or smash a rag?
    Suppose you duff? or nose and lag?
Or get the straight, and land your pot?
    How do you melt the multy swag?
Booze and the blowens cop the lot.

Fiddle, or fence, or mace, or mack;
    Or moskeneer, or flash the drag;
Dead-lurk a crib, or do a crack;
    Pad with a slang, or chuck a fag;
    Bonnet, or tout, or mump and gag;
Rattle the tats, or mark the spot;
    You cannot bag a single stag;
Booze and the blowens cop the lot.

Suppose you try a different tack,
  And on the square you flash your flag?
At penny-a-lining make your whack,
  Or with the mummers mug and gag?
  For nix, for nix the dibbs you bag!
At any graft, no matter what,
  Your merry goblins soon stravag:
Booze and the blowens cop the lot.

THE MORAL

It's up the spout and Charley Wag
With wipes and tickers and what not
  Until the squeezer nips your scrag,
Booze and the blowens cop the lot.

WILLIAM ERNEST HENLEY

OUR VILLAGE.—BY A VILLAGER

Our village, that's to say not Miss Mitford's village, but our
  village of Bullock Smithy,
Is come into by an avenue of trees, three oak pollards, two
  elders and a withy;
And in the middle there's a green of about not exceeding an
  acre and a half;
It's common to all, and fed off by nineteen cows, six ponies,
  three horses, five asses, two foals, seven pigs and a calf.
Besides a pond in the middle, which is held by a similar sort
  of common law lease,
And contains twenty ducks, six drakes, three ganders, two
  dead dogs, four drowned kittens, and twelve geese.
Of course the green's cropt very close, and does famous for
  bowling when the little village boys play at cricket;
Only some horse or pig, or cow, or great jackass, is sure to
  come and stand right before the wicket;
There's fifty-five private houses, let alone barns and work-
  shops and pigstyes and poultry huts and such-like sheds;
With plenty of public-houses—two Foxes, one Green Man,
  three Bunch of Grapes, one Crown, and six King's Heads.

The Green Man is reckoned the best, as the only one that
  for love or money can raise
A postilion, a blue jacket, two deplorable lame white horses,
  and a ramshackled "neat post-chaise."
There's one parish church for all the people, whatsoever may
  be their ranks in life or their degrees,
Except one very damp, small, dark, freezing-cold Methodist
  Chapel of Ease;
And close by the churchyard there's a stone-mason's yard,
  that when the time is seasonable
Will furnish with afflictions sore and marble urns and
  cherubims very cheap and reasonable;
There's a cage, comfortable enough, I've been in it with old
  Jack Jeffreys and Tom Pike;
For the Green Man next door will send you in ale, gin, or
  anything else you like;
I can't speak of the stocks, as nothing remains of them but
  the upright post,
But the Pound is kept in repair for the sake of Cob's horse,
  as is always there almost;
There's a smithy of course, where that queer sort of a chap
  in his way, old Joe Bradley,
Perpetually hammers and stammers, for he stutters and
  shoes horses very badly.
There's a shop of sorts, that sells everything, kept by the
  widow of Mr. Task.
But when you go there, it's ten to one she's out of everything
  you ask;
You'll know her house by the swarm of boys, like flies, about
  the old sugary cask;
There are six empty houses, and not so well papered inside
  as out;
For the billstickers won't beware, but stick notices of sales
  and election placards all about;
There's the Doctor's with a green door, where the garden
  pots in the windows are seen,
A weakly monthly rose that won't blow, and a dead geranium,
  and a tea-plant with five black leaves and one green.

As for hollyoaks at the cottage doors, and honey-suckles and
   jasmines, you may go and whistle;
But the Tailor's front garden grows two cabbages, a dock, a
   ha'porth of pennyroyal, two dandelions, and a thistle.
There are three small orchards—Mr. Busby's the school-
   master's is the chief—
With two pear-trees that don't bear; one plum and an apple,
   that every year is stripped by a thief.
There's another small day-school too, kept by the respectable
   Mrs. Gaby.
A select establishment, for six little boys and one big, and
   four little girls and a baby;
There's a rectory, with pointed gables and strange odd chim-
   neys that never smokes,
For the rector don't live on his living like other Christian
   kind of folks;
There's a barber's once a week filled with rough, black-
   bearded, shock-headed churls,
And a window with two feminine men's heads, and two
   masculine ladies in false curls;
There's a butcher's, and a carpenter's, and a plumbers's and
   a small green-grocer's and a baker,
But he won't bake on Sunday, and there's a sexton that's a
   coal-merchant besides, and an undertaker;
And a toyshop, but not a whole one, for a village can't compare with the London shops;
One window sells drums, dolls, kites, carts, bats, Clout's
   balls, and the other sells malt and hops.
And Mrs. Brown, in domestic economy not to be a bit behind
   her betters,
Lets her house to a milliner, a watchmaker, a rat-catcher, a
   cobbler, lives in it herself, and it's the post-office for
   letters.
Now I've gone through all the village—aye, from end to end,
   save and except one more house,
But I haven't come to that—and I hope I never shall—and
   that's the Village Poor House!

                                        THOMAS HOOD

THE WEDDING

Lady Clara Vere de Vere!
I hardly know what I must say,
But I'm to be Queen of the May, mother,
I'm to be Queen of the May!
I am half-crazed; I don't feel grave,
    Let me rave!

Whole weeks and months, early and late,
To win his love I lay in wait.
    Oh, the Earl was fair to see,
    As fair as any man could be;—
    The wind is howling in turret and tree

We two shall be wed tomorrow morn,
    And I shall be the Lady Clare,
And when my marriage morn shall fall,
    I hardly know what I shall wear.
    But I shan't say "my life is dreary,"
      And sadly hang my head,
    With the remark, "I'm very weary,
      And wish that I were dead."

But on my husband's arm I'll lean,
    And roundly waste his plenteous gold,
Passing the honeymoon serene
    In that new world which is the old.
For down we'll go and take the boat
Beside St. Katherine's docks afloat,
Which round about its prow has wrote—
    "The Lady of Shalotter"
(Mondays and Thursdays,—Captain Foat),
    Bound for the Dam of Rotter.
              THOMAS HOOD, JR.

PENNY WHISTLE BLUES

I haven't got a cent,
I haven't got a sou,
I haven't got a red,
I haven't got you.
I've lost my Mammy,
I've lost my Pappy,
I'm feeling very blue,
And unhappy.

E. H. L. ISLAND

ANSWER TO MASTER WITHER'S SONG, "SHALL I, WASTING IN DESPAIR?"

Shall I, mine affections slack,
'Cause I see a woman's black?
Or myself, with care cast down,
'Cause I see a woman brown?
Be she blacker than the night,
Or the blackest jet in sight!
    If she be not so to me,
    What care I how black she be?

Shall my foolish heart be burst,
'Cause I see a woman's curst?
Or a thwarting hoggish nature
Joinèd in as bad a feature?
Be she curst or fiercer than
Brutish beast, or savage man!
    If she be not so to me,
    What care I how curst she be?

Shall a woman's vices make
Me her vices quite forsake?
Or her faults to me made known,
Make me think that I have none?

Be she of the most accurst,
And deserve the name of worst!
  If she be not so to me,
  What care I how bad she be?

'Cause her fortunes seem too low,
Shall I therefore let her go?
He that bears an humble mind
And with riches can be kind,
Think how kind a heart he'd have,
If he were some servile slave!
  And if that same mind I see
  What care I how poor she be?

Poor, or bad, or curst, or black,
I will ne'er the more be slack!
If she hate me (then believe!)
She shall die ere I will grieve!
If she like me when I woo
I can like and love her too!
  If that she be fit for me!
  What care I what others be?

BEN JONSON

"AMERICA, I LOVE YOU"

Between fields of pop-corn,
'Twas just a little under
A hundred years or less,
A handful of people
They took lots of bother
To raise this country up.
It's now quite a village,
It's altogether separate
And free from every czar.
It's your place, it's my place,
A great place to die in.
I sing this song because:

CHORUS

United States, I like you.
You're like an uncle to I'm;
From mountain to river
To you my affection
Is touching each hemisphere.
Just like a new-born children
Climbing his father's lap,
America, how are you?
And there's a hundred people feeling the same.

The A stands for our navy,
The M for the soldiers we got,
The E for the heagle which flies up above you,
The R for you can't go wrong,
The I for hindependence,
The C stands for brave and bold—
The A for America, I like you!
Don't bite the hand that's feeding you.

BERT KALMAR AND HARRY RUBY

SPENSERIAN STANZAS ON CHARLES ARMITAGE BROWN

I

He is to weet a melancholy carle:
Thin in the waist, with bushy head of hair,
As hath the seeded thistle, when a parle
It holds with Zephyr, ere it sendeth fair
Its light balloons into the summer air;
Thereto his beard had not begun to bloom,
No brush had touched his chin, or razor sheer;
No care had touched his cheek with mortal doom,
But new he was, and bright, as scarf from Persian loom.

II

Ne carèd he for wine, or half and half;
Ne carèd he for fish, or flesh, or fowl;

And sauces held he worthless as the chaff,
He 'sdeigned the swine-head at the wassail-bowl:
Ne with lewd ribbalds sat he cheek by jowl;
Ne with sly lemans in the scorner's chair;
But after water-brooks this pilgrim's soul
Panted, and all his food was woodland air;
Though he would oft-times feast on gilliflowers rare

III

The slang of cities in no wise he knew,
Tipping the wink to him was heathen Greek;
He sipped no "olden Tom," or "ruin blue,"
Or Nantz, or cherry-brandy, drank full meek
By many a damsel brave, and rouge of cheek;
Nor did he know each aged watchman's beat,
Nor in obscurèd purlieus would he seek
For curlèd Jewesses, with ankles neat,
Who, as they walk abroad, make tinkling with their feet.

JOHN KEATS

IF I SHOULD DIE TO-NIGHT

If I should die to-night
And you should come to my cold corpse and say,
Weeping and heartsick o'er my lifeless clay—
If I should die to-night,
And you should come in deepest grief and woe—
And say: "Here's that ten dollars that I owe,"
I might arise in my large white cravat
And say, "What's that?"

If I should die to-night
And you should come to my cold corpse and kneel,
Clasping my bier to show the grief you feel,
I say, if I should die to-night
And you should come to me, and there and then

Just even hint 'bout paying me that ten,
  I might arise the while,
  But I'd drop dead again.

BEN KING

THE WIDE OPEN SPACES

The hot September sun shone down on the wide and peaceful
    bay,
Where the mighty fleet of England in warlike grandeur lay,
With its lines of black mouthed cannon, and its crews of
    white capped men,
But never a ship of all the fleet so staunch as the Jolly Jen.
But Marion, fair Marion, she had no thought of fear
As she leaped into the saddle with a loud and ringing cheer,
And then gave spur and rode away across the heathery plain,
And then turned round her palfrey, and rode back home
    again.

What then of the road to Mandalay and the boy with the
    twisted knee,
And other things men read about, but seldom or never see?
And why do the reapers in the fields and the toilers in the
    town
Give up their work with a troubled look, and, thinking, sit
    them down?

And dream of him with his caravan, as he toils the sandy way
Across the wastes of Africa, with never a word to say;
With one hand folded behind him and the other folded before,
And both of them folded together as they were in the days
    of yore?

So peace to the troubled spirit, peace to the heaving breast,
Peace to the Chinese thunder thing that rises in the West,
For the true born poet cares naught for sense and heeds nor
    tide nor time
As long as he makes his meters mete and a fairly passable
    rhyme.

OSCAR H. LEAR

THE REJECTED "NATIONAL HYMNS"

I

BY H - - - Y W. L - NGF - - - - W

Back in the years when Phlagstaff, the Dane, was monarch
　Over the sea-ribb'd land of the fleet-footed Norsemen,
Once there went forth young Ursa to gaze at the heavens—
　Ursa—the noblest of all the Vikings and horsemen.
Musing, he sat in his stirrups and viewed the horizon,
　Where the Aurora lapt stars in a North-polar manner,
Wildly he started,—for there in the heavens before him
　Flutter'd and flam'd the original Star Spangled Banner.

II

BY J - HN GR - - NL - - F WH - - T - - R

My Native Land, thy Puritanic stock
Still finds its roots firm-bound in Plymouth Rock,
And all thy sons unite in one grand wish—
To keep the virtues of Preservèd Fish.

Preservèd Fish, the Deacon stern and true,
Told our New England what her sons should do,
And if they swerve from loyalty and right,
Then the whole land is lost indeed in night.

III

BY DR. OL - V - R W - ND - - L H - LMES

A diagnosis of our hist'ry proves
Our native land a land its native loves;
Its birth a deed obstetric without peer,
Its growth a source of wonder far and near.

To love it more behold how foreign shores
Sink into nothingness beside its stores;
Hyde Park at best—though counted ultra-grand—
The "Boston Common" of Victoria's land.

IV

BY R - LPH W - LDO EM - R - - N

Source immaterial of material naught,
   Focus of light infinitesimal,
Sum of all things by sleepless Nature wrought,
   Of which the normal man is decimal.

Refract, in prism immortal, from thy stars
   To the stars bent incipient on our flag,
The beam translucent, neutrifying death,
   And raise to immortality the rag.

V

BY W - LL - - M C - LL - N B - Y - NT

The sun sinks softly to his Ev'ning Post,
   The sun swells grandly to his morning crown;
Yet not a star our Flag of Heav'n has lost,
   And not a sunset stripe with him goes down.

So thrones may fall, and from the dust of those
   New thrones may rise, to totter like the last;
But still our Country's nobler planet glows
   While the eternal stars of Heaven are fast.

VI

BY N. P. W - LL - IS

One hue of our Flag is taken
   From the cheeks of my blushing Pet,
And its stars beat time and sparkle
   Like the studs on her chemisette.

Its blue in the ocean shadow
   That hides in her dreamy eyes,
It conquers all men, like her,
   And still for a Union flies.

VII

BY TH - M - S B - IL - Y ALD - - CH

The little brown squirrel hops in the corn,
   The cricket quaintly sings,
The emerald pigeon nods his head,
   And the shad in the river springs,
The dainty sunflow'r hangs its head
   On the shore of the summer sea;
And better far that I were dead,
   If Maud did not love me.

I love the squirrel that hops in the corn,
   And the cricket that quaintly sings;
And the emerald pigeon that nods his head,
   And the shad that gaily springs.
I love the dainty sunflow'r, too,
   And Maud with her snowy breast;
I love them all;—but I love—I love—
   I love my country best.

ROBERT H. NEWELL

THE CONTENTED MAN

Happy the man whose wish and care
   A few paternal acres bound,
Content to breathe his native air
           In his own ground.

Whose herds with milk, whose fields with bread,
   Whose flocks supply him with attire;
Whose trees in summer yield him shade,
           In winter, fire.

Blest, who can unconcern'dly find
   Hours, days, and years slide soft away
In health of body, peace of mind,
           Quiet by day,

Sound sleep by night; study and ease
  Together mix'd, sweet recreation
And innocence, which most doth please
                    With meditation.

Thus let me live unseen, unknown;
  Thus, unlamented, let me die;
Steal from the world, and not a stone
                    Tell where I lie.

                                    ALEXANDER POPE

THE DOMICILE OF JOHN

Behold the mansion reared by Daedal Jack!
  See the malt stored in many a plethoric sack,
    In the proud cirque of Ivan's Bivouac!

Mark how the rat's felonious fangs invade
  The golden stores in John's pavilion laid!

Anon, with velvet foot and Tarquin strides,
  Subtle Grimalkin to his quarry glides;
Grimalkin grim, that slew the fierce rodent,
  Whose tooth insidious Johann's sackcloth rent!

Lo! Now the deep-mouthed canine foe's assault!
  That vexed the avenger of the stolen malt,
Stored in the hallowed precincts of that hall,
  That rose complete at Jack's creative call.

Here stalks the impetuous cow with the crumpled horn,
  Whereon the exacerbating hound was torn
Who bayed the feline slaughter-beast that slew
  The rat predaceous, whose keen fangs ran through
The textile fibres that involved the grain
  That lay in Hans' inviolate domain.

Here walks forlorn the damsel crowned with rue,
   Lactiferous spoils from vaccine dugs who drew
Of that corniculate beast whose tortuous horn
   Tossed to the clouds, in fierce vindictive scorn,
The baying hound whose braggart bark and stir
   Arched the lithe spine and reared the indignant fur
Of puss, that, with verminicidal claw,
   Struck the weird rat, in whose insatiate maw
Lay reeking malt, that erst in Juan's courts we saw.

Robed in senescent garb, that seems, in sooth,
   Too long a prey to Chronos' iron tooth,
Behold the man whose amorous lips incline
   Full with young Eros' osculative sign,
To the lorn maiden whose lactalbic hands
   Drew albulactic wealth from lacteal glands
Of that immortal bovine, by whose horn
   Distort, to realms ethereal was borne
The beast catulean, vexer of that sly
   Ulysses quadrupedal, who made die
The old mordaceous rat that dared devour
   Antecedaneous ale in John's domestic bower.

Lo! Here, with hirsute honors doffed, succinct
   Of saponaceous locks, the priest who linked
In Hymen's golden bands the man unthrift
   Whose means exiguous stared from many a rift,
E'en as he kissed the virgin all forlorn
   Who milked the cow with implicated horn,
Who in fierce wrath the canine torturer skied,
   That dared to vex the insidious muricide,
Who let auroral effluence through the pelt
   Of that sly rat that robbed the palace that Jack built.

The loud cantankerous Shanghai comes at last,
   Whose shouts aroused the shorn ecclesiast,
Who sealed the vows of Hymen's sacrament
   To him who, robed in garments indigent,

Exosculates the damsel lachrymose,
  The emulgator of the hornèd brute morose
That on gyrated horn, to heaven's high vault
  Hurled up, with many a tortuous somersault,
The low bone-cruncher, whose hot wrath pursued
  The scratching sneak, that waged eternal feud
With long-tailed burglar, who his lips would smack
  On farinaceous wealth, that filled the halls of Jack.

Vast limbed and broad the farmer comes at length,
  Whose cereal care supplied the vital strength
Of chanticleer, whose matutinal cry
  Roused the quiescent form and ope'd the eye
Of razor-loving cleric, who in bands
  Connubial linked the intermixèd hands
Of him, whose rent apparel gaped apart,
  And the lorn maiden with lugubrious heart,
Her who extraught the exuberant lactic flow
  Of nutriment from that cornigerent cow,
Eumenidal executor of fate,
  That to sidereal altitudes elate
Cerberus, who erst with fang lethiferous
  Left lacerate Grimalkin latebrose—
That killed the rat
  That ate the malt
    That lay in the house that Jack built.

                                    ALEXANDER POPE

LADY JANE

(Sapphics)

Down the green hill-side fro' the castle window
Lady Jane spied Bill Amaranth a-workin';
Day by day watched him go about his ample
                    Nursery garden.

Cabbages thriv'd there, wi' a mort o' green-stuff—
Kidney beans, broad beans, onions, tomatoes,
Artichokes, seakale, vegetable marrows,
Early potatoes.

Lady Jane cared not very much for all these:
What she cared much for was a glimpse o' Willum
Strippin' his brown arms wi' a view to horti-
Cultural effort.

Little guessed Willum, never extra-vain, that
Up the green hill-side, i' the gloomy castle,
Feminine eyes could so delight to view his
Noble proportions.

Only one day while, in an innocent mood,
Moppin' his brow (cos 'twas a trifle sweaty)
With a blue kerchief—lo, he spies a white 'un
Coyly responding.

Oh, delightsome Love! Not a jot do *you* care
For the restrictions set on human inter-
course by cold-blooded social refiners;
Nor do I, neither.

Day by day, peepin' fro' behind the bean-sticks,
Willum observed that scrap o' white a-wavin'
Till his hot sighs out-growin' all repression
Busted his weskit.

Lady Jane's guardian was a haughty Peer, who
Clung to old creeds and had a nasty temper;
Can we blame Willum that he hardly cared to
Risk a refusal?

Year by year found him busy 'mid the bean-sticks
Wholly uncertain how on earth to take steps.
Thus for eighteen years he beheld the maiden
Wave fro' her window.

But the nineteenth spring, i' the Castle post-bag,
Came by book-post Bill's catalogue o' seedlings
Mark'd wi' blue ink at "Paragraphs relatin'
　　　　　　　　Mainly to Pumpkins."

"W. A. can," so the Lady Jane read,
"Strongly commend that very noble Gourd, the
Lady Jane, first-class medal, ornamental;
　　　　　　　　Grows to a great height."

Scarce a year arter, by the scented hedgerows—
Down the mown hill-side, fro' the castle gateway—
Came a long train and, i' the midst, a black bier,
　　　　　　　　Easily shoulder'd.

"Whose is yon corse that, thus adorned wi' gourd-leaves
Forth ye bear with slow step?" A mourner answer'd,
"'Tis the poor clay-cold body Lady Jane grew
　　　　　　　　Tired to abide in."

"Delve my grave quick, then, for I die to-morrow.
Delve it one furlong fro' the kidney bean-sticks,
Where I may dream she's goin' on precisely
　　　　　　　　As she was used to."

Hardly died Bill when, fro' the Lady Jane's grave,
Crept to his white death-bed a lovely pumpkin:
Climb'd the house wall and over-arch'd his head wi'
　　　　　　　　Billowy verdure.

Simple this tale!—but delicately perfumed
As the sweet roadside honeysuckle. That's why,
Difficult though its metre was to tackle,
　　　　　　　　I'm glad I wrote it.
　　　　　　　　　　ARTHUR T. QUILLER-COUCH

ROMEO AND JULIET

Hark to the story of poor Romeo!
      Poor Romeo! Poor Romeo!
Cribbed out of Shakespeare and reeking with woe!
      Reeking with woe! 'king with woe!
If you have tears, now prepare to get at one;
Ne'er was a story so mournful as that one.
Juliet's the slim one and Romeo's the fat one,
      Poor Romeo! Romeo!

I am the hero of this little tale,
      I'm Romeo! I'm Romeo!
I am that highly susceptible male,
      I'm Romeo! Romeo!
Scarce did a lover e'er do as I did
When his girl into eternity slided;
I took cold poison and I suicided,
      I'm Romeo! Romeo!

I am the heroine of this tale of woe,
      I'm Juliet! I'm Juliet!
I am the darling that mashed Romeo,
      I'm Juliet! Juliet!
Locked in a tomb with no pickaxe to force it,
Gloomy old hole without room to stand *or* sit,
I up and stabbed myself right in the corset,
      I'm Juliet! Juliet!

This of our tale is the short and the long,
      I'm Romeo! I'm Juliet!
Here is the moral that goes with the song,
      I'm Romeo, Juliet!
Lovers, we warn you of daggers be wary,
Don't buy your drinks of an apothecary,
Don't stab yourselves in the left pulmonary,
      I'm Romeo, Juliet!

                    FRED NEWTON SCOTT

MARY AND THE LAMB

Mary,—what melodies mingle
    To murmur her musical name!
It makes all one's finger-tips tingle
    Like fagots, the food of the flame;
About her an ancient tradition
    A romance delightfully deep
Has woven in juxtaposition
    With one little sheep,—

One dear little lamb that would follow
    Her footsteps, unwearily fain.
Down dale, over hill, over hollow,
    To school and to hamlet again;
A gentle companion, whose beauty
    Consisted in snow-driven fleece,
And whose most imperative duty
    Was keeping the peace.

His eyes were as beads made of glassware,
    His lips were coquettishly curled,
His capers made many a lass swear
    His caper-sauce baffled the world;
His tail had a wag when it relished
    A sip of the milk in the pail,—
And this fact has largely embellished
    The wag of this tale.

One calm summer day when the sun was
    A great golden globe in the sky,
One mild summer morn when the fun was
    Unspeakably clear in his eye,
He tagged after exquisite Mary,
    And over the threshold of school
He tripped in a temper contrary,
    And splintered the rule.

A great consternation was kindled
  Among all the scholars, and some
Confessed their affection had dwindled
  For lamby, and looked rather glum;
But Mary's schoolmistress quick beckoned
  The children away from the jam,
And said, *sotto voce*, she reckoned
  That Mame loved the lamb.

Then all up the spine of the rafter
  There ran a most risible shock,
And sorrow was sweetened with laughter
  At this little lamb of the flock;
And out spoke the schoolmistress Yankee,
  With rather a New Hampshire whine,
"Dear pupils, sing Moody and Sankey,
  Hymn 'Ninety and Nine.'"

Now after this music had finished,
  And silence again was restored,
The ardor of lamby diminished,
  His quips for a moment were floored.
Then cried he, "Bah-ed children, you blundered
  When singing that psalmistry, quite.
I'm labelled by Mary, 'Old Hundred,'
  And I'm labelled right."

Then vanished the lambkin in glory,
  A halo of books round his head:
What furthermore happened the story,
  Alackaday! cannot be said.
And Mary, the musical maid, is
  To-day but a shadow in time;
Her epitaph, too, I'm afraid is
  Writ only in rhyme.

She's sung by the cook at her ladle
  That stirs up the capering sauce;

She's sung by the nurse at the cradle
    When ba-ba is restless and cross;
And lamby, whose virtues were legion,
    Dwells ever in songs that we sing,
He makes a nice dish in this region
    To eat in the spring!

FRANK DEMPSTER SHERMAN

THE OLD HOKUM BUNCOMBE

How dear to my heart are the grand politicians
    Who constantly strive for the popular votes,
Indulging in platitudes, trite repetitions,
    And time-honored bromides surrounded with quotes;
Though equally verbose opponents assail them
    With bitter invective, they never can quell
The force of the buncombe, which never will fail them—
    The old hokum buncombe we all know so well.
The old hokum buncombe,
The iron-clad buncombe,
    The moss-covered buncombe we all know so well.

They aim to make friends of the laboring classes—
    The trust of the people is sacred with them—
They swear that they're slaves to the will of the masses,
    They hem and they haw, and they haw and they hem;
They rave with a vehemence almost terrific,
    There isn't a doubt which they cannot dispel,
They revel in orgies of hope beatific—
    And serve us the buncombe we all know so well.
The old hokum buncombe,
The iron-clad buncombe,
    The moss-covered buncombe we all know so well.

Their torrents of words are a sure paregoric
    For all of the ills to which mankind is prey.
They pose as a Hamlet lamenting the Yorick
    Who typifies that which their rivals betray.

They picture perfection in every effusion;
  We gaze at Utopia under their spell,
And though it is only an optic illusion—
  We fall for the buncombe we all know so well.
The old hokum buncombe,
The iron-clad buncombe,
  The moss-covered buncombe we all love so well.
                              ROBERT E. SHERWOOD

HOW THEY DO IT

Mr. W. H. Davies

A poor old man
  Who has no bread,
He nothing can
  To get a bed.

He has a cough,
  Bad boots he has;
He takes them off
  Upon the grass.

He does not eat
  In cosy inns
But keeps his meat
  In salmon tins.

No oven hot,
  No frying-pan;
Thank God I'm not
  That poor old man.

Sir Henry Newbolt

It was eight bells in the forenoon and hammocks running sleek
  (*It's a fair sea flowing from the West*),
When the little Commodore came a-sailing up the Creek
  (*Heave Ho! I think you'll know the rest*).

Thunder in the halyards and horses leaping high,
Blake and Drake and Nelson are listenin' where they lie,
Four and twenty blackbirds a-bakin' in a pie,
　　And the *Pegasus* came waltzing from the West.

Now the little Commodore sat steady on his keel
　　(*It's a fair sea flowing from the West*),
A heart as stout as concrete reinforced with steel
　　(*Heave Ho! I think you'll know the rest*).
Swinging are the scuppers, hark, the rudder snores,
Plugging at the Frenchmen, downing 'em by scores.
Porto Rico, Vera Cruz, and also the Azores,
　　And the *Pegasus* came waltzing from the West.

So three cheers more for the little Commodore
　　(*It's a fair sea flowing from the West*).
I tell you so again as I've told you so before
　　(*Heigh Ho! I think you know the rest*).
Aged is the Motherland, old but she is young
(Easy with the tackle there—don't release the bung),
And I sang a song like all the songs that I have ever sung
　　When the *Pegasus* came sailing from the West.

J. C. SQUIRE

IMITATION OF ROBERT BROWNING

Birthdays? yes, in a general way;
For the most if not for the best of men:
You were born (I suppose) on a certain day:
So was I: or perhaps in the night: what then?

Only this: or at least, if more
You must know, not think it, and learn, not speak;
There is truth to be found on the unknown shore,
And many will find where few will seek.

For many are called and few are chosen,
And the few grow many as ages lapse:

But when will the many grow few: what dozen
Is fused into one by Time's hammer-taps?

A bare brown stone in a babbling brook:—
It was wanton to hurl it there, you say:
And the moss, which clung in the sheltered nook
(Yet the stream runs cooler) is washed away.

That begs the question: many a prater
Thinks such a suggestion a sound "stop thief!"
Which, may I ask, do you think the greater,
Sergeant-at-arms or a Robber Chief?

And if it were not so? still you doubt?
Ah! yours is a birthday indeed if so.
That were something to write a poem about,
If one thought a little. I only know.

P. S.

There's a Me Society down at Cambridge,
Where my works, *cum notis variorum*,
Are talked about; well, I require the same bridge
That Euclid took toll at as *Asinorum*.

And, as they have got through several ditties
I thought were as stiff as a brick-built wall,
I've composed the above, and a stiff one *it* is,
A bridge to stop asses at, once for all.

                                   JAMES KENNETH STEPHEN

SINCERE FLATTERY

Of W. W. (Americanus)

The clear cool note of the cuckoo which has ousted the
    legitimate nest-holder,
The whistle of the railway guard dispatching the train to the
    inevitable collision,
The maiden's monosyllabic reply to a polysyllabic proposal,
The fundamental note of the last trump, which is presum-
    ably D natural;
All of these are sounds to rejoice in, yea, to let your very
    ribs re-echo with:
But better than all of them is the absolutely last chord of the
    apparently inexhaustible pianoforte player.

JAMES KENNETH STEPHEN

THE MODERN HIAWATHA

From "The Song of Milkanwatha"

He killed the noble Mudjokivis,
With the skin he made him mittens,
Made them with the fur side inside,
Made them with the skin side outside,
He, to get the warm side inside,
Put the inside skin side outside:
He, to get the cold side outside,
Put the warm side fur side inside:
That's why he put the fur side inside,
Why he put the skin side outside,
Why he turned them inside outside.

GEORGE A. STRONG

NEPHELIDIA

From the depth of the dreamy decline of the dawn through
    a notable nimbus of nebulous moonshine,
  Pallid and pink as the palm of the flag-flower that flickers
    with fear of the flies as they float,
Are they looks of our lovers that lustrously lean from a
    marvel of mystic miraculous moonshine,
  These that we feel in the blood of our blushes that thicken
    and threaten with throbs through the throat?
Thicken and thrill as a theatre thronged at appeal of an
    actor's appalled agitation,
  Fainter with fear of the fires of the future than pale with
    the promise of pride in the past;
Flushed with the famishing fulness of fever that reddens
    with radiance of rathe recreation,
  Gaunt as the ghastliest of glimpses that gleam through
    the gloom of the gloaming when ghosts go aghast?
Nay, for the nick of the tick of the time is a tremulous touch
    on the temples of terror,
  Strained as the sinews yet strenuous with strife of the dead
    who is dumb as the dust-heaps of death;
Surely no soul is it, sweet as the spasm of erotic emotional
    exquisite error,
  Bathed in the balms of beatified bliss, beatific itself by
    beatitude's breath.
Surely no spirit or sense of a soul that was soft to the spirit
    and soul of our senses
  Sweetens the stress of surprising suspicion that sobs in the
    semblance and sound of a sigh;
Only this oracle opens Olympian, in mystical moods and
    triangular tenses,—
  "Life is the lust of a lamp for the light that is dark till the
    dawn of the day when we die."
Mild is the mirk and monotonous music of memory, melodi-
    ously mute as it may be,
  While the hope in the heart of a hero is bruised by the
    breach of men's rapiers, resigned to the rod;

Made meek as a mother whose bosom-beats bound with the
  bliss-bringing bulk of a balm-breathing baby,
As they grope through the grave-yard of creeds, under
  skies growing green at a groan for the grimness of God.
Blank is the book of his bounty beholden of old, and its
  binding is blacker than bluer:
Out of blue into black is the scheme of the skies, and their
  dews are the wine of the bloodshed of things:
Till the darkling desire of delight shall be free as a fawn
  that is freed from the fangs that pursue her,
Till the heart-beats of hell shall be hushed by a hymn from
  the hunt that has harried the kennel of kings.
                               ALGERNON CHARLES SWINBURNE

OLD FASHIONED FUN

When that old joke was new,
  It was not hard to joke,
And puns we now pooh-pooh,
  Great laughter would provoke.

True wit was seldom heard,
  And humor shown by few,
When reign'd King George the Third,
  And that old joke was new.

It passed indeed for wit,
  Did this achievement rare,
When down your friend would sit,
  To steal away his chair.

You brought him to the floor,
  You bruised him black and blue,
And this would cause a roar,
  When your old joke was new.
                               W. M. THACKERAY

"WHEN MOONLIKE ORE THE HAZURE SEAS"

When moonlike ore the hazure seas
  In soft effulgence swells,
When silver jews and balmy breaze
  Bend down the Lily's bells;
When calm and deap, the rosy sleap
  Has lapt your soal in dreems,
R Hangeline! R lady mine!
  Dost thou remember Jeames?

I mark thee in the Marble All,
  Where England's loveliest shine—
I say the fairest of them hall
  Is Lady Hangeline.
My soul, in desolate eclipse,
  With recollection teems—
And then I hask, with weeping lips,
  Dost thou remember Jeames?

Away! I may not tell thee hall
  This soughring heart endures—
There is a lonely sperrit-call
  That Sorrow never cures;
There is a little, little Star,
  That still above me beams;
It is the Star of Hope—but ar!
  Dost thou remember Jeames?

W. M. THACKERAY

THE WILLOW-TREE

ANOTHER VERSION

Long by the willow-trees
  Vainly they sought her,
Wild rang the mother's screams
  O'er the gray water:
Where is my lovely one?
  Where is my daughter?

"Rouse thee, Sir Constable—
    Rouse thee and look;
Fisherman, bring your net,
    Boatman, your hook.
Beat in the lily-beds,
    Dive in the brook!"

Vainly the constable
    Shouted and called her;
Vainly the fisherman
    Beat the green alder;
Vainly he flung the net,
    Never it hauled her!

Mother beside the fire
    Sat, her nightcap in;
Father, in easy chair,
    Gloomily napping,
When at the window-sill
    Came a light tapping!

And a pale countenance
    Looked through the casement,
Loud beat the mother's heart,
    Sick with amazement,
And at the vision which
    Came to surprise her,
Shrieked in an agony—
    "Lor'! it's Elizar!"

Yes, 'twas Elizabeth—
    Yes, 'twas their girl;
Pale was her cheek, and her
    Hair out of curl.
"Mother," the loving one,
    Blushing exclaimed,
"Let not your innocent
    Lizzy be blamed.

"Yesterday, going to Aunt
    Jones's to tea,
Mother, dear mother, I
    Forgot the door-key!
And as the night was cold
    And the way steep,
Mrs. Jones kept me to
    Breakfast and sleep."

Whether her Pa and Ma
    Fully believed her,
That we shall never know,
    Stern they received her;
And for the work of that
    Cruel, though short, night
Sent her to bed without
    Tea for a fortnight.

MORAL

Hey diddle diddlety,
    Cat and the fiddlety,
Maidens of England, take caution by she!
    Let love and suicide
    Never tempt you aside,
And always remember to take the door-key.
                       W. M. THACKERAY

JUSTICE TO SCOTLAND

AN UNPUBLISHED POEM BY BURNS

O mickle yeuks the keckle doup,
    An' a' unsicker girns the graith,
For wae and wae! the crowdies loup
    O'er jouk an' hallan, braw an' baith
Where ance the coggie hirpled fair,
    And blithesome poortith toomed the loof,
There's nae a burnie giglet rare
    But blaws in ilka jinking coof.

The routhie bield that gars the gear
   Is gone where glint the pawky een.
And aye the stound is birkin lear
   Where sconnered yowies wheeped yestreen,
The creeshie rax wi' skelpin' kaes
   Nae mair the howdie bicker whangs,
Nor weanies in their wee bit claes
   Glour light as lammies wi' their sangs.

Yet leeze me on my bonny byke!
   My drappie aiblins blinks the noo,
An' leesome luve has lapt the dyke
   Forgatherin' just a wee bit fou.
And Scotia! while thy rantin' lunt
   Is mirk and moop with gowans fine,
I'll stowlins pit my unco brunt,
   An' cleek my duds for auld lang syne.

UNKNOWN

YOUNG LOCHINVAR

THE TRUE STORY IN BLANK VERSE

Oh! young Lochinvar has come out of the West,
Thro' all the wide border his horse has no equal,
Having cost him forty-five dollars at the market,
Where good nags, fresh from the country,
With burrs still in their tails are selling
For a song; and save his good broad sword
He weapon had none, except a seven-shooter
Or two, a pair of brass knuckles, and an Arkansaw

Toothpick in his boot, so, comparatively speaking,
He rode all unarmed, and he rode all alone,
Because there was no one going his way.
He stayed not for brake, and he stopped not for
Toll-gates; he swam the Eske River where ford
There was none, and saved fifteen cents
In ferriage, but lost his pocket-book, containing
Seventeen dollars and a half, by the operation.

Ere he alighted at the Netherby mansion
He stopped to borrow a dry suit of clothes,
And this delayed him considerably, so when
He arrived the bride and consented—the gallant
Came late—for a laggard in love and a dastard in war
Was to wed the fair Ellen, and the guests had assembled.

So, boldly he entered the Netherby Hall
Among bridesmen and kinsmen and brothers and
Brothers-in-law and forty or fifty cousins;
Then spake the bride's father, his hand on his sword
(For the poor craven bridegroom ne'er opened his head)

"Oh, come ye in peace here, or come ye in anger,
Or to dance at our bridal, young Lord Lochinvar?"
"I long wooed your daughter, and she will tell you
I have the inside track in the free-for-all
For her affections! my suit you denied; but let
That pass, while I tell you, old fellow, that love
Swells like the Solway, but ebbs like its tide,
And now I am come with this lost love of mine
To lead but one measure, drink one glass of beer;
There are maidens in Scotland more lovely by far
That would gladly be bride to yours very truly."

The bride kissed the goblet, the knight took it up,
He quaffed off the nectar and threw down the mug,
Smashing it into a million pieces, while
He remarked that he was the son of a gun
From Seven-up and run the Number Nine.
She looked down to blush, but she looked up again
For she well understood the wink in his eye;
He took her soft hand ere her mother could
Interfere, "Now tread we a measure; first four
Half right and left; swing," cried young Lochinvar.

One touch to her hand and one word in her ear,
When they reached the hall door and the charger

Stood near on three legs eating post hay;
So light to the croup the fair lady he swung,
Then leaped to the saddle before her.
"She is won! we are gone! over bank, bush, and spar,
They'll have swift steeds that follow"—but in the

Excitement of the moment he had forgotten
To untie the horse, and the poor brute could
Only gallop in a little circus around the
Hitching-post; so the old gent collared
The youth and gave him the awfullest lambasting
That was ever heard of on Canobie Lee;
So dauntless in war and so daring in love,
Have ye e'er heard of gallant like young Lochinvar?

UNKNOWN

FRUSTRATE

(After an evening with Browning, Masefield, Lewis Carroll, and Gertrude
Stein)

I turned to the parlor in panic
    And blurted out, "What must you think?"
She rippled, "Then let me the canick-
        in clink!"

I soared to my feet; it was still dim. . . .
    The moon, like an opal in fright,
Leaned over and whispered, "I killed him
        Last night."

Not an hour to lose; I would save her—
    I fastened my spurs in the air
With the scent of the twilight I gave her
        To wear.

And I thought, with a shriek, of how Friday
    Would burst into corduroy pants—
And I drove like a fiend, and I cried "Day,
        Advance!"

The wind smacked its lips, "Here's a nice treat."
　　The sea was a forest of flame. . . .
And so to the billowy Bye Street
　　　　I came.

The stars at my shoulder were baying:
　　I surged through a hole i' the gate;
And I knew that the Bishop was saying,
　　　　"Too late."
　　　　　* * *
They tell me that no one believed me;
　　I *never* was asked to the feast. . . .
My dears, 'twas the cabby deceived me—
　　　　The beast!
　　　　　　　　　　Louis Untermeyer

THE POSTER GIRL

The blessed Poster girl leaned out
　　From a pinky-purple heaven.
One eye was red and one was green;
　　Her bang was cut uneven;
She had three fingers on her hand,
　　And the hairs on her head were seven.

Her robe, ungirt from clasp to hem,
　　No sunflowers did adorn,
But a heavy Turkish portiere
　　Was very neatly worn;
And the hat that lay along her back
　　Was yellow, like canned corn.

It was a kind of wobbly wave
　　That she was standing on,
And high aloft she flung a scarf
　　That must have weighed a ton;
And she was rather tall—at least
　　She reached up to the sun.

She curved and writhed, and then she said
   Less green of speech than blue:
"Perhaps I *am* absurd—perhaps
   I *don't* appeal to you;
But my artistic worth depends
   Upon the point of view."

I saw her smile, although her eyes
   Were only smudgy smears;
And then she swished her swirling arms,
   And wagged her gorgeous ears.
She sobbed a blue-and-green-checked sob,
   And wept some purple tears.

CAROLYN WELLS

Innocent Merriment

THE CENTIPEDE

I'm very, very glad indeed
I need not feed a centipede;
But I would rather, could I choose,
Feed him than buy his boots and shoes.

SAMUEL HOPKINS ADAMS

REASONS FOR DRINKING

If all be true that I do think,
There are five reasons we should drink;
Good wine—a friend—or being dry—
Or lest we should be by and by—
Or any other reason why.

DR. HENRY ALDRICH

OLD BILL'S MEMORY BOOK

Soundest of all literary legal tenders
Was Harry Leon Wilson's novel "The Spenders."
I was fonder of it—know what I mean?—
Than even of Merton or of Bunker Bean.
I read it at a time when we tiny tots
Were appalled by Thomas Dixon's "The Leopard's Spots";
And my young emotions were sliced and carvered
By Reginald Wright Kauffmann's "Jarvis of Harvard."
Purple with passion, red with strife,
Me and my pal thought, "Gee! That's life!"
But most of all we loved in our backyard shebeen
To smoke cubebs and read the Strand Magazine . . .
To the following statement there's no rebuttal
Swell stuff was Cutliffe Hyne's "Captain Cuttle,"
Though that is a point we can easily settle
Because actually the title was "Captain Kettle!"
But one of the greatest triumphs known to all nations
Were Stanley Wood's ferocious illustrations!

77

And ah, when life was just a-bornung
What a hero to me was E. W. Hornung!
On the stoop in the moonlight singing "Nelly Was a Lady"
Our minds would be dwelling on Old and Young King
    Brady—
And one's parents subscribed (though they'd books by the
    bin)
To the Booklovers' Library and the Tabard Inn;
And even today in the evening damp
I can smell the hot tin of my bicycle lamp;
Yes, and though today I may be dull and brainless,
Once I owned a Columbia Chainless!
A memory that cures my many ills
Is of reading in the bathtub "The Hound of the Baskervilles"
And the very same genius who thereby left me terrored
Also wrote "The Exploits of Brigadier Gerard"—
Also a book Earle Walbridge found for me, in those days
    displayed,
Was concerned with a hospital nurse named Hilda Wade;
And, of course, one of the best juveniles St. Nicholas ever
    gave
To a palpitant young public was dubbed "The White Cave,"
Wherein something was learned by my sister and me:
Which was the Australian hail and call of "Cooee!"
On the Fourth of July, as memory unreels,
I remember bunting around my bicycle wheels;
And in Bethlehem, Pennsylvania, (Moravian anointer
Of my youth) there was a picture of a horse called Star
    Pointer.
And it must have been at Bethlehem's famous hostel about
    that time
That my talented father delivered himself of the following
    rhyme:

> *All hail to the Eagle*
> *That hostelry regal*
> *Where happy we lived*
> *On the third story high—*
> *Where William grew pallid*

On too much shrimp salad,
And Laura had measles
And wanted to die!

WILLIAM ROSE BENÉT

THE WAY TO ARCADY

Oh, what's the way to Arcady,
To Arcady, to Arcady;
Oh, what's the way to Arcady,
Where all the leaves are merry?

Oh, what's the way to Arcady?
The spring is rustling in the tree—
The tree the wind is blowing through—
    It sets the blossoms flickering white.
I knew not skies could burn so blue
    Nor any breezes blow so light.
They blow an old-time way for me,
Across the world to Arcady.

Oh, what's the way to Arcady?
Sir Poet, with the rusty coat,
Quit mocking of the song-bird's note.
How have you heart for any tune,
You with the wayworn russet shoon?
Your scrip, a-swinging by your side,
Gapes with a gaunt mouth hungry-wide.
I'll brim it well with pieces red,
If you will tell the way to tread.

Oh, I am bound for Arcady,
And if you but keep pace with me
You tread the way to Arcady.

And where away lies Arcady,
And how long yet may the journey be?

Ah, that (quoth he) *I do not know—*
Across the clover and the snow—
Across the frost, across the flowers—
Through summer seconds and winter hours
I've trod the way my whole life long,
　　And know not now where it may be;
My guide is but the stir to song,
That tells me I cannot go wrong,
　　Or clear or dark the pathway be
　　Upon the road to Arcady.

But how shall I do who cannot sing?
　　I was wont to sing, once on a time—
There is never an echo now to ring
　　Remembrance back to the trick of rhyme.

'Tis strange you cannot sing (quoth he),
The folk all sing in Arcady.

But how may he find Arcady
Who hath not youth nor melody?

What know you not, old man (quoth he)—
　　Your hair is white, your face is wise—
　　That Love must kiss that Mortal's eyes
Who hopes to see fair Arcady?
No gold can buy you entrance there;
But beggared Love may go all bare—
No wisdom won with weariness;
But Love goes in with Folly's dress—
No fame that wit could ever win;
But only Love may lead Love in
　　To Arcady, to Arcady.

Ah, woe is me, through all my days
　　Wisdom and wealth I both have got,
And fame and name, and great men's praise;
　　But Love, ah, Love! I have it not.

There was a time, when life was new—
   But far away, and half forgot—
I only know her eyes were blue;
   But Love—I fear I knew it not.
We did not wed, for lack of gold,
And she is dead, and I am old.
All things have come since then to me,
Save Love, ah, Love! and Arcady.
Ah, then I fear we part (quoth he),
My way's for Love and Arcady.

But you, you fare alone, like me;
   The gray is likewise in your hair.
   What love have you to lead you there,
To Arcady, to Arcady?

Ah, no, not lonely do I fare;
   My true companion's Memory.
With Love he fills the Spring-time air;
   With Love he clothes the Winter tree.
Oh, past this poor horizon's bound
   My song goes straight to one who stands—
Her face all gladdening at the sound—
   To lead me to the Spring-green lands,
   To wander with enlacing hands.
The songs within my breast that stir
Are all of her, are all of her.
My maid is dead long years (quoth he),
She waits for me in Arcady.

Oh, yon's the way to Arcady,
   To Arcady, to Arcady;
Oh, yon's the way to Arcady,
   Where all the leaves are merry

H. C. BUNNER

LAMENT

Vowel Quintain in Gerunds

(CASENOVA AT DUX)

The ban of Time there is no disobeying;
  My acting's past, I must put up with being.
Old Age, remorseless, scorns my sickened suing.
  I'm reaping my wild oats, no longer sowing.
Accepting love has given way to buying.
Why waste my time in sentimental sighing?
  'Tis but an ancient wreck the girls are seeing;
And, should I strut, I hear them slyly saying,
  "Oh, quaint old fool, when will you cease your beauing?
Get off the stage ere we begin our booing!"

GELETT BURGESS

WRITTEN AFTER SWIMMING FROM SESTOS TO ABYDOS

If, in the month of dark December,
  Leander, who was nightly wont
(What maid will not the tale remember?)
  To cross thy stream broad Hellespont.

If, when the wint'ry tempest roar'd,
  He sped to Hero nothing loth,
And thus of old thy current pour'd,
  Fair Venus! how I pity both!

For *me*, degenerate, modern wretch,
  Though in the genial month of May,
My dripping limbs I faintly stretch,
  And think I've done a feat today.

But since he crossed the rapid tide,
  According to the doubtful story,
To woo—and—Lord knows what beside,
  And swam for Love, as I for Glory;

'T were hard to say who fared the best:
  Sad mortals! thus the gods still plague you!
He lost his labor, I my jest;
  For he was drowned, and I've the ague.

BYRON

LINES ON HEARING THE ORGAN

Grinder, who serenely grindest
  At my door the Hundredth Psalm,
Till thou ultimately findest
  Pence in thy unwashen palm:

Grinder, jocund-hearted Grinder,
  Near whom Barbary's nimble son,
Poised with skill upon his hinder
  Paws, accepts the proffered bun:

Dearly do I love thy grinding;
  Joy to meet thee on thy road
Where thou prowlest through the blinding
  Dust with that stupendous load,

'Neath the baleful stars of Sirius,
  When the postmen slowlier jog,
And the ox becomes delirious,
  And the muzzle decks the dog.

Tell me by what art thou bindest
  On thy feet those ancient shoon:
Tell me, Grinder, if thou grindest
  Always, always out of tune.

Tell me if, as thou art buckling
  On thy straps with eager claws,
Thou forecastest, inly chuckling,
  All the rage that thou wilt cause.

Tell me if at all thou mindest
   When folks flee, as if on wings,
From thee as at ease thou grindest:
   Tell me fifty thousand things.

Grinder, gentle-hearted Grinder!
   Ruffians who lead evil lives,
Soothed by thy sweet strains are kinder
   To their bullocks and their wives:

Children, when they see thy supple
   Form approach, are out like shots;
Half-a-bar sets several couple
   Waltzing in convenient spots;

Not with clumsy Jacks or Georges:
   Unprofaned by grasp of man
Maidens speed those simple orgies,
   Betsey Jane with Betsey Ann.

As they love thee in St. Giles's
   Thou art loved in Grosvenor Square:
None of those engaging smiles is
   Unreciprocated there.

Often, ere yet thou hast hammer'd
   Through thy four delicious airs,
Coins are flung thee by enamour'd
   Housemaids upon area stairs:

E'en the ambrosial-whisker'd flunkey
   Eyes thy boots and thine unkempt
Beard and melancholy monkey
   More in pity than contempt.

Far from England, in the sunny
   South, where Anio leaps in foam,
Thou wast rear'd, till lack of money
   Drew thee from thy vineclad home:

And thy mate, the sinewy Jocko,
   From Brazil or Afric came,
Land of simoom and sirocco—
   And he seems extremely tame.

There he quaffed the undefilèd
   Spring, or hung with apelike glee,
By his teeth or tail or eyelid,
   To the slippery mango-tree:

There he woo'd and won a dusky
   Bride, of instincts like his own;
Talk'd of love till he was husky
   In a tongue to us unknown:

Side by side 'twas theirs to ravage
   The potato ground, or cut
Down the unsuspecting savage
   With the well-aim'd cocoa-nut:—

Till the miscreant Stranger tore him
   Screaming from his blue-faced fair;
And they flung strange raiment o'er him,
   Raiment which he could not bear:

Sever'd from the pure embraces
   Of his children and his spouse,
He must ride fantastic races
   Mounted on reluctant sows:

But the heart of wistful Jocko
   Still was with his ancient flame
In the nutgroves of Morocco;
   Or if not it's all the same.

Grinder, winsome grinsome Grinder!
   They who see thee and whose soul
Melts not at thy charms, are blinder
   Than a trebly-bandaged mole:

They to whom thy curt (yet clever)
  Talk, thy music, and thine ape,
Seem not to be joys for ever,
  Are but brutes in human shape.

'Tis not that thy mien is stately,
  'Tis not that thy tones are soft;
'Tis not that I care so greatly
  For the same thing play'd so oft;

But I've heard mankind abuse thee;
  And perhaps it's rather strange,
But I thought that I would choose thee
  For encomium, as a change.

CHARLES STUART CALVERLEY

OUR TRAVELLER

If thou would'st stand on Etna's burning brow,
With smoke above, and roaring flame below;
And gaze adown that molten gulf reveal'd.
Till thy soul shudder'd and thy senses reel'd:
If thou wouldst beard Niag'ra in his pride,
Or stem the billows of Propontic tide;
Scale all alone some dizzy Alpine *haut*,
And shriek "Excelsior!" among the snow:
Would'st tempt all deaths, all dangers that may be—
Perils by land, and perils on the sea;
This vast round world, I say, if thou wouldst view it—
Then, why the dickens don't you go and do it?

HENRY CHOLMONDELEY-PENNELL

SEHNSUCHT; OR WHAT YOU WILL

The day is dark;
My mind is bleary;
The window pane
With mist is smeary;
Mine eyelids are
A little weary.

But when the sun
Shines bright and cheery,
Can life be sad
And dull and dreary?
The answer's yes
To that deep query.

CORINNA

THE TIDES OF LOVE

Flo was fond of Ebenezer—
  "Eb," for short she called her beau.
Talk of Tides of Love, great Caesar!
  You should see them—Eb and Flo.

T. A. DALY

HISTORICAL INCIDENTS

When they threw him overboard,
  Hoping to avoid
Being shipwrecked by the Lord,
  Jonah felt annoyed.

When he fell inside a whale,
  And, of course, perceived
Protests were of no avail,
  Jonah felt aggrieved.

When the whale, who hated gore,
  Went and catapulted
Jonah on a rocky shore,
  Jonah felt insulted.

After that, for twenty years,
  Jonah cruised around,
Muttering and poking spears
  At every fish he found.

CLARENCE DAY

RISE AND FALL OF VALENTINES

When Claudius was emperor and grandeur still was Roman,
He framed an edict hard upon each legionary yeoman.
He ruled that all who marched away in warfare grim to
    mingle
Must, if not previously wed, remain entirely single.
'Twas Caesar's thought barbarians might be much better
    harried
By legionaries who were fierce, unbridled, and unmarried.
The thought was quite imperial, impressive and ingenious,
But in the opposition stood the Bishop Valentinius.

That insubordination met this law of Claudius's
May go without the saying, for all human nature thus is.
Each maiden wrote a missive in her very warmest Latin;
The verb, to love, in all its moods—she failed not to put
    that in.
Each soldier seized a stylus and set down his sturdy promise
And also conjugated all *amo, amas, amamus.*
'Twas Valentine exchanged their notes. He helped them get
    acquainted.
And happily he saw them wed. No wonder he was sainted.

And thus it came that off to war to take a charge and siege on
Paraded what was probably the world's most married legion.
"The Girl I Left Behind Me" was the marching song
    unanimous.
And soldiers anxious to return attacked the foe with animus.

* * *

So that's the tale of how we owe to Valentine, the bishop,
The cards of loving sentiment we buy in that or this shop,
And why in piping times of peace and in an age more wary
We never sign the valentines we send in February.

FAIRFAX DOWNEY

EPITAPH INTENDED FOR HIS WIFE

Here lies my wife: here let her lie!
Now she's at rest, and so am I.

JOHN DRYDEN

THE NEW HELLAS

Granville Barker is to produce Greek plays in New York City.—*News Item*

The tragedies that entertained the burghers of antiquity,
The legends of the demi-gods, and purple-souled iniquity,
The plays they once produced in Greek, in Sanskrit and in
    Latin
Are soon to be revived upon the island of Manhattan.

And we, like Attic citizens, shall go in prayer and piety,
To see how Fate has juggled with Olympian society;
While Aeschylus and Sophocles shall play with our emotions,
And fill the modern Metropole with sad Hellenic notions.

From office and from counting house, from college and
    emporium
Shall come the new Athenian to Gotham's auditorium,
Where shall be played a tragedy, whose unfamiliar chorus
Shall strangely serve to help the plot, and analyze it for us.

We shall behold the ancient themes, eternally triangular,
Dispose of heroes tastefully by artifices strangular;
The Monologuing Messenger shall come ere we've departed,
And tell how all the epic-making complications started.

The mournful music and the eerie shock of Greek epiphany,
The jewels of Grecian drama by a dramaturgic Tiffany,
Shall wean us for a moment from our petty, passing worry,
To Granville Barker and the Anglo-Greek of Gilbert Murray.

Our souls shall soon be purged by pain and passionate
    sublimity,

While vulgar cars and taxicabs are howling in proximity;
The town in toto shall be thrilled by classic love and slaying—
That is, unless the Yankees happen also to be playing.

IRWIN EDMAN

MY SABINE FARM

At last I have a Sabine farm
    Abloom with shrubs and flowers;
And garlands gay I weave by day
    Amid those fragrant bowers;
And yet, O fortune hideous,
I have no blooming Lydias;
And what, ah, what's a Sabine farm to us without its Lydias?

Within my cottage is a room
    Where I would fain be merry;
Come one and all unto that hall,
    Where you'll be welcome, very!
I've a butler who's Hibernian—
But no, I've no Falernian!
And what, ah, what's a Sabine farm to you without Falernian?

Upon this cosey Sabine farm
    What breeds my melancholy?
Why is my Muse down with the blues
    Instead of up and jolly?
A secret this between us:
I'm shy of a Maecenas!
And what's, oh, what's a Sabine farm to me without Maecenas!

EUGENE FIELD

WHEN WEST COMES EAST

I hail from high in the alkali
    Where the desert bones lie rotten;
Where men set their faces to the open spaces,
    Forgetting and being forgotten.

I was at my best, as I say, out West
   And my coming East was rash,
For my strength is vain in a railway train—
   I never can raise the sash.

I can tell—who knows—of a desert rose
   That bloomed where the coyote starts;
Where the only sound for miles around
   Was the clash of primitive hearts.
I can tell, of course, how my faithful horse
   Was my truest of pals—all that,
But I never can tell, in a large hotel,
   Just when to remove my hat.

Oh, ship me West in a leather vest
   With chaps on my corduroy pants;
Back to the rows of baked plateaus
   Where the strongheart has a chance!
Clean-limbed, clear-eyed, I'd be satisfied
   With the life I led before,—
For I can never collect my self-respect
   When I use a revolving door.

                             COREY FORD

THE CONVERSATIONAL REFORMER

When Theo: Roos: unfurled his bann:
   As Pres: of an immense Repub:
And sought to manufact: a plan
   For saving people troub:
His mode of spelling (termed phonet:)
Affec: my brain like an emet:

And I evolved a scheme (*pro-tem*)
   To simplify my mother-tongue,
That so in fame I might resem:
   Upt: Sinc:, who wrote "The Jung:,"
And rouse an interest enorm:
In conversational reform.

I grudge the time my fellows waste
   Completing words that are so comm:
Wherever peop: of cult: and taste
   Habitually predom:,
'Twould surely tend to simpl: life
Could they but be curtailed a trif:

For is not "Brev: the Soul of Wit"?
   (Inscribe the mott: upon your badge).
The sense will never suff: a bit
   If left to the imag:
Since any pers: can see what's meant
By words so simp: as "husb:" or "gent:"

When at some meal (at dinn: for inst:)
   You hand your unc: an empty plate,
Or ask your aunt (that charming spinst:)
   To pass you the potat:,
They have too much sagac:, I trust,
To give you sug: or pep: or must:.

If you require a slice of mutt:,
   You'll find the selfsame princ: hold good,
Nor get, instead of bread and butt:,
   Some tapioca pudd:,
Nor vainly bid some boon compan:
Replen: with Burg: his vacant can.

At golf, if your oppon: should ask
   Why in a haz: your nib: is sunk
And you explain your fav'rite Hask:
   Lies buried in a bunk:,
He cannot very well misund:
That you (poor fooz:) have made a blund:

If this is prob:—nay, even cert:—
   My scheme at once becomes attrac:

And I (pray pard: a litt: impert:)
　A public benefac:
Who saves his fellow-man and neighb:
A large amount of needless lab:.

Gent: Reader, if to me you'll list:
　And be not irritab: or peev:,
You'll find it of tremend: assist:
　This habit of abbrev:,
Which grows like some infec: disease,
Like chron: paral: or German meas:.

And every living human bipe:
　Will feel his heart grow grate: and warm
As he becomes the loy: discip:
　Of my partic: reform,
(Which don't confuse with that, I beg,
Of Brander Math: or And: Carneg:).

"'Tis not in mort: to comm: success,"
　As Addison remarked; but if my meth:
Does something to dimin: or less:
　The waste of public breath,
My country, overcome with grat:
Should in my hon: erect a stat:.

My bust by Rod: (what matt: the cost?)
　Shall be exhib: devoid of charge,
With (in the Public Lib: at Bost:)
　My full-length port: by Sarge:,
That thous: from Pitts: or Wash: may swarm
To worsh: the Found: of this Reform.

*　*　*

Meanwhile I seek with some avid:
The fav: of your polite consid:.

HARRY GRAHAM

ELEGY

The jackals prowl, the serpents hiss
In what was once Persepolis.
Proud Babylon is but a trace
Upon the desert's dusty face.
The topless towers of Ilium
Are ashes. Judah's harp is dumb.
The fleets of Nineveh and Tyre
Are down with Davy Jones, Esquire
And all the oligarchies, kings,
And potentates that ruled these things
Are gone! But cheer up; don't be sad;
Think what a lovely time they had!

ARTHUR GUITERMAN

WHAT LITERATURE NEEDS:

*Lines on Municipal Transportation, Including the Bus,
the Trolley, and the Subway and Elevated Trains,
both Local and Express*

I hate
To wait.

* * *

Verses Explanatory of the Literary Works of a Certain Mariner

William McFee
Was born at sea.

* * *

Mathematics of Felicity, or a Simple Sum in Showmanship

To Noel Coward
Add Leslie Howard.

* * *

Autobiography of Alice B. Toklas, or Plain Truth
from the Atlantic Monthly

Gertrude Stein
Is a friend of mine.

* * *

Testimonial in Hours of Stress from Statesmen, Bankers,
Philosophers, and Other Perplexed Mortals

Edgar Wallace
Is my solace.

* * *

Lines on What Happens Just When the Immediate Present Is
About as Bad as It Could Be

H. G. Wells
Invents new hells.

* * *

Esthetic Consideration of Anatomy as Represented in Certain
Modern Art

Rockwell Kent
Draws men bent.

* * *

On Learning That a Leading Dramatist Has Sketched Plots
of Thirty Plays to Come

I stagger and reel
From Eugene O'Neill.

* * *

The Sweet Uses of Solid Reading, or How I Felled the Burglar

I hit him squarely on the nose
With "The Oxford Book of English Prose.'

* * *

Lines Portraying a Nordic Reaction to the Mysticism of the East

It makes me sweat at every pore
To read Rabindranath Tagore.

JOHN A. HOLMES

A FAMILIAR LETTER TO SEVERAL CORRESPONDENTS

Yes, write if you want to—there's nothing like trying;
  Who knows what a treasure your casket may hold?
I'll show you that rhyming's as easy as lying,
  If you'll listen to me while the art I unfold.

Here's a book full of words: one can choose as he fancies,
  As a painter his tint, as a workman his tool;
Just think! all the poems and plays and romances
  Were drawn out of this, like the fish from a pool!

You can wander at will through its syllabled mazes,
  And take all you want—not a copper they cost;
What is there to hinder your picking out phrases
  For an epic as clever as "Paradise Lost"?

Don't mind if the index of sense is at zero;
  Use words that run smoothly, whatever they mean;
Leander and Lillian and Lillibullero
  Are much the same thing in the rhyming machine.

There are words so delicious their sweetness will smother
  That boarding-school flavour of which we're afraid;
There is "lush" is a good one and "swirl" is another;
  Put both in one stanza, its fortune is made.

With musical murmurs and rhythmical closes
  You can cheat us of smiles when you've nothing to tell;
You hand us a nosegay of milliner's roses,
  And we cry with delight, "Oh, how sweet they do smell!"

Perhaps you will answer all needful conditions
   For winning the laurels to which you aspire,
By docking the tails of the two prepositions
   I' the style o' the bards you so greatly admire.

As for subjects of verse, they are only too plenty
   For ringing the changes on metrical chimes;
A maiden, a moonbeam, a lover of twenty,
   Have filled that great basket with bushels of rhymes.

Let me show you a picture—'tis far from irrelevant—
   By a famous old hand in the arts of design;
'Tis only a photographed sketch of an elephant;
   The name of the draughtsman was Rembrandt of Rhine.

How easy! no troublesome colours to lay on;
   It can't have fatigued him, no, not in the least;
A dash here and there with a haphazard crayon,
   And there stands the wrinkled-skinned, baggy-limbed
      beast.

Just so with your verse—'tis as easy as sketching;
   You can reel off a song without knitting your brow,
As lightly as Rembrandt a drawing or etching;
   It is nothing at all, if you only know how.

Well, imagine you've printed your volume of verses;
   Your forehead is wreathed with the garland of fame;
Your poem the eloquent school-boy rehearses;
   Her album the school-girl presents for your name.

Each morning the post brings you autograph letters;
   You'll answer them promptly—an hour isn't much
For the honour of sharing a page with your betters,
   With magistrates, members of Congress, and such.

Of course you're delighted to serve the committees
   That come with requests from the country all round;

You would grace the occasion with poems and ditties
    When they've got a new school-house, or poor-house, or
        pound.

With a hymn for the saints, and a song for the sinners,
    You go and are welcome wherever you please;
You're a privileged guest at all manner of dinners;
    You've a seat on the platform among the grandees

At length your mere presence becomes a sensation;
    Your cup of enjoyment is filled to its brim
With the pleasure Horatian of digitmonstration,
    As the whisper runs round of "That's he!" or "That's
        him!"

But, remember, O dealer in phrases sonorous,
    So daintily chosen, so tunefully matched,
Though you soar with the wings of the cherubim o'er us,
    The ovum was human from which you were hatched.

No will of your own, with its puny compulsion,
    Can summon the spirit that quickens the lyre;
It comes, if at all, like the sibyl's convulsion,
    And touches the brain with a finger of fire.

So, perhaps, after all, it's as well to be quiet,
    If you've nothing you think is worth saying in prose,
As to furnish a meal of their cannibal diet
    To the critics, by publishing, as you propose.

But it's all of no use, and I'm sorry I've written;
    I shall see your thin volume some day on my shelf;
For the rhyming tarantula surely has bitten,
    And music must cure you, so pipe it yourself.
                                    OLIVER WENDELL HOLMES

TO MINERVA

My temples throb, my pulses boil,
   I'm sick of Song and Ode and Ballad—
So Thyrsis, take the midnight oil,
   And pour it on a lobster salad.

My brain is dull, my sight is foul,
   I cannot write a verse, or read—
Then Pallas, take away thine Owl,
   And let us have a Lark instead.

THOMAS HOOD

SONG FOR A CRACKED VOICE

When I was young and slender, a spender, a lender,
   What gentleman adventurer was prankier than I,
Who lustier at passes with glasses—and lasses,
   How pleasant was the look of 'em as I came jaunting by!
   (But now there's none to sigh at me as I come creaking by.)

Then Pegasus went loping 'twixt hoping and toping,
   A song in every dicky-bird, a scent in every rose;
What moons for lovelorn glances, romances, and dances,
   And how the spirit of the waltz went thrilling to my toes!
   (Egad, it's now a gouty pang goes thrilling to my toes!)

Was I that lover frantic, romantic, and antic,
   Who found the lute in Molly's voice, the heaven in her
     eyes?
Who, madder than a hatter, talked patter? No matter
   Call not that little, youthful ghost, but leave it where it
     lies!
   (Dear, dear, how many winter snows have drifted where
     she lies!)

But now I'm old and humble, why mumble and grumble
   At all the posy-linkèd rout that hurries laughing by?

Framed in my gold-rimmed glasses each lass is who passes
And Youth is still a-twinkling in the corner of my eye.
(How strange you cannot see it in the corner of my eye!)
WALLACE IRWIN

THE PESSIMIST

Nothing to do but work,
  Nothing to eat but food,
Nothing to wear but clothes,
  To keep one from going nude.

Nothing to breathe but air,
  Quick as a flash 't is gone;
Nowhere to fall but off,
  Nowhere to stand but on.

Nothing to comb but hair,
  Nowhere to sleep but in bed,
Nothing to weep but tears,
  Nothing to bury but dead.

Nothing to sing but songs,
  Ah, well, alas! alack!
Nowhere to go but out,
  Nowhere to come but back.

Nothing to see but sights,
  Nothing to quench but thirst,
Nothing to have but what we've got
  Thus through life we are cursed.

Nothing to strike but a gait;
  Everything moves that goes.
Nothing at all but common sense
  Can ever withstand these woes.

BEN KING

THE INFLAMED DISCIPLE

On seeing an eminent Judge in the Bar Association's library on a warm
Saturday afternoon

Whoso the path of law would tread
　With glory and with high renown,
Must, while his fellows lie abed,
　Over his mound of cases frown.

While others lounge he may not rest;
　He may not frolic while they play;
The vestal flame within his breast
　Must blaze at night, and blaze at day.

Jagged and sheer his course, and long;
　And he were faithless to his goal
To pause to join a wayside song,
　Or nap upon a shady knoll.

Pondering thus I saw him trudge
　From shelf to shelf, a pad in hand,
Learning, that he might better judge,
　That he might better understand.

And I was glad that one should guide
　Our courts by whom the beckoning June
So resolutely was denied
　Throughout that fulgent afternoon.

And I was proud to march among
　An army whose inspiring chief
To his appointed duty clung,
　Nor respite asking, nor relief.

And you, I thought, you, too, might climb
　To equal heights if you would stop
Squandering days of precious time
　Watching a silly golf ball hop.

Give up your nights of aimless ease!
  With cocktail-drinking friends dispense!
Who stares too long at show girls' knees
  Will write no famous precedents.

For, with those golden hours regained,
  Great gaps of knowledge can be filled;
That mind enlightened, strengthened, trained,
  Which is now barren and untilled.

Indeed, the thought enthralled me so,
  That minutes went with leaps and bounds
And I almost missed the opening throw
  (A perfect strike) at the Polo Grounds.

ARTHUR KRAMER

TIME TO BE WISE

Yes; I write verses now and then,
But blunt and flaccid is my pen,
No longer talked of by young men
      As rather clever:
In the last quarter are my eyes,
You see it by their form and size;
Is it not time then to be wise?
      Or now or never.

Fairest that ever sprang from Eve!
While Time allows the short reprieve,
Just look at me! would you believe
      'Twas once a lover?
I cannot clear the five-bar gate;
But, trying first its timber's state,
Climb stiffly up, take breath, and wait
      To trundle over.

Through gallopade I cannot swing
The entangling blooms of Beauty's spring:

I cannot say the tender thing,
    Be't true or false,
And am beginning to opine
Those girls are only half-divine
Whose waists yon wicked boys entwine
    In giddy waltz.

I fear that arm above that shoulder;
I wish them wiser, graver, older,
Sedater, and no harm if colder,
    And panting less.
Ah! people were not half so wild
In former days, when, starchly mild,
Upon her high-heeled Essex smiled
    The brave Queen Bess.
           WALTER SAVAGE LANDOR

THE BALLAD OF CHARITY

It was in a pleasant deepô, sequestered from the rain,
That many weary passengers were waitin' for the train;
Piles of quite expensive baggage, many a gorgeous portmantô,
Ivory-handled umberellas made a most touristic show.

Whereunto there came a person, very humble was his mien,
Who took an observation of the interestin' scene;
Closely scanned the umberellas, watched with joy the mighty
    trunks,
And observed that all the people were securin' Pullman
    bunks:

Who was followed shortly after by a most unhappy tramp,
Upon whose features poverty had jounced her iron stamp;
And to make a clear impression as bees sting you while they
    buzz,
She had hit him rather harder than she generally does.

For he was so awful ragged, and in parts so awful bare,
That the folks were quite repulsioned to behold him begging
       there;
And instead of drawing currency from out their pocket-books,
They drew themselves asunder with aversionary looks.

Sternly gazed the first newcomer on the unindulgent crowd.
Then in tones which pierced the deepô he solilicussed
       aloud:—
"I hev trevelled o'er this cont'nent from Quebec to Bogotáw,
But sech a set of scallawags as these I never saw.

"Ye are wealthy, ye are gifted, ye have house and lands and
       rent,
Yet unto a suff'rin' mortal ye will not donate a cent;
Ye expend your missionaries to the heathen and the Jew,
But there isn't any heathen that is half as small as you.

"Ye are lucky—ye hev cheque-books and deeposits in the
       bank,
And ye squanderate your money on the titled folks of rank;
The onyx and the sardonyx upon your garments shine,
An' ye drink at every dinner p'r'aps a dollar's wuth of wine.

"Ye are goin' for the summer to the islands by the sea,
Where it costs four dollars daily—setch is not for setch as
       me;
Iv'ry-handled umberellas do not come into my plan,
But I kin give a dollar to this suff'rin' fellow-man.

"Hand-bags made of Rooshy leather are not truly at my
       call,
Yet in the eyes of Mussy I am richer 'en you all,
For I kin give a dollar wher' you dare not stand a dime,
And never miss it nother, nor regret it ary time."

Sayin' this he drew a wallet from the inner of his vest,
And gave the tramp a daddy, which it was his level best;

Other people havin' heard him soon to charity inclined—
One giver soon makes twenty if you only get their wind.

The first who gave the dollar led the other one about,
And at every contribution he a-raised a joyful shout,
Exclaimin' how 'twas noble to relieviate distress,
And remarkin' that our duty is our present happiness.

Thirty dollars altogether were collected by the tramp,
When he bid 'em all good evenin' and went out into the
   damp,
And was followed briefly after by the one who made the
   speech,
And who showed by good example how to practise as to
   preach.

Which soon around the corner the couple quickly met,
And the tramp produced the specie for to liquidate his debt;
And the man who did the preachin' took his twenty of the
   sum,
Which you see that out of thirty left a tenner for the bum.

And the couple passed the summer at Bar Harbor with the
   rest,
Greatly changed in their appearance and most elegently
   dressed.
Any fowl with change of feathers may a brilliant bird
   become:
Oh, how hard is life for many! oh, how sweet it is for some!
                              CHARLES GODFREY LELAND

THE REPORTERS

They are ordinary men like you and me;
You'd find it hard to spot them in a mob;
But when anything occurs on land or sea
They're pretty sure to be right on the job.

They're ready for a wedding or a war,
A murder, an election, or a cruise.
They feed on trouble, then come back for more,
The snappy lads who gather in the news.

Oh, in England they call 'em the pressmen,
The boys with the pencils and pads,
Those pushing, ubiquitous, sometimes iniquitous
Fresh, irrepressible lads.
We call them, on this side, reporters,
But what is a name more or less,
To those dashing, spectacular, wise and oracular,
Clever young men of the press?

If the British should unearth a Russian plot,
Or the Turks should start a rumpus with the Greeks,
You will find a bright reporter on the spot
Who has known about the thing for weeks and weeks.
If a chorus girl should shoot a millionaire,
Or a foreign Prince should wed a movie queen,
You can bet your life that some reporter's there
Collecting facts and pictures of the scene.

Where angels fear to tread they rush right in.
They do not dread the devil nor his wife.
You snub 'em and they greet you with a grin,
Then they ask you for the story of your life.
They can scent a crime or scandal miles away;
They can hear through walls of iron if they choose;
But we couldn't do without 'em for a day—
The snappy lads who gather in the news.

So here's to the gallant reporters,
The boys with the pencils and pads,
The calm, undisturbable, cool, imperturbable
Nervy, inquisitive lads.
Each time that we pick up a paper

Their valorous deeds we should bless,
The bold, reprehensible, brave, indispensable
Sensible lads of the press.

NEWMAN LEVY

A TERRIBLE INFANT

I recollect a nurse call'd Ann,
    Who carried me about the grass,
And one fine day a fine young man
    Came up, and kiss'd the pretty lass.
She did not make the least objection!
    Thinks I, "*Aha!*
    When I can talk I'll tell Mamma"
—And that's my earliest recollection.

FREDERICK LOCKER-LAMPSON

KING COPHETUA AND THE BEGGAR MAID

Cophetua was a merry King,
    And slightly sentimental;
His morals were (if anything)
    What some call "Oriental."

Zenelophon, the Beggar Goil,
    Was innocent and careful;
She had been reared to Honest Toil
    By parents poor and prayerful,

For Papa peddled lemonade
    While Mamma laundered laundry,
And she had been a solder maid
    Within a muzzle foundry;

But, oh! the foreman of the staff
    Had tried to Make Advances . . .
The Villain used to smirk and chaff
    And ask her out to dances!

And so she quit the Hellish Place
  And went salvationarming
A careful smile upon her face
  So innocent and charming.

While begging in a Beer Saloon
  Right opposite the palace
She saw the King one afternoon
  Drink chalice after chalice—

(He dallied daily with the Jug,
  He hit the pipe and gambled,
He introduced the bunny-hug
  As round his realm he rambled)—

Eftsoons the Monarch, reeling by
  Imperially laden,
Remarked, iniquitous and sly,
  "Pray, buss me, Beggar Maiden!"

"Not I!" she cried, "I'd rather go
  Right back to making muzzles
Than kiss a King that roisters so
  And gambles, flirts, and guzzles!"

The Regal Cut-up, in a mood
  Majestically reckless,
Then offered her a samite snood,
  A duchy, and a necklace.

"Oh, keep your Royal Gauds," she said,
  "And buss your legal spouses!
I won't kiss none until I'm wed,
  Especial if they're souses!"

With that he laid his sceptre down
  Beneath her footsy-wootsies—
"Oh, wed me, and I'll fling muh crown
  Before them pretty tootsies!"

"O King!" says she, "you *have* some queens!"
  Says he, "They're soon beheaded!"
That day his headsman reaped their beans,
  The next the King was wedded.

And Mrs. King Cophetua made
  All parties quit their vices,
And Papa's private lemonade
  Soon rose to fancy prices,

And Mamma laundered for the King
  As happy as a linnet—
Oh, Virtue always wins, I sing,
  If Wisdom's mingled in it!

DON MARQUIS

ALLEGRO

King Alexander led the van
O'er hill and dale to Hindostan,
  Heavy his heart and sad;
Mid battle crash, mid battle-plan,
He wished by Zeus he were the man
  That wrote the Iliad!

A poet followed in his train,
For share of wine, for share of grain,
  For share of anything;
With weary heart, with weary brain,
His menial service gave him pain,
  He wished he were the king!

The cup was deep, the wine was red,
The morning came, the King was dead,
  Half-wrought his dream of fame.
Haply the poet died in bed,
Or haply knocked upon the head;
  I do not know his name.

So monarchs envy poesy,
And poets fain would Princes be
To dwell in lordly hall.
Examine well this revery,
Make what you will thereof: to me
It has no sense at all.

McM.

PYGMALION

Pygmalion thought that women were a great abomination.
  What little charm they had, he thought, was always on vacation.
He swore he'd never say "I do" before the bridal altar
  And said he'd rather hammer stones than wear a husband's halter.

He took a block of ivory and many months he sculped,
  And what he had when he got done impressed him so he gulped.
For Pyg had carved a woman, an extremely lovely creature,
  And doggone realistic, every hillock, curve, and feature.

The figure was his masterpiece. He kissed it and caressed it
  And gave it pearls and emeralds, but first of course, he dressed it.
He spoke of her as "Mrs." and he played the good provider.
  He tucked her into bed at night and hopped right in beside her.

The folks at Venus' Festival heard young Pygmalion urgin'
  The Goddess to create a woman like his ivory virgin.
He rated high with Venus, so she simply up and took
  Her wand and mumbled something, and said, "Go right home and look."

But why go any further? It would be undignified,
  For Venus blessed the nuptials, and the family multiplied.

Now this is pretty fiction, but don't let your Mrs. catch
    you
  In the parlor after midnight making sheep's-eyes at a
    statue.

                                    ALBERT G. MILLER

FROM A FULL HEART

In days of peace my fellow-men
    Rightly regarded me as more like
A Bishop than a Major-Gen.,
    And nothing since has made me warlike;
But when this age-long struggle ends
    And I have seen the Allies dish up
The goose of Hindenburg—oh, friends!
    I shall out-bish the mildest Bishop.

When the War is over and the Kaiser's out of print
I'm going to buy some tortoises and watch the beggars sprint;
When the War is over and the sword at last we sheathe
I'm going to keep a jelly-fish and listen to it breathe.

I never really longed for gore,
    And any taste for red corpuscles
That lingered with me left before
    The German troops had entered Brussels.
In early days the Colonel's " 'Shun!"
    Froze me; and as the war grew older
The noise of some one else's gun
    Left me considerably colder.

When the War is over and the battle has been won
I'm going to buy a barnacle and take it for a run;
When the War is over and the German fleet we sink
I'm going to keep a silkworm's egg and listen to it think.

The Captains and the Kings depart—
  It may be so, but not lieutenants;
Dawn after weary dawn I start
  The never ending round of penance;
One rock amid the welter stands
  One which my gaze is fixed intently:
An after-life in quiet lands
  Lived very lazily and gently.

When the War is over and we've done the Belgians proud
I'm going to keep a chrysalis and read to it aloud;
When the War is over and we've finished up the show
I'm going to plant a lemon pip and listen to it grow.

Oh, I'm tired of the noise and turmoil of battle,
And I'm even upset by the lowing of cattle,
And the clang of the bluebells is death to my liver,
And the roar of the dandelion gives me a shiver,
And a glacier, in movement, is much too exciting,
And I'm nervous, when standing on one, of alighting—
Give me Peace; that is all, that is all that I seek. . . .
        Say, starting on Saturday week.
                                    A. A. MILNE

DEAR FANNY

"She has beauty, but still you must keep your heart cool;
  She has wit, but you must not be caught so";
Thus Reason advises, but Reason's a fool,
  And 'tis not the first time I have thought so,
    Dear Fanny.

"She is lovely!" Then love her, nor let the bliss fly;
  'Tis the charm of youth's vanishing season:
Thus love has advised me, and who will deny
  That Love reasons much better than Reason,
    Dear Fanny?
                                    THOMAS MOORE

UNSATISFIED YEARNING

Down in the silent hallway
  Scampers the dog about,
And whines, and barks, and scratches,
  In order to get out.

Once in the glittering starlight,
  He straightway doth begin
To set up a doleful howling
  In order to get in.

R. K. MUNKITTRICK

THE GROANING BOARD

A buttery, sugary, syrupy waffle—
Gee, but I love it somep'n awful.
Ginger-cakes dripping with chocolate goo,
Oo! How I love 'em! Oo! *Oo!* OO!

PINK

THE VICAR

Some years ago, ere Time and Taste
  Had turned our parish topsy-turvy,
When Darnel Park was Darnel Waste,
  And roads as little known as scurvy,
The man who lost his way between
  St. Mary's Hill and Sandy Thicket,
Was always shown across the Green,
  And guided to the Parson's wicket.

Back flew the bolt of lissom lath;
  Fair Margaret, in her tidy kirtle,
Led the lorn traveller up the path
  Through clean-clipt rows of box and myrtle;
And Don and Sancho, Tramp and Tray,
  Upon the parlor steps collected,
Wagged all their tails, and seemed to say,
  "Our master knows you; you're expected!"

Up rose the Reverend Doctor Brown,
  Up rose the Doctor's "winsome marrow";
The lady laid her knitting down,
  Her husband clasped his ponderous Barrow;
Whate'er the stranger's caste or creed,
  Pundit or papist, saint or sinner,
He found a stable for his steed,
  And welcome for himself, and dinner.

If, when he reached his journey's end,
  And warmed himself in court or college,
He had not gained an honest friend,
  And twenty curious scraps of knowledge;—
If he departed as he came,
  With no new light on love or liquor,—
Good sooth, the traveller was to blame,
  And not the Vicarage, nor the Vicar.

His talk was like a stream which runs
  With rapid change from rocks to roses;
It slipped from politics to puns;
  It passed from Mahomet to Moses;
Beginning with the laws which keep
  The planets in their radiant courses,
And ending with some precept deep
  For dressing eels or shoeing horses.

He was a shrewd and sound divine,
  Of loud Dissent the mortal terror;
And when, by dint of page and line,
  He 'stablished Truth, or startled Error,
The Baptist found him far too deep,
  The Deist sighed with saving sorrow,
And the lean Levite went to sleep
  And dreamed of tasting pork to-morrow.

His sermon never said or showed
  That Earth is foul, that Heaven is gracious,

Without refreshment on the road
   From Jerome, or from Athanasius;
And sure a righteous zeal inspired
   The hand and head that penned and planned them,
For all who understood, admired,
   And some who did not understand them.

He wrote, too, in a quiet way,
   Small treatises, and smaller verses,
And sage remarks on chalk and clay,
   And hints to noble lords and nurses;
True histories of last year's ghost;
   Lines to a ringlet or a turban;
And trifles to the Morning Post,
   And nothings for Sylvanus Urban.

He did not think all mischief fair,
   Although he had a knack of joking;
He did not make himself a bear,
   Although he had a taste for smoking;
And when religious sects ran mad,
   He held, in spite of all his learning,
That if a man's belief is bad,
   It will not be improved by burning.

And he was kind, and loved to sit
   In the low hut or garnished cottage,
And praise the farmer's homely wit,
   And share the widow's homelier pottage,
At his approach complaint grew mild,
   And when his hand unbarred the shutter,
The clammy lips of Fever smiled
   The welcome which they could not utter.

He always had a tale for me
   Of Julius Caesar or of Venus;
From him I learned the rule of three,
   Cat's-cradle, leap-frog, and *Quae genus*.

I used to singe his powdered wig,
    To steal the staff he put such trust in,
And make the puppy dance a jig
    When he began to quote Augustine.

Alack, the change! In vain I look
    For haunts in which my boyhood trifled;
The level lawn, the trickling brook,
    The trees I climbed, the beds I rifled.
The church is larger than before,
    You reach it by a carriage entry:
It holds three hundred people more,
    And pews are fitted up for gentry.

Sit in the Vicar's seat; you'll hear
    The doctrine of a gentle Johnian,
Whose hand is white, whose voice is clear,
    Whose phrase is very Ciceronian.
Where is the old man laid? Look down,
    And construe on the slab before you:
"*Hic jacet Gulielmus Brown,*
    Vir nullâ non donandus lauru."

                    WINTHROP MACKWORTH PRAED

ODE TO EVE

O Mother Eve, I do believe that after all you're glad you ate
That fruity prize that made you wise as any college graduate;
I think you thought (I'm sure you ought) the taste that
    made you win a sense
Of what you are, is better far than vegetative innocence!

O Mother Eve, I do not grieve though to our primal Pop
    you lent
That fatal bite that put a blight on Eden's treasures opulent;
Though cold and wide, the world outside was big with
    possibilities,
While for a wife the Sheltered Life is packed with puerilities.

O Mother Eve, you gained reprieve from commonplace
    transparency,
Although you trod on thorny sod, and sailed on many a
    barren sea;
Yet you might fly from spots too dry, or move from spots
    too saturate—
No Paradise so newly nice as any furnished flat you rate!

O Mother Eve, you now deceive our eyes with dress and
    drapery;
Around your waist are garments laced to make it small
    and tapery.
(If I had time to write the rhyme, I think I could contrive
    a list
Of gains unsought your apple brought, to stagger a re-
    vivalist!)

                              EDWIN MEADE ROBINSON

BALLADE OF THE ANCIENT WHEEZE

I wonder if, sunning in Eden's vales,
Fielding and Smollett still hold sway;
And Gaffer Chaucer sits swapping tales
With Old Sam Clemens and Rabelais?
And then I can hear, 'mid the merry play
Of wit and laughter's jovial din,
One or the other guffaw and say:
"A traveling salesman came to an inn—."

Over the scented Elysian swales
Pan strides piping to nymph and fay;
But down the depths of the woodland dales
A whisper goes round where the men folk stay.
There's mischief abroad, or my wit's astray—
Shepherds a-chuckle and fauns a-grin—
Theocritus starts in the same old way;
"A traveling salesman came to an inn—."

This is the password of brother males,
Linking together the grave and gay,
Story that never grows old nor stales,
Jest that is stranger to Time's decay,
Life-scarred veterans, old and gray,
Skinny of arm and lank of shin,
Cackle at thoughts of the old brave fray—
"A traveling salesman came to an inn—."

L'ENVOI

Prince, you are fashioned of mortal clay,
Tarry a little and quaff a skin;
I heard a good one the other day—
"A traveling salesman came to an inn—."

NATE SALSBURY
NEWMAN LEVY

PROSIT NEUJAHR

Be the New Year sweet and short,
    As the days of girl and boy are
Full of friendship, full of sport—
    Prosit Neujahr!

Be it beautiful and great
    As the days of grief and joy are
Full of wonder and of fate—
    Prosit Neujahr!

GEORGE SANTAYANA

THE SEAMY SIDE OF MOTLEY

Lady, when we sat together,
    And your flow of talk that turned
On the Park, the Play, the Weather,
    Left me frankly unconcerned,
I could see how hard you labour'd
    Till your brain was stiff and sore,
Never having yet been neighbour'd
    By so dull a bore.

Later on, from information
  Gathered elsewhere after lunch,
You had got at my vocation,
  Learned that I belonged to *Punch*,
And in tones of milk and honey
  You invited me to speak
On the art of being funny,
  Funny once a week.

'Tis a task that haunts me waking,
  Like a vampire on the chest,
Spoils my peace, prevents my taking
  Joyance in another's jest;
Makes me move abroad distracted,
  Trailing speculative feet;
Makes me wear at home a rack'd head
  In a dripping sheet.

Women hint that I am blinded
  To their chaste, but obvious, charms;
Sportsmen deem me absent-minded
  When addressed to feats of arms:
If the sudden partridge rises
  I but rend the neighbouring air,
And the rabbit's rude surprises
  Take me unaware.

Life for me's no game of skittles
  As at first you might opine;
I have lost my love of victuals
  And a pretty taste in wine;
When at lunch your talk was wasted,
  Did you notice what occurred,—
How I left the hock untasted,
  How I passed the bird?

So, if you would grant a favour,
  In your orisons recall

One whose smile could scarce be graver
   If his mouth were full of gall;
Let your lips (that shame the ruby)
   Pray for mine all wan and bleak
With the strain of trying to be
   Funny every week.

OWEN SEAMAN

MAMA'S ADVICE

Die Mutter sagt, "Nau Lieschen listen here.
Es tun für dich die Wedding Bells heut pealeh,
Und's iss mei Pflicht und Duty dass ich dir
Die Facts von Life mitaus Reserf revealeh.
Ich hab in Innocence dich aufgebracht
But nau lässt sich die Sach' net länger shirkeh.
So keep mei Words in Mind bei Tag und Nacht:
A gute Noodlesupp' tut Wunders workeh.

"Wie shweet geflavort iss der Honeymoon!
But leider kann et net fürever lasteh.
Bald giebt's aplenty Chores in Haus zu tun
Wo likely sein Loff's süssen Traum zu blasteh.
A Mann gemarried iss a Mann gebored.
In Intimacy da tut Danger lurkeh.
But sei net bang wenn er a Kiss ignored:
A gute Noodlesupp' tut Wunders workeh.

"Die cut'sten Charms, die faden mit der Zeit.
Die Shkin ver yellowed und commenzt zu saggeh;
Das Harr wird dünn, der Back in Shpots zu breit
Und Conversation tut auch öfters laggeh.
Man foolt mit Canfield, und turnt's Radio an,
Und tried all kinds von Schemes um aufzuperkeh.
Mei Child, remember speshelly dass dann:
A gute Noodlesupp' tut Wunders workeh."

KURT M. STEIN

AN UNSERER BEACH

An der Beach, an der Beach,
Da iss plenty Fun for Each,
Da gibt's Sights, die gäb a Blinder viel zu sehn.
Da iss Nature wundervoll,
Da iss net a Minute dull,
Wer a Eyefull will, das iss der Platz zu gehn.

Es steht an uns'rer Beach im Sand
Der Missis Meier's Popkorn Stand.
Da gibt's all Kinds von Vittels:
Hot Dogs, und Pop, und Icecreamcones,
Und Bags mit Peanutbrittles.

Frau Meier hat da einen Pot
In dem sie English Mustard hat.
Den tut sie highly preissen.
But unverschämte Flies die tun
Mit Preference dort speissen.

Frau Meier hat auch ein Paar Twins
Die sind im Winter Manikins,
But an der Beach da schmieren
Sie Butter auf die Buns und tun
Die Facts von Life studieren.

Frau Meier hat auch einen Suit
In dem sie schwimmen gehen tut.
Sie hat ihn selbst geknittet.
Und wenn was bustet dran, da wird's
Mit Chewing Gum verkittet.

Frau Meier macht auch Lemonade
Wo aus dem following besteht:
Neun Lemon disks, die floateh
On Top in so a Goldfishbowl,
Und Zucker stickt am Bode'.

Frau Meier hatt' auch eine Tante
Die all die Firemen gut kannte.
Und tat zu heiss sie fuhlen,
So ging sie in das Station house
Und lies sich dort abkuhlen.

Frau Meier hat auch einen Freund,
A Barber, der sie Abends joint.
Before iss er zu busy.
Er specializet in Wasserwaves,
Und seine Frau heisst Lizzie.

Frau Meier hat auch einen Poodle
Den feedet sie mit Apfelstrudel.
Das tut den Cur so bloateh
Dass wenn er schwimmt wo's shallow iss
Er an sei Back muss floateh.

                              KURT M. STEIN

TO BE CONTINUED

Said Opie Read to E. P. Roe;
"How do you like Gaboriau?"
"I like him very much indeed,"
Said E. P. Roe to Opie Read.

                      JULIAN STREET AND
                      JAMES MONTGOMERY FLAGG

THE LITTLE STAR

Scintillate, scintillate, globule orific,
Fain would I fathom thy nature's specific.
Loftily poised in ether capacious,
Strongly resembling a gem carbonaceous.

When torrid Phoebus refuses his presence
And ceases to lamp with fierce incandescence,
Then you illumine the regions supernal,
Scintillate, scintillate, semper nocturnal.

Then the victim of hospiceless peregrination
Gratefully hails your minute coruscation.
He could not determine his journey's direction
But for your bright scintillating protection.

UNKNOWN

THE ORIGINAL LAMB

Oh, Mary had a little lamb, regarding whose cuticular
The fluff exterior was white and kinked in each particular.
On each occasion when the lass was seen perambulating,
The little quadruped likewise was there a gallivating.

One day it did accompany her to the knowledge dispensary,
Which to every rule and precedent was recklessly contrary.
Immediately whereupon the pedagogue superior,
Exasperated, did eject the lamb from the interior.

Then Mary, on beholding such performance arbitrary,
Suffused her eyes with saline drops from glands called
    lachrymary,
And all the pupils grew thereat tumultuously hilarious,
And speculated on the case with wild conjectures various.

"What makes the lamb love Mary so?" the scholars asked
    the teacher.
He paused a moment, then he tried to diagnose the creature.
"Oh pecus amorem Mary habit omnia temporum."
"Thanks, teacher dear," the scholars cried, and awe crept
    darkly o'er 'em.

UNKNOWN

MANILA

Oh, dewy was the morning, upon the first of May,
And Dewey was the admiral, down in Manila Bay;
And dewy were the Regent's eyes, them royal orbs of blue,
And do we feel discouraged? We do not think we do!

EUGENE F. WARE

Love, Etc.

TO A LADY TROUBLED BY INSOMNIA

Let the waves of slumber billow
Gently, softly o'er thy pillow;
Let the darkness wrap thee round
Till in slumber thou art drowned;
Let my tenderest lullabies
Guard the closing of thine eyes;
If *these* fail to make thee weary,
Then I cannot help thee, dearie.

FRANKLIN P. ADAMS

THE BROKEN PITCHER

It was a Moorish maiden was sitting by a well,
And what the maiden thought of I cannot, cannot tell,
When by there rode a valiant knight from the town of
Oviedo—
Alphonso Guzman was he hight, the Count of Desparedo.

"Oh, maiden, Moorish maiden! why sitt'st thou by the
spring?
Say, dost thou seek a lover, or any other thing?
Why gazest thou upon me, with eyes so large and wide,
And wherefore doth the pitcher lie broken by thy side?"

"I do not seek a lover, thou Christian knight so gay,
Because an article like that hath never come my way;
And why I gaze upon you, I cannot, cannot tell,
Except that in your iron hose you look uncommon swell.

"My pitcher it is broken, and this the reason is,—
A shepherd came behind me, and tried to snatch a kiss;
I would not stand his nonsense, so ne'er a word I spoke,
But scored him on the costard, and so the jug was broke.

"My uncle, the Alcaydè, he waits for me at home,
And will not take his tumbler until Zorayda come.
I cannot bring him water—the pitcher is in pieces—
And so I'm sure to catch it, 'cos he wallops all his nieces."

"Oh, maiden, Moorish maiden! wilt thou be ruled by me!
So wipe thine eyes and rosy lips, and give me kisses three;
And I'll give thee my helmet, thou kind and courteous lady,
To carry home the water to thy uncle, the Alcaydè."

He lighted down from off his steed—he tied him to a tree—
He bowed him to the maiden, and took his kisses three:
"To wrong thee, sweet Zorayda, I swear would be a sin!"
He knelt him at the fountain, and he dipped his helmet in.

Up rose the Moorish maiden—behind the knight she steals,
And caught Alphonso Guzman up tightly by the heels;
She tipped him in, and held him down beneath the bubbling
      water,—
"Now, take thou that for venturing to kiss Al Hamet's
      daughter!"

A Christian maid is weeping in the town of Oviedo;
She waits the coming of her love, the Count of Desparedo.
I pray you all in charity, that you will never tell,
How he met the Moorish maiden beside the lonely well.

WILLIAM E. AYTOUN

BELIEF

Tell me that the snow is red,
  And dandelions blue,
I will believe what you have said,
  I *must* believe in you.

Tell me that the earth is flat,
  And a peacock coos like a dove,
Why should I question this or that?
  I have not doubted love.

RUTH FITCH BARTLETT

A WINTER MADRIGAL

Chloris made my heart to stop
    And turn'd my joy to acid,
For I was working in the shop
    And she was in Lake Placid.

In my despair I could not bear
    Her gladsome letters, prating
Of frolic in the sparkling air,
    And skiing, sleighing, skating.
        Hey nonny, nonny, etc.

It fill'd my soul with woe and hate
    To hear about her ski-jumps,
For in proportion to her weight
    She jump'd far as a flea jumps;

But now the dart has ceas'd to smart,
    My pain has ceas'd to rankle,
For though my Beauty broke my heart
    My Beauty broke her ankle.
        Hey nonny, nonny, etc.
                    MORRIS BISHOP

THENOT PROTESTS

Her eyes that might be filled with wishes,
Stare back at me like empty dishes;
I've seen more warmth in little fishes.
    It's Spring. And no one's told Clorinda.

Her lips whose sweetness I might rob,
Are little loafers on the job;
So chastely pure they make me sob.
    It's Spring. And no one's told Clorinda

Her heart that might be soft and sweet
Is hard and sour and void of heat;
I doubt if it can even beat.
  It's Spring. And no one's told Clorinda.

Her body, soft as overtones,
Is naught to her but flesh and bones,
Sweet Venus! Heed my prayers and groans.
It's Spring. And no one's told Clorinda.
                                    C. N. S.

FIRST LOVE

O my earliest love, who, ere I number'd
  Ten sweet summers, made my bosom thrill!
Will a swallow—or a swift, or some bird—
  Fly to her and say, I love her still?

Say my life's a desert drear and arid,
  To its one green spot I aye recur:
Never, never—although three times married—
  Have I cared a jot for aught but her.

No, mine own! though early forced to leave you,
  Still my heart was there where first we met;
In those "Lodgings with an ample sea-view,"
  Which were, forty years ago, "To Let."

There I saw her first, our landlord's oldest
  Little daughter. On a thing so fair
Thou, O Sun,—who (so they say) beholdest
  Everything,—hast gazed, I tell thee, ne'er.

There she sat—so near me, yet remoter
  Than a star—a blue-eyed, bashful imp:
On her lap she held a happy bloater.
  'Twixt her lips a yet more happy shrimp.

And I loved her, and our troth we plighted
  On the morrow by the shingly shore:
In a fortnight to be disunited
  By a bitter fate forevermore.

O my own, my beautiful, my blue-eyed!
  To be young once more, and bite my thumb
At the world and all its cares with you, I'd
  Give no inconsiderable sum.

Hand in hand we tramp'd the golden seaweed,
  Soon as o'er the gray cliff peep'd the dawn:
Side by side, when came the hour for tea, we'd
  Crunch the mottled shrimp and hairy prawn:—

Has she wedded some gigantic shrimper,
  That sweet mite with whom I loved to play?
Is she girt with babes that whine and whimper,
  That bright being who was always gay?

Yes—she has at least a dozen wee things!
  Yes—I see her darning corduroys,
Scouring floors, and setting out the tea-things,
  For a howling herd of hungry boys,

In a home that reeks of tar and sperm-oil!
  But at intervals she thinks, I know,
Of those days which we, afar from turmoil,
  Spent together forty years ago.

O my earliest love, still unforgotten,
  With your downcast eyes of dreamy blue!
Never, somehow, could I seem to cotton
  To another as I did to you!
                 CHARLES STUART CALVERLEY

LINES SUGGESTED BY THE FOURTEENTH
OF FEBRUARY

Ere the morn the East has crimsoned,
   When the stars are twinkling there,
(As they did in Watts's Hymns, and
   Made him wonder what they were:)
When the forest-nymphs are beading
   Fern and flower with silvery dew—
My infallible proceeding
   Is to wake and think of you.

When the hunter's ringing bugle
   Sounds farewell to field and copse,
And I sit before my frugal
   Meal of gravy-soup and chops:
When (as Gray remarks) "the moping
   Owl doth to the moon complain,"
And the hour suggests eloping—
   Fly my thoughts to you again.

May my dreams be granted never?
   Must I aye endure affliction
Rarely realised, if ever,
   In our wildest works of fiction?
Madly Romeo loved his Juliet;
   Copperfield began to pine
When he hadn't been to school yet—
   But their loves were cold to mine.

Give me hope, the least, the dimmest,
   Ere I drain the poisoned cup:
Tell me I may tell the chymist
   Not to make that arsenic up!
Else the heart must cease to throb in
   This my breast; and when, in tones
Hushed, men ask, "Who killed Cock Robin?"
   They'll be told, "Miss Clara J - - - s."

CHARLES STUART CALVERLEY

BUXOM JOAN

A soldier and a sailor,
A tinker and a tailor,
Had once a doubtful strife, sir,
To make a maid a wife, sir,
   Whose name was Buxom Joan.
For now the time was ended,
When she no more intended
To lick her lips at men, sir,
And gnaw the sheets in vain, sir,
   And lie o' nights alone.

The soldier swore like thunder,
He loved her more than plunder;
And showed her many a scar, sir,
That he had brought from far, sir,
   With fighting for her sake.
The tailor thought to please her,
With offering her his measure.
The tinker too with mettle,
Said he could mend her kettle,
   And stop up every leak.

But while these three were prating,
The sailor slily waiting,
Thought if it came about, sir,
That they should all fall out, sir,
   He then might play his part.
And just e'en as he meant, sir,
To loggerheads they went, sir,
And then he let fly at her
A shot 'twixt wind and water,
   That won this fair maid's heart.

WILLIAM CONGREVE

SONG

Pious Selinda goes to prayers,
    If I but ask a favour;
And yet the tender fool's in tears,
    When she believes I'll leave her.

Would I were free from this restraint,
    Or else had hope to win her!
Would she could make of me a saint,
    Or I of her a sinner!

                    WILLIAM CONGREVE

THE JOYS OF MARRIAGE

How uneasy is his life,
Who is troubled with a wife!
Be she ne'er so fair or comely,
Be she ne'er so foul or homely,
Be she ne'er so young and toward,
Be she ne'er so old and froward,
Be she kind, with arms enfolding,
Be she cross, and always scolding,
Be she blithe or melancholy,
Have she wit, or have she folly,
Be she wary, be she squandering,
Be she staid, or be she wandering,
Be she constant, be she fickle,
Be she fire, or be she ickle;
Be she pious or ungodly,
Be she chaste, or what sounds oddly:
Lastly, be she good or evil,
Be she saint, or be she devil,—
Yet, uneasy is his life
Who is married to a wife.

                    CHARLES COTTON

MIA CARLOTTA

Giuseppe, da barber, ees greata for "mash,"
He gotta da bigga, da blacka moustache,
Good clo'es an' good styla an' playnta good cash.

W'enevra Giuseppe ees walk on da street,
Da peopla dey talka, "how nobby! how neat!
How softa da handa, how smalla da feet."

He leefta hees hat an' he shaka hees curls,
An' smila weeth teetha so shiny like pearls;
Oh, manny da heart of da seelly young girls
He gotta.
Yes, playnta he gotta
But notta
Carlotta.

Giuseppe, da barber, he maka da eye,
An' lika da steam engine puffa an' sigh,
For catcha Carlotta w'en she ees go by.

Carlotta she walka weeth nose in da air,
An' look through Giuseppe weeth far-away stare,
As eef she no see dere ees somebody dere.

Giuseppe, da barber, he gotta da cash,
He gotta da clo'es an' da bigga moustache,
He gotta da seelly young girls for da "mash,"
But notta
You bat my life, notta—
Carlotta.
I gotta.

T. A. DALY

THE CONSERVATIVE SHEPHERD TO HIS LOVE

Tell me, dear, in terms laconic,
If my dreams will e'er come true.
You're so secret and Masonic;

Tell me how I stand with you.
If it's true you really love me,
Tell me so; nor try to bluff.
Then by all the powers above me,
I'll know how to do my stuff.

But if, on the other hand, dear,
I'm a friend and nothing more,
Don't soft pedal on the grand, dear,
Tell me and I won't get sore.
If with you I'm not a winner,
That means little in my life.
I'll buy you a farewell dinner
And take you home to meet the wife.

JACK D'ARCY

RURAL BLISS

The poet is, or ought to be, a hater of the city,
   And so, when happiness is mine, and Maud becomes my
      wife,
We'll look on town inhabitants with sympathetic pity,
   For we shall lead a peaceful and serene Arcadian life.

Then shall I sing in eloquent and most effective phrases
   The grandeur of geraniums and the beauty of the rose;
Immortalise in deathless strains the buttercups and daisies—
   For even I can hardly be mistaken as to those.

The music of the nightingale will ring from leafy hollow,
   And fill us with a rapture indescribable in words;
And we shall also listen to the robin and the swallow
   (I wonder if a swallow sings?), and . . . well, the other
      birds.

Too long I dwelt in ignorance of all the countless treasures
   Which dwellers in the country have in such abundant store;
To give a single instance from the multitude of pleasures—
   The music of the nighting—oh, I mentioned that before.

And shall I prune potato-trees and artichokes, I wonder,
 And cultivate the silo-plant, which springs (I *hope* it
  springs?)
In graceful foliage overhead?—Excuse me if I blunder,
 It's really inconvenient not to know the name of things!

No matter; in the future, when I celebrate the beauty
 Of country life in glowing terms, and "build the lofty
  rhyme,"
Aware that every Englishman is bound to do his duty,
 I'll learn to give the stupid things their proper names in
  time!

Meanwhile, you needn't wonder at the view I've indicated,
 The country life appears to me indubitably blest,
For, even if its other charms are somewhat over-rated,
 As long as Maud is there, you see—what matters all the
  rest?

ANTHONY C. DEANE

OF BEAUTY

Let us use it while we may
Snatch those joys that haste away!
Earth her Winter coat may cast,
And renew her beauty past:
But our Winter come, in vain
We solicit Spring again;
And, when our furrows snow shall cover,
Love may return, but never lover.

SIR RICHARD FANSHAWE

JESSIE

When I remark her golden hair
 Swoon on her glorious shoulders,
I marvel not that sight so rare
 Doth ravish all beholders;

For summon hence all pretty girls
  Renowned for beauteous tresses,
And you shall find among their curls
  There's none so fair as Jessie's.

And Jessie's eyes are, oh, so blue
  And full of sweet revealings—
They seem to look you through and through
  And read your inmost feelings;
Nor black emits such ardent fires,
  Nor brown such truth expresses—
Admit it, all ye gallant squires—
  There are no eyes like Jessie's.

Her voice (like liquid beams that roll
  From moonland to the river)
Steals subtly to the raptured soul,
  Therein to lie and quiver;
Or falls upon the grateful ear
  With chaste and warm caresses—
Ah, all concede the truth (who hear):
  There's no such voice as Jessie's.

Of other charms she hath such store
  All rivalry excelling,
Though I used adjectives galore,
  They'd fail me in the telling;
But now discretion stays my hand—
  Adieu, eyes, voice, and tresses.
Of all the husbands in the land
  There's none so fierce as Jessie's.

EUGENE FIELD

THE BUSY BODY

Now fields are striped in green and brown,
  And every dooryard's sweet,
So I will take the road to town
  And nod to all I meet.

I'll smile and say—"A pleasant day."
　　I'll praise the sky's far blue,
And none will guess, I'll be so gay,
　　My heart is set on you.

I'll pile my wicker basket high
　　With parcels at the store.
Green peas and buns and eggs I'll buy,
　　Raisins and nuts galore.
Each one I'll choose with such a care,
　　As if we two should dine
From bowl and plate of willow-ware,
　　By fire and candle shine.

But when the cups and plates are dried
　　And set upon the shelf—
I will put off this foolish pride,
　　This sprightly, hard-earned self.
I'll miss you to my heart's content
　　And not be dubbed a fool—
For who pretends to ticking clocks,
　　Or wooden chair and stool?

RACHEL FIELD

THE IDEAL HUSBAND TO HIS WIFE

We've lived for forty years, dear wife,
　　And walked together side by side,
And you to-day are just as dear
　　As when you were my bride.
I've tried to make life glad for you,
　　One long, sweet honeymoon of joy,
A dream of marital content,
　　Without the least alloy.
I've smoothed all boulders from our path,
　　That we in peace might toil along,
By always hastening to admit
　　That I was right and you were wrong.

No mad diversity of creed
 Has ever sundered me from thee;
For I permit you evermore
 To borrow your ideas of me.
And thus it is, through weal or woe,
 Our love forevermore endures;
For I permit that you should take
 My views and creeds and make them yours.
And thus I let you have my way,
 And thus in peace we toil along,
For I am willing to admit
 That I am right and you are wrong.

And when our matrimonial skiff
 Strikes snags in love's meandering stream,
I lift our shallop from the rocks,
 And float as in a placid dream.
And well I know our marriage bliss
 While life shall last will never cease;
For I shall always let thee do,
 In generous love, just what I please.
Peace comes, and discord flies away,
 Love's bright day follows hatred's night;
For I am ready to admit
 That you are wrong and I am right.

      SAM WALTER FOSS

TO PHOEBE

"Gentle, modest little flower,
 Sweet epitome of May,
Love me but for half an hour,
 Love me, love me, little fay."
Sentences so fiercely flaming
 In your tiny, shell-like ear,
I should always be exclaiming
 If I loved you, Phoebe dear.

"Smiles that thrill from any distance
　　Shed upon me while I sing!
Please ecstaticize existence,
　　Love me, oh, thou fairy thing!"
Words like these, outpouring sadly,
　　You'd perpetually hear,
If I loved you fondly, madly;—
　　But I do not, Phoebe dear.

W. S. GILBERT

DELIGHT IN DISORDER

A sweet disorder in the dress
Kindles in clothes a wantonness:
A lawn about the shoulders thrown
Into a fine distraction:
An erring lace, which here and there
Enthralls the crimson stomacher:
A cuff neglectful, and thereby
Ribbons to flow confusedly:
A winning wave, deserving note,
In the tempestuous petticoat:
A careless shoe-string, in whose tie
I see a wild civility:
Do more bewitch me, than when art
Is too precise in every part.

ROBERT HERRICK

THE ROCK OF RUBIES

Some ask'd me where the rubies grew?
　　And nothing I did say;
But with my finger pointed to
　　The lips of Julia.
Some ask'd how pearls did grow, and where?
　　Then spoke I to my girle,
To part her lips, and shew'd them there
　　The quarelets of pearl.

ROBERT HERRICK

THE ROSARIE

One ask'd me where the roses grew?
  I bade him not goe seek;
But forthwith bade my Julia shew
  A bud in either cheek.

ROBERT HERRICK

TO THE VIRGINS

TO MAKE MUCH OF TIME

Gather ye rose-buds while ye may,
  Old Time is still a-flying:
And this same flower that smiles to-day,
  To morrow will be dying.

The glorious lamp of heaven, the sun,
  The higher he's a getting;
The sooner will his race be run,
  And neerer he's to setting.

That age is best, which is the first,
  When youth and blood are warmer;
But being spent, the worse, and worst
  Times still succeed the former.

Then be not coy, but use your time;
  And while ye may, goe marry;
For having lost but once your prime,
  You may for ever tarry.

ROBERT HERRICK

POEMS OF PASSION, CAREFULLY RESTRAINED SO AS TO OFFEND NOBODY

I

You have a most attractive pan,
And I'm a very foolish man,
And, what between the two, I fell

As deep as Dante into hell.
But do you, in your triumph, think
I'll stay forever on the blink,
And pine and pale and waste away
And grow cadaverous and gray—
A wreck, a rum, a shard? Well, maybe
You are right about it, baby!

II

When you're away, I'm restless, lonely,
Wretched, bored, dejected; only
Here's the rub, my darling dear,
I feel the same when you are here.

III

Psycho-analyzed, I stand
And meditate your little hand—
Your lost, evasive eyes, that seem
To lean upon me while they scheme.
And thus contemplative, I know
Why I adore and need you so:
When I was six or seven or eight,
In that divine, pre-nubile state,
I had a horror, vent in yelpings,
Of what were known as single helpings;
When I was nine, or maybe ten,
I nursed an unrequited yen:
I loved her, middle-aged and shrewish,
That she was Christian, I but Jewish—
Though now I marvel at it all,
Who am devout Episcopal.
When I was in my teens, I dreamed
Green apples were not what they seemed,
But beasts, inimical to rest,
Who sat upon a fellow's chest;
When I achieved the peak of twenty,
Bad breaks with dames I had aplenty,
Who left my burning love behind,

And each, a complex in my mind.
Now, to these inhibitions true,
I am a-Freud of losing you,
And, though I fully understand,
I meditate your little hand,
Your eyes that lie as like as not,
And love you, whom I ought to swat.

SAMUEL HOFFENSTEIN

LOVE IS LIKE A DIZZINESS

I lately lived in quiet case,
    An' ne'er wish'd to marry, O!
But when I saw my Peggy's face,
    I felt a sad quandary, O!
Though wild as ony Athol deer,
    She has trepann'd me fairly, O!
Her cherry cheeks an' een sae clear
    Torment me late an' early O!
        O, love, love, love!
            Love is like a dizziness;
        It winna let a poor body
            Gang about his biziness!

To tell my feats this single week
    Wad mak a daft-like diary, O!
I drave my cart out ow'r a dike,
    My horses in a miry, O!
I wear my stockings white an' blue,
    My love's sae fierce an' fiery, O!
I drill the land that I should pleugh,
    An' pleugh the drills entirely, O!
        O, love, love, love! etc.

Ae morning, by the dawn o' day,
    I rase to theek the stable, O!
I keust my coat, and plied away
    As fast as I was able, O!

I wrought that morning out an' out,
  As I'd been redding fire, O!
When I had done an look'd about,
  Gudefaith, it was the byre, O!
    O, love, love, love! etc.

Her wily glance I'll ne'er forget,
  The dear, the lovely blinkin o't
Has pierced me through an' through the heart,
  An' plagues me wi' the prinking o't.
I tried to sing, I tried to pray,
  I tried to drown't wi' drinkin' o't,
I tried with sport to drive't away,
  But ne'er can sleep for thinkin' o't.
    O, love, love, love! etc.

Nae man can tell what pains I prove,
  Or how severe my pliskie, O!
I swear I'm sairer drunk wi' love
  Than ever I was wi' whiskey, O!
For love has raked me fore an' aft,
  I scarce can lift a leggie, O!
I first grew dizzy, then gaed daft,
  An' soon I'll dee for Peggy, O!
    O, love, love, love!
      Love is like a dizziness;
      It winna let a poor body
        Gang about his biziness!

                          JAMES HOGG

JENNY KISSED ME

Jenny kissed me when we met,
  Jumping from the chair she sat in;
Time, you thief, who love to get
  Sweets into your list, put that in!
Say I'm weary, say I'm sad,
  Say that health and wealth have missed me,
Say I'm growing old, but add,
  Jenny kissed me.

                          LEIGH HUNT

THE NUN

Suggested by part of the Italian Song, beginning "Se Moneca Ti Fai."

I

If you become a nun, dear,
  A friar I will be;
In any cell you run, dear,
  Pray look behind for me.
The roses all turn pale, too;
The doves all take the veil, too;
  The blind will see the show:
What! you become a nun, my dear!
  I'll not believe it, no.

II

If you become a nun, dear,
  The bishop Love will be;
The Cupids every one, dear,
  Will chaunt "We trust in thee";
The incense will go sighing,
The candles fall a dying,
  The water turn to wine:
What! you go take the vows, my dear!
  You may—but they'll be mine.

LEIGH HUNT

SNOWFALL

Wires strung with diamonds,
Shanties decked in white,
Our shabby little village
Turned lovely overnight.

If I were dressed in satin,
With diamonds in my hair,
Do you think, perhaps, that some one
Would say that I was fair?

I. V. S. W.

SHOPPING DAY

Beauty blue and beauty white,
Beauty of the day and night,
Be of her the flesh and bone,
Be her beauty and your own.

Make her step be light and proud
Going in a gown of cloud,
Make her scarves of trailing blue
Cut from each day's sky anew.

Beauty, rob as for a goddess
Autumn of her brightest bodice;
Be she true or be she flirt,
Of a green tree make the skirt.

Weave from dusk and dawn to measure
Fairy frocks when she's in pleasure,
Or if she must walk in pain
Drape about her silver rain.

If she walks in heaven or hell,
Beauty dress her body well.
Beauty blue and beauty white
Be her own by day and night.

ORRICK JOHNS

SPRING

I

You haven't got so very far
    From here down the hill;
Grab branches when you reach the rocks
    Unless you want a spill.

Once you're down you'll find a creek—
    We girls have crossed it dry;
It's lonely there, the hidden grass . . .
    Show you the way? But why?

II

It's always harder coming up . . .
 You're going now, you say?
But you'll be back? Oh, much you mean!
 I'll never see the day.

Walk with you half the way to town?
 I should go further still . . .
Yes, there's a clerk and parson there—
 Show you the way? I will!

ORRICK JOHNS

CUPID

Beauties, have ye seen this toy,
Calléd love, a little boy
Almost naked, wanton, blind,
Cruel now, and then as kind?
If he be amongst ye, say!
He is Venus' runaway.

He hath of marks about him plenty;
Ye shall know him among twenty;
All his body is a fire,
And his breath a flame entire,
That, being shot like lightning in,
Wounds the heart, but not the skin.

He doth bear a golden bow,
And a quiver, hanging low,
Full of arrows, that outbrave
Dian's shaft, where, if he have
Any head more sharp than other,
With that first he strikes his mother.

Trust him not: his words, though sweet,
Seldom with his heart do meet;
All his practice is deceit,
Every gift is but a bait;
Not a kiss but poison bears,
And most treason in his tears.

If by these ye please to know him,
Beauties, be not nice, but show him,
Though ye had a will to hide him.
Now, we hope, ye'll not abide him,
Since ye hear his falser play,
And that he's Venus' runaway.

BEN JONSON

EVIDENCE

(To M. F.)

Sometimes when I think of things
A little bell within me rings.

Ding!

Sometimes when I lie awake
I wish to God that things were jake.

Whew!

Sometimes when I'm fast asleep
I still can see the jumping sheep.

Baaa!

Sometimes when I'm feeling good
I find my knuckles tapping wood.

Knock!

Sometimes when I'm deep in love
I don't know what I'm thinking of.

Oh, don't I, though!
ARTHUR KOBER

PROPINQUITY NEEDED

Celestine Silvousplait Justine de Mouton Rosalie,
A coryphée who lived and danced in naughty, gay Paree,
Was every bit as pretty as a French girl e'er can be
(Which isn't saying much).

Maurice Boulanger (there's a name that would adorn a
    king),
But Morris Baker was the name they called the man I sing.
He lived in New York City in the Street that's labeled
    Spring
        (Chosen because it rhymed).

Now Baker was a lonesome youth and wanted to be wed,
And for a wife, all over town he hunted, it is said;
And up and down Fifth Avenue be ofttimes wanderéd
        (He was a peripatetic Baker, he was).

And had he met Celestine, not a doubt but Cupid's darts
Would in a trice have wounded both of their fond, loving
    hearts;
But he has never left New York to stray in foreign parts
        (Because he hasn't the price).

And she has never left Paree and so, of course, you see
There's not the slightest chance at all she'll marry Morris B.
For love to get well started, really needs propinquity
        (Hence my title).
                                CHARLES BATTELL LOOMIS

SONG

Why should you swear I am forsworn,
    Since thine I vowed to be?
Lady, it is already morn,
    And 'twas last night I swore to thee
    That fond impossibility.

Have I not loved thee much and long,
    A tedious twelve hours' space?
I must all other beauties wrong,
    And rob thee of a new embrace,
    Could I still dote upon thy face.

Not but all joy in thy brown hair
   By others may be found;
But I must search the black and fair,
   Like skilful mineralists that sound
   For treasure in unploughed-up ground

Then, if when I have loved my round,
   Thou prov'st the pleasant she;
With spoils of meaner beauties crowned
   I laden will return to thee,
   Even sated with variety.

RICHARD LOVELACE

THE COURTIN'

God makes sech nights, all white an' still
   Fur 'z you can look or listen,
Moonshine an' snow on field an' hill,
   All silence an' all glisten.

Zekle crep' up quite unbeknown
   An' peeked in thru' the winder,
An' there sot Huldy all alone,
   'Ith no one nigh to hender.

A fireplace filled the room's one side
   With half a cord o' wood in—
There warn't no stoves (tell comfort died)
   To bake ye to a puddin'.

The wa'nut logs shot sparkles out
   Towards the pootiest, bless her,
An' leetle flames danced all about
   The chiny on the dresser.

Agin the chimbley crook-necks hung,
   An' in amongst 'em rusted
The ole queen's-arm that Gran'ther Young
   Fetched back f'om Concord busted.

The very room, coz she was in,
　　Seemed warm f'om floor to ceilin',
An' she looked full ez rosy agin
　　Ez the apples she was peelin'.

'Twas kin' o' kingdom-come to look
　　On sech a blessed cretur;
A dogrose blushin' to a brook
　　Ain't modester nor sweeter.

He was six foot o' man, A 1,
　　Clear grit an' human natur';
None couldn't quicker pitch a ton,
　　Nor dror a furrer straighter.

He'd sparked it with full twenty gals,
　　He'd squired 'em, danced 'em, druv 'em,
Fust this one, an' then thet, by spells—
　　All is, he couldn't love 'em.

But long o' her his veins 'ould run
　　All crinkly like curled maple;
The side she breshed felt full o' sun
　　Ez a south slope in Ap'il.

She thought no v'ice hed sech a swing
　　Ez hisn in the choir;
My! when he made Ole Hundred ring,
　　She *knowed* the Lord was nigher.

An' she'd blush scarlit, right in prayer,
　　When her new meetin'-bunnet
Felt somehow thru' its crown a pair
　　O' blue eyes sot upun it.

Thet night, I tell ye, she looked *some!*
　　She seemed to 've gut a new soul,
For she felt sartin-sure he'd come,
　　Down to her very shoe-sole.

She heered a foot, an' knowed it tu,
  A-raspin' on the scraper,—
All ways to once her feelins flew
  Like sparks in burnt-up paper.

He kin' o' l'itered on the mat,
  Some doubtfle o' the sekle;
His heart kep' goin' pitty-pat,
  But hern went pity Zekle.

An' yit she gin her cheer a jerk
  Ez though she wished him furder,
An' on her apples kep' to work,
  Parin' away like murder.

"You want to see my Pa, I s'pose?"
  "Wal . . . no . . . I come dasignin'—"
"To see my Ma? She's sprinklin' clo'es
  Agin to-morrer's i'nin'."

To say why gals act so or so,
  Or don't, 'ould be presumin';
Mebbe to mean *yes* an' say *no*
  Comes nateral to women.

He stood a spell on one foot fust,
  Then stood a spell on t'other,
An' on which one he felt the wust
  He couldn't ha' told ye nuther.

Says he, "I'd better call agin";
  Says she, "Think likely, Mister";
Thet last word pricked him like a pin,
  An' . . . Wal, he up an' kissed her.

When Ma bimeby upon 'em slips,
  Huldy sot pale ez ashes,
All kin' o' smily roun' the lips
  An' teary roun' the lashes.

For she was jes' the quiet kind
  Whose naturs never vary,
Like streams that keep a summer mind
  Snowhid in Jenooary.

The blood clost roun' her heart felt glued
  Too tight for all expressin',
Tell mother see how metters stood,
  An' gin 'em both her blessin'.

Then her red come back like the tide
  Down to the Bay o' Fundy,
An' all I know is they was cried
  In meetin' come nex' Sunday.

                JAMES RUSSELL LOWELL

THE PASSIONATE ENCYCLOPEDIA BRITANNICA READER TO HIS LOVE

  As And to Aus, and Aus to Bis;
  As Hus to Ita, and Ita to Kys;
  As Pay to Pol, and Pol to Ree;
  Ah, that is how vou are to me!

  As Bis to Cal, and Cal to Cha;
  As Edw to Eva, and Eva to Fra;
  As Ref to Sai, and Sai to Shu;
  That is, I hope, how I'm to you.

                    MAGGIE

COMPROMISE

"Vacation is coming, where shall we go?"
  A month ago to my wife said I.
"If you're asking me, I prefer the sea,
  And these," she said, "are the reasons why:

"I like the smell of the salty air
  And the scorch of the off-shore breeze.
I think it's swell to get sand in my hair
  And burn the backs of my knees;
To return to town a mahogany brown
  So dark that your friends don't know you—
And the bathing suit that I've bought is cute—
  Shall I run upstairs and show you?
But any place is all right with me,
You are the one to decide," said she.

"Then give me the crunch of a mountain trail
  With its shadows, soft and cool,
And the quiet hunch that the flashing tail
  Of a trout is deep in that pool;
Those nights in a tent, when my spine gets bent—
  The joy of my oldest clothes—
And the half-cooked steak for outdoor's sake
  With smoke in my eyes and nose,"
I said, "That's what appeals to me."

* * *

So here we are by the sounding sea.

LAURENCE McKINNEY

SONG TO MY LOVE

(A poet writes in the language of wild flowers)

The Vipers Bugloss beckons me
  Across the flowery lea,
And a glorious stretch of blue Cow Vetch,
  (Where the Skunk Cabbage used to be.)
Where the Devil's Paint Brush nestles,
  And the Harebells sadly peal,
I'll send to my love an armful of
  Hardback and False Solomon's Seal.

CHORUS

My Sneezeweed, my Chickweed, Joe Pye Weed,
My Milkweed, My Ragweed (Achoo!!),
My Fireweed, Ironweed, Jewelweed,
(Say you'll be my cruel little Jewelweed)
Each flower reminds me of you.

The Dutchman's Breeches call to me
  The Corn Cockle guides my way,
And I'll seek me a bed of Turtlehead
  Where the Corpse Plant holds its sway.
Where the Toadflax sports with the Goat's Rue
  And the bees round the Cow Lilies hum,
My spirits feed on Rattlesnake Weed,
  As I wait for my love to come,

CHORUS

My Moneywort, Liverwort, Soapwort,
My Stitchwort, My Toothwort, my child,
My Spiderwort, Mitrewort, Motherwort,
(My dear little, queer little Motherwort)
The flowers are driving me wild.

LAURENCE McKINNEY

SHE IS OVERHEARD SINGING

Oh, Prue she has a patient man,
  And Joan a gentle lover,
And Agatha's Arth' is a hug-the-hearth,—
  But my true love's a rover!

Mig, her man's as good as cheese
  And honest as a briar,
Sue tells her love what he's thinking of,—
  But my dear lad's a liar!

Oh, Sue and Prue and Agatha
  Are thick with Mig and Joan!

They bite their threads and shake their heads
   And gnaw my name like a bone;

And Prue says, "Mine's a patient man,
   As never snaps me up,"
And Agatha, "Arth' is a hug-the-hearth,
   Could live content in a cup";

Sue's man's mind is like good jell—
   All one color, and clear—
And Mig's no call to think at all
   What's to come next year,

While Joan makes boast of a gentle lad,
   That's troubled with that and this;—
But they all would give the life they live
   For a look from the man I kiss!

Cold he slants his eyes about,
   And few enough's his choice,—
Though he'd slip me clean for a nun, or a queen,
   Or a beggar with knots in her voice,—

And Agatha will turn awake
   When her good man sleeps sound,
And Mig and Sue and Joan and Prue
   Will hear the clock strike round;

For Prue she has a patient man,
   As asks not when or why,
And Mig and Sue have naught to do
   But peep who's passing by,

Joan is paired with a putterer
   That bastes and tastes and salts,
And Agatha's Arth' is a hug-the-hearth,—
   But my true love is false!

EDNA ST. VINCENT MILLAY

THURSDAY

And if I loved you Wednesday,
  Well, what is that to you?
I do not love you Thursday—
  So much is true.

And why you come complaining
  Is more than I can see.
I loved you Wednesday,—yes—but what
  Is that to me?

EDNA ST. VINCENT MILLAY

TRAVEL

The railroad track is miles away,
  And the day is loud with voices speaking,
Yet there isn't a train goes by all day
  But I hear its whistle shrieking.

All night there isn't a train goes by,
  Though the night is still for sleep and dreaming,
But I see its cinders red on the sky,
  And hear its engine steaming.

My heart is warm with the friends I make,
  And better friends I'll not be knowing,
Yet there isn't a train I wouldn't take,
  No matter where it's going.

EDNA ST. VINCENT MILLAY

THE GOSPEL OF MR. PEPYS

"Among the others pretty Mrs. Margaret; who indeed is a very pretty lady; and though by my vow it costs me 12*d.* a kiss yet I did adventure upon a couple."—*Pepys's Diary*, Feb. 8, 1665

Good Mr. Peeps or Peps or Pips
  (However he should be yclept),
Clerk of the King's Bureau of Ships,
  A snappy, spicy journal kept.

He knew a Lemon from a Peach,
    And, witting that, he also knew
When kisses are a shilling each
    We should adventure on a few.

He was a connoisseur of lips,
    And though I cannot quite accept
Some of his rather shady tips
    (I grant he often overstepped
The bounds of taste)—still he can teach
    Misogynists a thing or two—
When kisses are a shilling each
    We should adventure on a few.

He drank the wine of life by sips;
    He roundly ate and soundly slept;
His spirits suffered no eclipse;
    But Lord! How sore he would have wept
To see his private linen bleach
    And flutter in the public view . . .
For kisses were a shilling each
    And he adventured on a few!

I love to read about his trips
    With Nell or Knipp; how home he crept
And told his wife a lot of quips,
    Albeit many were inept.
And yet, although he loved to preach,
    Than this he never spake more true:
When kisses are a shilling each
    We should adventure on a few.
                    CHRISTOPHER MORLEY

BALLADE OF BIG PLANS

She loved him. He knew it. And love was a game that two could play at.—
                    Julia Cane, p. 280

Once the orioles sang in chorus,
Once the skies were a cloudless blue.

Spring bore blossoms expressly for us.
Stars lined up to spell "Y-O-U."
All the world wore a golden hue,
Life was a thing to be bold and gay at;
Love was the only game I knew,
And love is a game for two to play at.

Now the heavens are scowling o'er us,
Now the blossoms are pale and few.
Love was a rose with thorns that tore us,
Love was a ship without a crew.
Love is untender, and love is untrue,
Love is a moon for a dog to bay at,
Love is the Lady-That's-Known-As-Lou,
And love is a game for two to play at.

Recollections can only bore us;
Now it's over, and now it's through
Our day is dead as a dinosaurus.
Other the paths that you pursue.
What is the girl in the case to do?
What is she doing to spend her day at?
Fun demands, at a minimum, two—
And love is a game that two can play at.

L'ENVOI

Prince, I'm packing away the rue.
I'll show them something to shout "Hooray" at.
I've got somebody else in view:
And love is a game that two can play at.

DOROTHY PARKER

THE COUNSELOR

I met a man the other day—
    A kindly man, and serious—
Who viewed me in a thoughtful way,
    And spoke me so, and spoke me thus:

"Oh, dallying's a sad mistake;
  'Tis craven to survey the morrow!
Go give your heart, and if it break—
  A wise companion is Sorrow.

"Oh, live, my child, nor keep your soul
  To crowd your coffin when you're dead. . . . "
I asked his work; he dealt in coal,
  And shipped it up the Tyne, he said.
                        DOROTHY PARKER

THE DANGER OF WRITING DEFIANT VERSE

And now I have another lad!
  No longer need you tell
How all my nights are slow and sad
  For loving you too well.

His ways are not your wicked ways;
  He's not the like of you!
He treads his path of reckoned days—
  A sober man, and true.

They'll never see him in the town,
  Another on his knee.
He'd cut his laden orchards down
  If that would pleasure me.

He'd give his blood to paint my lips
  If I should wish them red.
He prays to touch my finger-tips,
  Or stroke my prideful head.

He never weaves a glinting lie,
  Nor brags the hearts he'll keep.
I have forgotten how to cry—
  Remembered how to sleep.

He's none to come and wrench a kiss
　　Nor pull me to his lap . . .
Oh, Lord! I see, on reading this,
　　He is an awful sap!

DOROTHY PARKER

THE DARK GIRL'S RHYME

Who was there had seen us
　　Wouldn't bid him run?
Heavy lay between us
　　All our sires had done.

There he was, a-springing
　　Of a pious race,
Setting hags a-swinging
　　In a market-place;

Sowing turnips over
　　Where the poppies lay;
Looking past the clover,
　　Adding up the hay;

Shouting through the Spring song,
　　Clumping down the sod;
Toadying, in sing-song,
　　To a crabbèd god.

There I was, that came of
　　Folk of mud and flame—
I that had my name of
　　Them without a name.

Up and down a mountain
　　Streeled my silly stock;
Passing by a fountain,
　　Wringing at a rock;

Devil-gotten sinners,
  Throwing back their heads;
Fiddling for their dinners,
  Kissing for their beds.

Not a one had seen us
  Wouldn't help him flee.
Angry ran between us
  Blood of him and me.

How shall I be mating
  Who have looked above—
Living for a hating,
  Dying of a love?

DOROTHY PARKER

DILEMMA

If I were mild, and I were sweet,
And laid my heart before your feet,
And took my dearest thoughts to you,
And hailed your easy lies as true;
Were I to murmur "Yes," and then
"How true, my dear," and "Yes," again,
And wear my eyes discreetly down,
And tremble whitely at your frown,
And keep my words unquestioning—
My love, you'd run like anything!

Should I be frail, and I be mad,
And share my heart with every lad,
But beat my head against the floor
What times you wandered past my door;
Were I to doubt, and I to sneer,
And shriek "Farewell!" and still be here,
And break your joy, and quench your trust—
I should not see you for the dust!

DOROTHY PARKER

THE LITTLE OLD LADY IN LAVENDER SILK

I was seventy-seven, come August,
    I shall shortly be losing my bloom;
I've experienced zephyr and raw gust
    And (symbolical) flood and simoom.

When you come to this time of abatement,
    To this passing from Summer to Fall,
It is manners to issue a statement
    As to what you got out of it all.

So I'll say, though reflection unnerves me
    And pronouncements I dodge as I can,
That I think (if my memory serves me)
    There was nothing more fun than a man!

In my youth, when the crescent was too wan
    To embarass with beams from above,
By the aid of some local Don Juan
    I fell into the habit of love.

And I learned how to kiss and be merry—an
    Education left better unsung.
My neglect of the waters Pierian
    Was a scandal, when Grandma was young.

Though the shabby unbalanced the splendid,
    And the bitter outmeasured the sweet,
I should certainly do as I then did,
    Were I given the chance to repeat.

For contrition is hollow and wraithful,
    And regret is no part of my plan,
And I think (if my memory's faithful)
    There was nothing more fun than a man!

DOROTHY PARKER

LOVE SONG

My own dear love, he is strong and bold
  And he cares not what comes after.
His words ring sweet as a chime of gold,
  And his eyes are lit with laughter.
He is jubilant as a flag unfurled—
  Oh, a girl, she'd not forget him.
My own dear love, he is all my world—
  And I wish I'd never met him.

My love, he's mad, and my love, he's fleet,
  And a wild young wood-thing bore him!
The ways are fair to his roaming feet,
  And the skies are sunlit for him.
As sharply sweet to my heart he seems
  As the fragrance of acacia.
My own dear love, he is all my dreams—
  And I wish he were in Asia.

My love runs by like a day in June,
  And he makes no friends of sorrows.
He'll tread his galloping rigadoon
  In the pathway of the morrows.
He'll live his days where the sunbeams start,
  Nor could storm or wind uproot him.
My own dear love, he is all my heart—
  And I wish somebody'd shoot him.

DOROTHY PARKER

STORY

"And if he's gone away," said she,
"Good riddance, if you're asking me.
I'm not a one to lie awake
And weep for anybody's sake.
There's better lads than him about!
I'll wear my buckled slippers out
A-dancing till the break of day.

I'm better off with him away!
And if he never come," said she,
"Now what on earth is that to me?
I wouldn't have him back!"
                              I hope
Her mother washed her mouth with soap.
                              DOROTHY PARKER

THRENODY

Lilacs blossom just as sweet
    Now my heart is shattered.
If I bowled it down the street,
    Who's to say it mattered?
If there's one that rode away
    What would I be missing?
Lips that taste of tears, they say,
    Are the best for kissing.

Eyes that watch the morning star
    Seem a little brighter;
Arms held out to darkness are
    Usually whiter.
Shall I bar the strolling guest,
    Bind my brow with willow,
When, they say, the empty breast
    Is the softer pillow?

That a heart falls tinkling down,
    Never think it ceases.
Every likely lad in town
    Gathers up the pieces.
If there's one gone whistling by
    Would I let it grieve me?

Let him wonder if I lie;
    Let him half believe me.
                              DOROTHY PARKER

THE BELLE OF THE BALL-ROOM

Years, years ago, ere yet my dreams
  Had been of being wise and witty;
Ere I had done with writing themes,
  Or yawn'd o'er this infernal Chitty;—
Years, years ago, while all my joy
  Was in my fowling-piece and filly;
In short, while I was yet a boy,
  I fell in love with Laura Lily.

I saw her at the County Ball;
  There, when the sounds of flute and fiddle
Gave signal sweet in that old hall
  Of hands across and down the middle,
Hers was the subtlest spell by far
  Of all that set young hearts romancing:
She was our queen, our rose, our star;
  And then she danced—oh, Heaven, her dancing!

Dark was her hair, her hand was white;
  Her voice was exquisitely tender;
Her eyes were full of liquid light;
  I never saw a waist so slender;
Her every look, her every smile,
  Shot right and left a score of arrows;
I thought 'twas Venus from her isle,
  And wonder'd where she'd left her sparrows.

She talk'd,—of politics or prayers,—
  Of Southey's prose, or Wordsworth's sonnets,
Of danglers or of dancing bears,
  Of battles, or the last new bonnets;
By candle-light, at twelve o'clock,
  To me it matter'd not a tittle,
If those bright lips had quoted Locke,
  I might have thought they murmured Little.

Through sunny May, through sultry June,
  I loved her with a love eternal;
I spoke her praises to the moon,
  I wrote them to the *Sunday Journal.*
My mother laugh'd; I soon found out
  That ancient ladies have no feeling:
My father frown'd; but how should gout
  See any happiness in kneeling?

She was the daughter of a dean,
  Rich, fat, and rather apoplectic;
She had one brother just thirteen,
  Whose color was extremely hectic;
Her grandmother, for many a year
  Had fed the parish with her bounty;
Her second cousin was a peer,
  And lord-lieutenant of the county.

But titles and the three-per-cents,
  And mortgages, and great relations,
And India bonds, and tithes and rents,
  Oh! what are they to love's sensations?
Black eyes, fair forehead, clustering locks,—
  Such wealth, such honors, Cupid chooses;
He cares as little for the stocks,
  As Baron Rothschild for the Muses.

She sketched; the vale, the wood, the beach,
  Grew lovelier from her pencil's shading;
She botanized; I envied each
  Young blossom in her boudoir fading;
She warbled Händel; it was grand,—
  She made the Catalina jealous;
She touch'd the organ; I could stand
  For hours and hours to blow the bellows.

She kept an album, too, at home,
  Well fill'd with all an album's glories;

Paintings of butterflies, and Rome,
  Patterns for trimming, Persian stories,
Soft songs to Julia's cockatoo,
  Fierce odes to Famine and to Slaughter;
And autographs of Prince Lèboo,
  And recipes for elder-water.

And she was flatter'd, worshipp'd, bored;
  Her steps were watch'd, her dress was noted;
Her poodle-dog was quite adored,
  Her sayings were extremely quoted.
She laugh'd, and every heart was glad,
  As if the taxes were abolish'd;
She frown'd, and every look was sad,
  As if the Opera were demolished.

She smil'd on many just for fun,—
  I knew that there was nothing in it;
I was the first, the only one
  Her heart had thought of for a minute.
I knew it, for she told me so,
  In phrase which was divinely moulded;
She wrote a charming hand, and oh,
  How sweetly all her notes were folded!

Our love was like most other loves,—
  A little glow, a little shiver,
A rosebud and a pair of gloves,
  And "Fly Not Yet," upon the river;
Some jealousy of some one's heir,
  Some hopes of dying broken-hearted;
A miniature, a lock of hair,
  The usual vows—and then we parted.

We parted—months and years roll'd by;
  We met again four summers after;
Our parting was all sob and sigh—
  Our meeting was all mirth and laughter;

For in my heart's most secret cell,
  There had been many other lodgers;
And she was not the ball-room's belle,
  But only—Mrs. Something Rogers.
                    WINTHROP MACKWORTH PRAED

A SONG OF IMPOSSIBILITIES

Lady, I loved you all last year,
  How honestly and well—
Alas! would weary you to hear,
  And torture me to tell;
I raved beneath the midnight sky,
  I sang beneath the limes—
Orlando in my lunacy,
  And Petrarch in my rhymes.
But all is over! When the sun
  Dries up the boundless main,
When black is white, false-hearted one,
  I may be yours again!

When passion's early hopes and fears
  Are not derided things;
When truth is found in falling tears,
  Or faith in golden rings;
When the dark Fates that rule our way
  Instruct me where they hide
One woman that would ne'er betray,
  One friend that never lied;
When summer shines without a cloud,
  And bliss without a pain;
When worth is noticed in a crowd,
  I may be yours again!

When science pours the light of day
  Upon the lords of lands;
When Huskisson is heard to say
  That Lethbridge understands;

When wrinkles work their way in youth
    Or Eldon's in a hurry;
When lawyers represent the truth,
    Or Mr. Sumner Surrey;
When aldermen taste eloquence
    Or bricklayers champagne;
When common law is common sense,
    I may be yours again!

When learned judges play the beau,
    Or learned pigs the tabor;
When traveller Bankes beats Cicero,
    Or Mr. Bishop Weber;
When sinking funds discharge a debt,
    Or female hands a bomb;
When bankrupts study the *Gazette*,
    Or colleges *Tom Thumb*;
When little fishes learn to speak,
    Or poets not to feign;
When Dr. Geldart construes Greek,
    I may be yours again!

When Pole and Thornton honour cheques,
    Or Mr. Const a rogue;
When Jericho's in Middlesex,
    Or minuets in vogue;
When Highgate goes to Devonport,
    Or fashion to Guildhall;
When argument is heard at Court,
    Or Mr. Wynn at all;
When Sydney Smith forgets to jest,
    Or farmers to complain;
When kings that are are not the best,
    I may be yours again!

When peers from telling money shrink,
    Or monks from telling lies;
When hydrogen begins to sink,
    Or Grecian scrip to rise;

When German poets cease to dream,
  Americans to guess;
When Freedom sheds her holy beam
  On Negroes, and the Press;
When there is any fear of Rome,
  Or any hope of Spain;
When Ireland is a happy home,
  I may be yours again!

When you can cancel what has been,
  Or alter what must be,
Or bring once more that vanished scene,
  Those withered joys to me;
When you can tune the broken lute,
  Or deck the blighted wreath,
Or rear the garden's richest fruit,
  Upon a blasted heath;
When you can lure the wolf at bay
  Back to his shattered chain,
To-day may then be yesterday—
  I may be yours again!

              Winthrop Mackworth Praed

CUPID MISTAKEN

As after noon one Summer's day,
  Venus stood bathing in a river,
Cupid a-shooting went that way,
  New strung his bow, new fill'd his quiver.

With skill he chose his sharpest dart;
  With all his might his bow he drew;
Swift to his beauteous parent's heart
  The too-well-guided arrow flew.

I faint! I die! the goddess cried;
  O cruel, couldst thou find none other
To wrack thy spleen on? Parricide!
  Like Nero, thou hast slain thy mother.

Poor Cupid sobbing scarce could speak:
　　Indeed, mamma, I did not know ye:
Alas! how easy my mistake,
　　I took you for your likeness, Cloe!
MATTHEW PRIOR

THE ANNUAL SOLUTION

Now apprehension, with terrible dragon-eyes,
　　Pierces my soul and reveals it unsightly;
Now do I cogitate daily, and agonize
　　Nightly.

Yes, I am brooding on what I shall get her for
　　Christmas—it strains my acutest endeavor;
What would be nice, yet not leave me a debtor for-
　　Ever?

Shall it be some little trinket of platinum,
　　Something in leather or silk or prunella?
Ivory stew-pan, perhaps, or a satin um-
　　Brella?

Nay, I am shy of apparel or ornament—
　　Oh, I should suffer acutely and direly,
If when I purchased such gew-gaws she'd scorn 'em ent-
　　Irely!

Likewise I doubt my selection of furniture—
　　Period stuff finds me perfectly dopeless;
Oh, I can hear her exclaiming, "Gol durn it, you're
　　Hopeless!"

Here is a check for you, dearest—and this must tide
　　Both of us over this season so snappy;
Spend it, and render our mutual Christmastide
　　Happy!
EDWIN MEADE ROBINSON

HARVESTING

Be quick, be quick, my eyes, my ears,
   My senses five, remember
Before it wholly disappears
   This vanishing September.

Gather it into vivid sheaves
   That I may have again
The sound of the wind as it whips the leaves,
   Like the sound of heavy rain.

The rusty grass and the purple rocks,
   With patches of yellow moss,
The second blossoming of the phlox
   With spider webs flung across,

Sumac burning along the walls,
   Fires on every hearth,
Even the tracks of the sightless moles
   Tunnelling through the earth.

The jars of jam on the kitchen shelf,
   Apple and plum and peach,
Cherry and pear, and me, myself,
   Pasting a name on each.

SELMA ROBINSON

PENDULUM RHYME

(To be sung in time with a clock)

Crawl, crawl, clock on the wall,
   Eternity is shorter
Than waiting for an errant love
   An hour and a quarter.

Hour and minute hand
   Drag around again.
He said he'd come at nine o'clock
   And now it's after ten;

Tic-toc. Please, Clock,
   Beat a little softer.
I'll wait until eleven strikes—
   Perhaps a little after.

SELMA ROBINSON

FOR A LITTLE LADY

THE MONEY PROBLEM

Shelley's loves
   On fancies ripened;
But he got
   A family stipend.

Thus providing
   Frocks and collars,
He watched the lark's flight—
   I, the dollar's.

FRED SAIDY

SONG

Phillis is my only joy,
   Faithless as the winds or seas;
Sometimes coming, sometimes coy,
   Yet she never fails to please;
     If with a frown
     I am cast down,
     Phillis smiling,
     And beguiling,
Makes me happier than before.

Though, alas, too late I find,
   Nothing can her fancy fix;
Yet the moment she is kind,
   I forgive her all her tricks;

Which though I see
I can't get free;
She deceiving,
I believing;
What need lovers wish for more?

SIR CHARLES SEDLEY

O MISTRESS MINE

O mistress mine, where are you roaming?
O stay and hear! your true love's coming,
　That can sing both high and low;
Trip no further, pretty sweeting,
Journeys end in lovers' meeting
　Every wise man's son doth know.

What is love? 'tis not hereafter;
Present love hath present laughter;
　What's to come is still unsure;
In delay there lies no plenty,—
Then come kiss me, Sweet-and-twenty,
　Youth's a stuff will not endure.

WILLIAM SHAKESPEARE

SIGH NO MORE, LADIES

From "Much Ado about Nothing"

Sigh no more, ladies, sigh no more,
　Men were deceivers ever;
One foot in sea, and one on shore;
　To one thing constant never.
　　Then sigh not so,
　　But let them go,
　And be you blithe and bonny,
Converting all your sounds of woe
Into Hey nonny, nonny.

Sing no more ditties, sing no moe
　Of dumps so dull and heavy;

The fraud of men was ever so,
  Since summer first was leavy.
    Then sigh not so,
    But let them go,
  And be you blithe and bonny,
Converting all your sounds of woe
  Into Hey nonny, nonny.
WILLIAM SHAKESPEARE

THE SORROWS OF WERTHER

Werther had a love for Charlotte
  Such as words could never utter;
Would you know how first he met her?
  She was cutting bread and butter.

Charlotte was a married lady,
  And a moral man was Werther,
And for all the wealth of Indies,
  Would do nothing for to hurt her.

So he sigh'd and pined and ogled,
  And his passion boil'd and bubbled,
Till he blew his silly brains out,
  And no more was by it troubled.

Charlotte, having seen his body
  Borne before her on a shutter,
Like a well-conducted person,
  Went on cutting bread and butter.
W. M. THACKERAY

THE REVERSIBLE METAPHOR
(To Jean)

Is it the beauty of the rose,
  Unfolding to my view,
That stirs again this heart of mine
  To gentle thoughts of you?

Or is it that the thought of you,
  Which sweetly in me glows,
Can make me see each time anew
  The beauty of the rose?

TROUBADOUR

THE CHEMIST TO HIS LOVE

I love thee, Mary, and thou lovest me—
Our mutual flame is like th' affinity
That doth exist between two simple bodies:
I am Potassium to thine Oxygen.
'Tis little that the holy marriage vow
Shall shortly make us one. That unity
Is, after all, but metaphysical
Oh, would that I, my Mary, were an acid,
A living acid; thou an alkali
Endow'd with human sense, that, brought together,
We both might coalesce into one salt,
One homogeneous crystal. Oh, that thou
Wert Carbon, and myself were Hydrogen;
We would unite to form olefiant gas,
Or common coal, or naphtha—would to heaven
That I were Phosphorus, and thou wert Lime!
And we of Lime composed a Phosphuret.
I'd be content to be Sulphuric Acid,
So that thou might be Soda. In that case
We should be Glauber's Salt. Wert thou Magnesia
Instead we'd form the salt that's named from Epsom.
Couldst thou Potassa be, I Aqua-fortis,
Our happy union should that compound form,
Nitrate of Potash—otherwise Saltpetre.
And thus our several natures sweetly blent,
We'd live and love together, until death
Should decompose the fleshly *tertium quid*,
Leaving our souls to all eternity
Amalgamated.   Sweet, thy name is Briggs

And mine is Johnson. Wherefore should not we
Agree to form a Johnsonate of Briggs?

UNKNOWN

"WHEN I LOVED YOU"

When I loved you
And you loved me,
You were the sea,
The sky, the tree.

Now skies are skies,
And seas are seas,
And trees are brown
And they are trees.

CHARLES A. WAGNER

ON A GIRDLE

That which her slender waist confined,
Shall now my joyful temples bind;
No monarch but would give his crown,
His arms might do what this has done.
   It was my heaven's extremest sphere,
The pale which held that lovely deer.
My joy, my grief, my hope, my love,
Did all within this circle move
   A narrow compass! and yet there
Dwelt all that's good, and all that's fair;
Give me but what this ribband bound,
Take all the rest the sun goes round.

EDMUND WALLER

AFFIDAVIT IN PLATITUDES

Love is the cause of war and death in battle,
   Of public woe and private indigestion;
Love is a bore, a nuisance, and a chattel,
   Love is the wrong reply to every question.

Stealing the eye, Love leaves the mind in darkness;
   Stealing the mind, Love leaves the heart in pain;
Stripping the flesh to all its fearful starkness,
   Love wanders calmly off to make a train.

Love is a word unfaithful wives have need of,
   Seeking a vindication for their course;
Love is a bond no man was ever freed of,
   Love is a beggar riding on a horse.

Love is the clip that binds in clumsy fashion
   Who never should be bound at all, 'twould seem;
Love is a thing young men confuse with passion;
   Love is a thing young girls confuse with Dream.

For Love alone one does or does not marry,
   Being an ill whose cure is worse than illness;
For Love there is no weight one does not carry,
   For Love the heart endures an Arctic stillness.

In every instance Love is all one-sided;
   Love is a joke so old it isn't funny.
Who loves most deep, most deep for Love is chided;
   Love is a thing you buy with rubber money.

Love is a tree whose top is so much higher
   Than are the tops of any other trees,
A man in love becomes perforce a liar
   Merely describing all the things he sees.

Love makes each hill, each cloud, each tumbling ocean
   Seem incomplete till Love's delight shall share it;
Love makes contempt the payment for devotion,
   And then unfits the human mind to bear it.

Love is absurd, uncouth, a grim delusion;
   Love is a boat unsafe to go to sea in;
And yet, from what I know of Love's confusion,
   I don't know any state I'd rather *be* in.

                       E. B. WHITE

THE CIRCUS

I did not see the pachyderms—
  Which every one expects to;
I saw instead a dark-haired girl
  Whom I sat next to.

I did not hear the clowning acts,
  The jangle, or the roar;
And yet I heard a whispering
  I'd heard twice before.

They say there was a tight-rope man
  Balanced athwart the air;
I counted more precarious
  My sitting there.

I cannot now remember one—
  The smells, the shouts, the laughter;
Why must I still remember her
  From whom I parted after?

E. B. WHITE

RESOLUTION

I was in the Harbor
  Snug as I could be—
Pierrot whistled down the wind—
  "Oh, come out to Sea!"

I was bruised and weary
  With sailing on the Sea:
The Harbor held me in its arms
  And safely cradled me.

I knew all about the Sea
  And what a Harbor meant;
Pierrot whistled down the wind—
  And of course I went!

WIOLAR

THE LOVER'S RESOLUTION

Shall I, wasting in despair,
Die because a woman's fair?
Or make pale my cheeks with care
'Cause another's rosy are?
Be she fairer than the day,
Or the flowery meads in May,
  If she think not well of me,
  What care I how fair she be?

Shall my silly heart be pined
'Cause I see a woman kind?
Or a well disposèd nature
Joinèd with a lovely feature?
Be she meeker, kinder, than
Turtle-dove or pelican,
  If she be not so to me,
  What care I how kind she be?

Shall a woman's virtues move
Me to perish for her love?
Or her well-deservings known
Make me quite forget my own?
Be she with that goodness blest
Which may merit name of Best,
  If she be not such to me,
  What care I how good she be?

'Cause her fortune seems too high,
Shall I play the fool and die?
She that bears a noble mind,
If not outward helps she find,
Thinks what with them he would do
That without them dares her woo;
  And unless that mind I see,
  What care I how great she be?

Great, or good, or kind, or fair,
I will ne'er the more despair;
If she love me, this believe,
I will die ere she shall grieve;
If she slight me when I woo,
I can scorn and let her go;
  For if she be not for me,
  What care I for whom she be?

GEORGE WITHER

SONG

O, inexpressible as sweet,
  Love takes my voice away;
I cannot tell thee when we meet
  What most I long to say.

But hadst thou hearing in thy heart,
  To know what beats in mine,
Then shouldst thou walk, where'er thou art.
  In melodies divine.

So warbling birds lift higher notes
  Than to our ears belong;
The music fills their throbbing throats,
  But silence steals the song.

GEORGE E. WOODBERRY

Nonsense

ON AN INTAGLIO HEAD OF MINERVA

Beneath the warrior's helm, behold
   The flowing tresses of the woman!
Minerva, Pallas, what you will—
   A winsome creature, Greek or Roman.

Minerva? No! 'tis some sly minx
   In cousin's helmet masquerading;
If not—then Wisdom was a dame
   For sonnets and for serenading!

I thought the goddess cold, austere,
   Not made for love's despairs and blisses:
Did Pallas wear her hair like that?
   Was Wisdom's mouth so shaped for kisses?

The Nightingale should be her bird,
   And not the Owl, big-eyed and solemn:
How very fresh she looks, and yet
   She's older far than Trajan's Column!

The magic hand that carved this face,
   And set this vine-work round it running,
Perhaps ere mighty Phidias wrought,
   Had lost its subtle skill and cunning.

Who was he? Was he glad or sad,
   Who knew to carve in such a fashion?
Perchance he graved the dainty head
   For some brown girl that scorned his passion.

Perchance, in some still garden-place,
   Where neither fount nor tree to-day is,
He flung the jewel at the feet
   Of Phryne, or perhaps 'twas Laïs.

But he is dust; we may not know
   His happy or unhappy story:
Nameless, and dead these centuries,
   His work outlives him,—there's his glory!

Both man and jewel lay in earth
   Beneath a lava-buried city;
The countless summers came and went,
   With neither haste, nor hate, nor pity.

Years blotted out the man, but left
   The jewel fresh as any blossom,
Till some Visconti dug it up,—
   To rise and fall on Mabel's bosom!

O nameless brother! see how Time
   Your gracious handiwork has guarded:
See how your loving, patient art
   Has come, at last, to be rewarded.

Who would not suffer slights of men,
   And pangs of hopeless passion also,
To have his carven agate-stone
   On such a bosom rise and fall so!
THOMAS BAILEY ALDRICH

KINDNESS TO ANIMALS

Speak gently to the herring and kindly to the calf,
Be blithesome with the bunny, at barnacles don't laugh!
Give nuts unto the monkey, and buns unto the bear,
Ne'er hint at currant jelly if you chance to see a hare!
Oh, little girls, pray hide your combs when tortoises draw
   nigh,
And never in the hearing of a pigeon whisper Pie!
But give the stranded jelly-fish a shove into the sea,—
Be always kind to animals wherever you may be!

Oh, make not game of sparrows, nor faces at the ram,
And ne'er allude to mint sauce when calling on a lamb.
Don't beard the thoughtful oyster, don't dare the cod to
    crimp,
Don't cheat the pike, or ever try to pot the playful shrimp.
Tread lightly on the turning worm, don't bruise the butterfly,
Don't ridicule the wry-neck, nor sneer at salmon-fry;
Oh, ne'er delight to make dogs fight, nor bantams disagree,—
Be always kind to animals wherever you may be!

Be lenient with lobsters, and ever kind to crabs,
And be not disrespectful to cuttle-fish or dabs;
Chase not the Cochin-China, chaff not the ox obese,
And babble not of feather-beds in company with geese.
Be tender with the tadpole, and let the limpet thrive,
Be merciful to mussels, don't skin your eels alive;
When talking to a turtle don't mention calipee—
Be always kind to animals wherever you may be!

J. Ashby-Sterry

EASTERN SERENADE

The minarets wave on the plains of Stamboul,
And the breeze of the evening blows freshly and cool;
The voice of the musnud is heard from the west,
And kaftan and kalpac have gone to their rest.
The notes of the kislar re-echo no more,
And the waves of Al Sirat fall light on the shore.

Where art thou, my beauty: where art thou, my bride?
Oh, come and repose by thy dragoman's side!
I wait for thee still by the flowery tophaik—
I have broken my eiblis for Zuleima's sake.
But the heart that adores thee, is faithful and true,
Though it beats, neath the folds of a Greek Allah-hu!

Oh, wake thee, my dearest! the muftis are still,
And the tschocadars sleep on the Frabgestan hill;
No sullen aleikoum—no derveesh is here.

And the mosques are all watching by lonely Kashmere!
Oh, come in the gush of thy beauty so full,
I have waited for thee, my adored attar-gul!

I see thee—I hear thee—thy antelope foot
Treads lightly and softly on the velvet cheroot;
The jewelled amaun of thy zemzem is bare,
And the folds of thy palampore wave in the air.
Come, rest on the bosom that loves thee so well,
My dove! my phingari! my gentle gazelle!

Nay, tremble not, dearest! I feel thy heart throb,
'Neath the sheltering shroud of thy snowy kiebaub;
Lo, there shines Muezzin, the beautiful star!
Thy lover is with thee, and danger afar:
Say, is it the glance of the haughty vizier,
Or the bark of the distant effendi, you fear?

Oh, swift fly the hours in the garden of bliss!
And sweeter than balm of Gehenna, thy kiss!
Wherever I wander—wherever I roam,
My spirit flies back to its beautiful home:
It dwells by the lake of the limpid Stamboul,
With thee, my adored one! my own attar-gul!

WILLIAM E. AYTOUN AND
SIR THEODORE MARTIN

THE FROG

Be kind and tender to the Frog,
    And do not call him names,
As "Slimy-Skin," or "Polly-wog,"
    Or likewise, "Uncle James,"
Or "Gape-a-grin," or "Toad-gone-wrong,"
    Or "Billy-Bandy-knees;"
The Frog is justly sensitive
    To epithets like these.

No animal will more repay
    A treatment kind and fair,
At least, so lonely people say
Who keep a frog (and, by the way,
    They are extremely rare).

HILAIRE BELLOC

THE YAK

As a friend to the children commend me the yak.
    You will find it exactly the thing:
It will carry and fetch, you can ride on its back,
    Or lead it about with a string.

A Tartar who dwells on the plains of Thibet
    (A desolate region of snow)
Has for centuries made it a nursery pet,
    And surely the Tartar should know!

Then tell your papa where the Yak can be got,
    And if he is awfully rich,
He will buy you the creature—or else he will *not*.
    (I cannot be positive which).

HILAIRE BELLOC

ODE TO THE HUMAN HEART

Blind Thamyris, and blind Maeonides,
    Pursue the triumph and partake the gale!
Drop tears as fast as the Arabian trees,
    To point a moral or adorn a tale.

Full many a gem of purest ray serene,
    Thoughts that do often lie too deep for tears,
Like angels' visits, few and far between,
    Deck the long vista of departed years.

Man never is, but always to be bless'd;
    The tenth transmitter of a foolish face,
Like Aaron's serpent, swallows up the rest,
    And makes a sunshine in the shady place.

For man the hermit sigh'd, till woman smiled,
    To waft a feather or to drown a fly,
(In wit a man, simplicity a child,)
    With silent finger pointing to the sky.

But fools rush in where angels fear to tread,
    Far out amid the melancholy main;
As when a vulture on Imaus bred,
    Dies of a rose in aromatic pain.

                                LAMAN BLANCHARD

P IS FOR PALEONTOLOGY

Consider the sages who pulverize boulders,
And burrow for elbows and shinbones and shoulders,
And shovel the loot from a hill or a dale of it,
And lovingly carry off pail after pail of it.

Anon a remarkable Tyrannosaurus
As tall as a steeple is standing before us,
Rebuilt from a bit of the skin or a scale of it
Or maybe as much as a single toe-nail of it.

Curators are handy to speak of its habits,
To say that it fed on the forebears of rabbits,
To mimic the whine or the whistle or wail of it
And tell (in a whisper) the female or male of it.

But though in the quest for some primitive lemur,
They fish out a fragment of petrified femur,
I wish they'd not fashion a four-footed whale of it
Without ever knowing the head or the tail of it.*

                                MILTON BRACKER

* And I don't give a darn for the Harvard or Yale of it.

THE WALRUS AND THE CARPENTER

The sun was shining on the sea,
  Shining with all his might:
He did his very best to make
  The billows smooth and bright—
And this was odd, because it was
  The middle of the night.

The moon was shining sulkily,
  Because she thought the sun
Had got no business to be there
  After the day was done—
"It's very rude of him," she said,
  "To come and spoil the fun!"

The sea was wet as wet could be,
  The sands were dry as dry.
You could not see a cloud, because
  No cloud was in the sky:
No birds were flying overhead—
  There were no birds to fly.

The Walrus and the Carpenter
  Were walking close at hand;
They wept like anything to see
  Such quantities of sand:
"If this were only cleared away,"
  They said, "it *would be* grand!"

"If seven maids with seven mops
  Swept it for half a year,
Do you suppose," the Walrus said,
  "That they could get it clear?"
"I doubt it," said the Carpenter,
  And shed a bitter tear.

"O Oysters, come and walk with us!"
  The Walrus did beseech.

"A pleasant walk, a pleasant talk,
   Along the briny beach:
We cannot do with more than four,
   To give a hand to each."

The eldest Oyster looked at him,
   But not a word he said:
The eldest Oyster winked his eye,
   And shook his heavy head—
Meaning to say he did not choose
   To leave the oyster-bed.

But four young Oysters hurried up,
   All eager for the treat:
Their coats were brushed, their faces washed,
   Their shoes were clean and neat—
And this was odd, because, you know,
   They hadn't any feet.

Four other Oysters followed them,
   And yet another four;
And thick and fast they came at last,
   And more, and more, and more—
All hopping through the frothy waves,
   And scrambling to the shore.

The Walrus and the Carpenter
   Walked on a mile or so,
And then they rested on a rock
   Conveniently low:
And all the little Oysters stood
   And waited in a row.

"The time has come," the Walrus said,
   "To talk of many things:
Of shoes—and ships—and sealing-wax—
   Of cabbages—and kings—
And why the sea is boiling hot—
   And whether pigs have wings."

"But wait a bit," the Oysters cried,
  "Before we have our chat;
For some of us are out of breath,
  And all of us are fat!"
"No hurry!" said the Carpenter.
  They thanked him much for that.

"A loaf of bread," the Walrus said,
  "Is what we chiefly need:
Pepper and vinegar besides
  Are very good indeed—
Now, if you're ready, Oysters dear,
  We can begin to feed."

"But not on us!" the Oysters cried,
  Turning a little blue.
"After such kindness that would be
  A dismal thing to do!"
"The night is fine," the Walrus said,
  "Do you admire the view?"

"It was so kind of you to come,
  And you are very nice!"
The Carpenter said nothing but
  "Cut us another slice.
I wish you were not quite so deaf—
  I've had to ask you twice!"

"It seems a shame," the Walrus said,
  "To play them such a trick.
After we've brought them out so far
  And made them trot so quick!"
The Carpenter said nothing but
  "The butter's spread too thick!"

"I weep for you," the Walrus said,
  "I deeply sympathize."

With sobs and tears he sorted out
   Those of the largest size,
Holding his pocket-handkerchief
   Before his streaming eyes.

"O Oysters," said the Carpenter,
   "You've had a pleasant run!
Shall we be trotting home again?"
   But answer came there none—
And this was scarcely odd, because
   They'd eaten every one.

                            LEWIS CARROLL

ROBINSON CRUSOE'S STORY

The night was thick and hazy
   When the *Piccadilly Daisy*
Carried down the crew and captain in the sea;
   And I think the water drowned 'em,
   For they never, never found 'em,
And I know they didn't come ashore with me.

   Oh! 'twas very sad and lonely
   When I found myself the only
Population on this cultivated shore;
   But I've made a little tavern
   In a rocky little cavern,
And I sit and watch for people at the door.

   I spent no time in looking
   For a girl to do my cooking,
As I'm quite a clever hand at making stews;
   But I had that fellow Friday
   Just to keep the tavern tidy,
And to put a Sunday polish on my shoes.

   I have a little garden
   That I'm cultivating lard in,

As the things I eat are rather tough and dry;
  For I live on toasted lizards,
  Prickly pears and parrot gizzards,
And I'm really very fond of beetle-pie.

  The clothes I had were furry,
  And it made me fret and worry
When I found the moths were eating off the hair;
  And I had to scrape and sand 'em,
  And I boiled 'em and I tanned 'em,
Till I got the fine morocco suit I wear.

  I sometimes seek diversion
  In a family excursion,
With the few domestic animals you see;
  And we take along a carrot
  As refreshment for the parrot,
And a little can of jungleberry tea.

  Then we gather, as we travel,
  Bits of moss and dirty gravel,
And we chip off little specimens of stone;
  And we carry home as prizes
  Funny bugs, of handy sizes,
Just to give the day a scientific tone.

  If the roads are wet and muddy
  We remain at home and study,—
For the Goat is very clever at a sum,—
  And the Dog, instead of fighting,
  Studies ornamental writing,
While the Cat is taking lessons on the drum.

  We retire at eleven,
  And we rise again at seven;
And I wish to call attention, as I close,
  To the fact that all the scholars
  Are correct about their collars,
And particular in turning out their toes.
                 CHARLES EDWARD CARRYL

THE WALLOPING WINDOW-BLIND

A capital ship for an ocean trip
   Was *The Walloping Window-blind*—
No gale that blew dismayed her crew
   Or troubled the captain's mind.
The man at the wheel was taught to feel
   Contempt for the wildest blow,
And it often appeared, when the weather had cleared,
   That he'd been in his bunk below.

The boatswain's mate was very sedate,
   Yet fond of amusement, too;
And he played hop-scotch with the starboard watch,
   While the captain tickled the crew.
And the gunner we had was apparently mad,
   For he sat on the after-rail,
And fired salutes with the captain's boots,
   In the teeth of the booming gale.

The captain sat in a commodore's hat
   And dined, in a royal way,
On toasted pigs and pickles and figs
   And gummery bread, each day.
But the cook was Dutch and behaved as such;
   For the food that he gave the crew
Was a number of tons of hot-cross buns
   Chopped up with sugar and glue.

And we all felt ill as mariners will,
   On a diet that's cheap and rude;
And we shivered and shook as we dipped the cook
   In a tub of his gluesome food.
Then nautical pride we laid aside,
   And we cast the vessel ashore
On the Gulliby Isles, where the Poohpooh smiles,
   And the Anagazanders roar.

Composed of sand was that favored land,
  And trimmed with cinnamon straws;
And pink and blue was the pleasing hue
  Of the Tickletoeteaser's claws.
And we sat on the edge of a sandy ledge
  And shot at the whistling bee;
And the Binnacle-bats wore water-proof hats
  As they danced in the sounding sea.

On rubagub bark, from dawn to dark,
  We fed, till we all had grown
Uncommonly shrunk,—when a Chinese junk
  Came by from the torriby zone.
She was stubby and square, but we didn't much care,
  And we cheerily put to sea;
And we left the crew of the junk to chew
  The bark of the rubagub tree.
CHARLES EDWARD CARRYL

HOW THE HELPMATE OF BLUE-BEARD MADE FREE WITH A DOOR

A maiden from the Bosphorus,
With eyes as bright as phosphorus,
  Once wed the wealthy bailiff
      Of the caliph
        Of Kelat.
Though diligent and zealous, he
Became a slave to jealousy.
  (Considering her beauty,
      'Twas his duty
        To be that!)

When business would necessitate
A journey, he would hesitate,
  But, fearing to disgust her,
      He would trust her
        With his keys,

Remarking to her prayerfully:
"I beg you'll use them carefully.
  Don't look what I deposit
      In that closet,
         If you please."

It may be mentioned, casually,
That blue as lapis lazuli
  He dyed his hair, his lashes,
      His mustaches,
        And his beard.
And, just because he did it, he
Aroused his wife's timidity:
  Her terror she dissembled,
      But she trembled
        When he neared.

This feeling insalubrious
Soon made her most lugubrious,
  And bitterly she missed her
      Elder sister
        Marie Anne:
She asked if she might write her to
Come down and spend a night or two,
  Her husband answered rightly
      And politely:
        "Yes, you can!"

Blue-Beard, the Monday following,
His jealous feeling swallowing,
  Packed all his clothes together
      In a leather—
        Bound valise,
And, feigning reprehensibly,
He started out, ostensibly
  By traveling to learn a
      Bit of Smyrna
        And of Greece.

His wife made but a cursory
Inspection of the nursery;
  The kitchen and the airy
      Little dairy
         Were a bore,
As well as big or scanty rooms,
And billiard, bath, and ante-rooms,
  But not that interdicted
      And restricted
         Little door!

For, all her curiosity
Awakened by the closet he
  So carefully had hidden,
      And forbidden
         Her to see,
This damsel disobedient
Did something inexpedient,
  And in the keyhole tiny
      Turned the shiny
         Little key:

Then started back impulsively,
And shrieked aloud convulsively—
  Three heads of girls he'd wedded
      And beheaded
         Met her eye!
And turning round, much terrified,
Her darkest fears were verified,
  For Blue-Beard stood behind her,
      Come to find her
         On the sly!

Perceiving she was fated to
Be soon decapitated, too,
  She telegraphed her brothers
      And some others
         What she feared.

And Sister Anne looked out for them,
In readiness to shout for them
  Whenever in the distance
      With assistance
         They appeared.

But only from her battlement
She saw some dust that cattle meant.
  The ordinary story
      Isn't gory,
         But a jest.
But here's the truth unqualified.
The husband *wasn't* mollified
  Her head is in his bloody
      Little study
         With the rest!

The Moral: Wives, we must allow,
Who to their husbands will not bow,
A stern and dreadful lesson learn
When, as you've read, they're cut in turn.
                GUY WETMORE CARRYL

THE SYCOPHANTIC FOX AND
THE GULLIBLE RAVEN

A raven sat upon a tree,
  And not a word he spoke, for
His beak contained a piece of Brie,
  Or, maybe, it was Roquefort:
    We'll make it any kind you please—
    At all events, it was a cheese.

Beneath the tree's umbrageous limb
  A hungry fox sat smiling;
He saw the raven watching him,
  And spoke in words beguiling.
    "*J'admire*," said he, "*ton beau plumage.*"
    (The which was simply persiflage.)

Two things there are, no doubt you know,
  To which a fox is used:
A rooster that is bound to crow,
  A crow that's bound to roost,
    And whichsoever he espies
    He tells the most unblushing lies.

"Sweet fowl," he said, "I understand
  You're more than merely natty,
I hear you sing to beat the band
  And Adelina Patti.
    Pray render with your liquid tongue
    A bit from 'Götterdämmerung.'"

This subtle speech was aimed to please
  The crow, and it succeeded:
He thought no bird in all the trees
  Could sing as well as he did.
    In flattery completely doused,
    He gave the "Jewel Song" from "Faust."

But gravitation's law, of course,
  As Isaac Newton showed it,
Exerted on the cheese its force,
  And elsewhere soon bestowed it.
    In fact, there is no need to tell
    What happened when to earth it fell.

I blush to add that when the bird
  Took in the situation
He said one brief, emphatic word,
  Unfit for publication.
    The fox was greatly startled, but
    He only sighed and answered "Tut."

The moral is: A fox is bound
  To be a shameless sinner.

And also: When the cheese comes round
  You know it's after dinner.
    But (what is only known to few)
    The fox is after dinner, too.
GUY WETMORE CARRYL

LAY OF THE DESERTED INFLUENZAED

Doe, doe!
  I shall dever see her bore!
Dever bore our feet shall rove
  The beadows as of yore!
Dever bore with byrtle boughs
  Her tresses shall I twide—
Dever bore her bellow voice
  Bake bellody with bide!
Dever shall we lidger bore,
  Abid the flow'rs at dood,
Dever shall we gaze at dight
  Upon the tedtder bood!
    Ho, doe, doe!
  Those berry tibes have flowd,
Ad I shall dever see her bore,
  By beautiful! by owd!
    Ho, doe, doe!
  I shall dever see her bore,
She will forget be id a bonth,
  (Bost probably before)—
She will forget the byrtle boughs,
  The flow'rs we plucked at dood,
Our beetigs by the tedtder stars.
  Our gazigs at the bood.
Ad I shall dever see agaid
  The Lily and the Rose;
The dabask cheek! the sdowy brow!
  The perfect bouth ad dose!
    Ho, doe, doe!
  Those berry tibes have flowd—

Ad I shall dever see her bore,
By beautiful! by owd!!
HENRY CHOLMONDELEY-PENNELL

BOSTON NURSERY RHYMES

RHYME FOR A GEOLOGICAL BABY

Trilobite, Grapholite, Nautilus pie;
Seas were calcareous, oceans were dry.
Eocene, miocene, pliocene Tuff,
Lias and Trias and that is enough.

RHYME FOR ASTRONOMICAL BABY

Bye Baby Bunting,
Father's gone star-hunting;
Mother's at the telescope
Casting baby's horoscope.
Bye Baby Buntoid,
Father's found an asteroid;
Mother takes by calculation
The angle of its inclination.

RHYME FOR BOTANICAL BABY

Little bo-peepals
Has lost her sepals,
And can't tell where to find them;
In the involucre
By hook or by crook or
She'll make up her mind not to mind them.

RHYME FOR A CHEMICAL BABY

Oh, sing a song of phosphates,
Fibrine in a line,
Four-and-twenty follicles
In the van of time.

When the phosphorescence
Evoluted brain,
Superstition ended,
Men began to reign.

REV. JOSEPH COOK

HALF HOURS WITH THE CLASSICS

Ah, those hours when by-gone sages
    Led our thoughts through Learning's ways,
When the wit of sunnier ages,
    Called once more to Earth the days
When rang through Athens' vine-hung lanes
Thy wild, wild laugh, Aristophanes!

Pensive through the land of Lotus,
    Sauntered we by Nilus' side;
Garrulous old Herodotus
    Still our mentor, still our guide,
Prating of the mystic bliss
Of Isis and of Osiris.

All the learn'd ones trooped before us,
    All the wise of Hellas' land,
Down from mythic Pythagoras,
    To the hemlock drinker grand.
Dark the hour that closed the gates
Of gloomy Dis on thee, Socrates.

Ah, those hours of tend'rest study,
    When Electra's poet told
Of Love's cheek once warm and ruddy,
    Pale with grief, with death chill cold!
Sobbing low like summer tides
Flow thy verses, Euripides!

High our hearts beat when Cicero
    Shook the Capitolian dome;

How we shuddered, watching Nero
'Mid the glare of blazing Rome!
How those records all affright us
On thy gloomy page, Tacitus!

Back to youth I seem to glide, as
I recall those by-gone scenes,
When we conned o'er Thucydides,
Or recited Demosthenes.

L'ENVOI

Ancient sages, pardon these
Somewhat doubtful quantities.

H. J. DeBurgh

ELLEN M'JONES ABERDEEN

MacPhairson Clonglocketty Angus M'Clan
Was the son of an elderly labouring man,
You've guessed him a Scotchman, shrewd reader, at sight,
And p'raps altogether, shrewd reader, you're right.

From the bonnie blue Forth to the hills of Deeside,
Round by Dingwall and Wrath to the mouth of the Clyde,
There wasn't a child or a woman or man
Who could pipe with Clonglocketty Angus M'Clan.

No other could wake such detestable groans,
With reed and with chaunter—with bag and with drones:
All day and all night he delighted the chiels
With sniggering pibrochs and jiggety reels.

He'd clamber a mountain and squat on the ground,
And the neighbouring maidens would gather around
To list to his pipes and to gaze in his e'en,
Especially Ellen M'Jones Aberdeen.

All loved their M'Clan, save a Sassenach brute,
Who came to the Highlands to fish and to shoot;
He dressed himself up in a Highlander way,
Though his name it was Pattison Corby Torbay.

Torbay had incurred a good deal of expense
To make him a Scotchman in every sense;
But this is a matter, you'll readily own,
That isn't a question of tailors alone.

A Sassenach chief may be bonily built,
He may purchase a sporran, a bonnet, and kilt;
Stick a skean in his hose—wear an acre of stripes—
But he cannot assume an affection for pipes.

Clonglocketty's pipings all night and all day
Quite frenzied poor Pattison Corby Torbay;
The girls were amused at his singular spleen,
Especially Ellen M'Jones Aberdeen.

"MacPhairson Clonglocketty Angus, my lad,
With pibrochs and reels you are driving me mad;
If you really must play on that cursed affair,
My goodness! play something resembling an air."

Boiled over the blood of MacPhairson M'Clan—
The clan of Clonglocketty rose as one man;
For all were enraged at the insult, I ween—
Especially Ellen M'Jones Aberdeen.

"Let's show," said M'Clan, "to this Sassenach loon
That the bagpipes can play him a regular tune.
Let's see," said M'Clan, as he thoughtfully sat,
"'In My Cottage' is easy—I'll practise at that."

He blew at his "Cottage," and blew with a will,
For a year, seven months, and a fortnight, until
(You'll hardly believe it) M'Clan, I declare,
Elicited something resembling an air.

It was wild—it was fitful—as wild as the breeze—
It wandered about into several keys;
It was jerky, spasmodic, and harsh, I'm aware,
But still it distinctly suggested an air.

The Sassenach screamed, and the Sassenach danced,
He shrieked in his agony—bellowed and pranced;
And the maidens who gathered rejoiced at the scene,
Especially Ellen M'Jones Aberdeen.

"Hech gather, hech gather, hech gather around;
And fill a' yer lugs wi' the exquisite sound.
An air frae the bagpipes—beat that if ye can!
Hurrah for Clonglocketty Angus M'Clan!"

The fame of his piping spread over the land:
Respectable widows proposed for his hand,
And maidens came flocking to sit on the green—
Especially Ellen M'Jones Aberdeen.

One morning the fidgety Sassenach swore
He'd stand it no longer—he drew his claymore,
And (this was, I think, in extremely bad taste),
Divided Clonglocketty close to the waist.

Oh! loud were the wailings for Angus M'Clan—
Oh! deep was the grief for that excellent man—
The maids stood aghast at the horrible scene,
Especially Ellen M'Jones Aberdeen.

It sorrowed poor Pattison Corby Torbay
To find them "take on" in this serious way,
He pitied the poor little fluttering birds,
And solaced their souls with the following words:—

"Oh, maidens," said Pattison, touching his hat,
"Don't snivel, my dears, for a fellow like that;
Observe, I'm a very superior man,
A much better fellow than Angus M'Clan."

They smiled when he winked and addressed them as "dears,"
And they all of them vowed, as they dried up their tears,
A pleasanter gentleman never was seen—
Especially Ellen M'Jones Aberdeen.

W. S. GILBERT

EMILY, JOHN, JAMES, AND I

A DERBY LEGEND

Emily Jane was a nursery maid—
   James was a bold Life Guard,
And John was a constable, poorly paid
   (And I am a doggerel bard).

A very good girl was Emily Jane,
   Jimmy was good and true,
And John was a very good man in the main
   (And I am a good man, too).

Rivals for Emmie were Johnny and James,
   Though Emily liked them both;
She couldn't tell which had the strongest claims
   (And *I* couldn't take my oath).

But sooner or later you're certain to find
   Your sentiments can't lie hid—
Jane thought it was time that she made up her mind
   (And I think it was time she did).

Said Jane, with a smirk, and a blush on her face,
   "I'll promise to wed the boy
Who takes me to-morrow to Epsom Race!"
   (Which *I* would have done, with joy).

From Johnny escaped an expression of pain,
   But Jimmy said, "Done with you!
I'll take you with pleasure, my Emily Jane"
   (And I would have said so too).

John lay on the ground, and he roared like mad
  (For Johnny was sore perplexed),
And he kicked very hard at a very small lad
  (Which *I* often do, when vexed).

For John was on duty next day with the Force,
  To punish all Epsom crimes;
Some people *will* cross, when they're clearing the course
  (I do it myself, sometimes).

           * * *

The Derby Day sun glittered gaily on cads,
  On maidens with gamboge hair,
On sharpers and pickpockets, swindlers and pads
  (For I, with my harp, was there).

And Jimmy went down with his Jane that day,
  And John by the collar or nape
Seized everybody who came in this way
  (And *I* had a narrow escape).

He noticed his Emily Jane with Jim,
  And envied the well-made elf;
And people remarked that he muttered "Oh, dim!"
  (I often say "dim!" myself).

John dogged them all day, without asking their leaves;
  For his sergeant he told, aside,
That Jimmy and Jane were notorious thieves
  (And I think he was justified).

But James wouldn't dream of abstracting a fork,
  And Jenny would blush with shame
At stealing so much as a bottle or cork
  (A bottle I think fair game).

But, ah! there's another more serious crime!
  They wickedly strayed upon
The course, at a critical moment of time
  (I pointed them out to John).

The crusher came down on the pair in a crack—
   And then, with a demon smile,
Let Jenny cross over, but sent Jimmy back
   (I played on my harp the while).

Stern Johnny their agony loud derides
   With a very triumphant sneer—
They weep and they wail from the opposite sides
   (And *I* shed a silent tear).

And Jenny is crying away like mad,
   And Jimmy is swearing hard;
And Johnny is looking uncommonly glad
   (And I am a doggerel bard).

But Jimmy he ventured on crossing again
   The scenes of our Isthmian Games—
John caught him and collared him, giving him pain
   (I felt very much for James).

John led him away with a victor's hand,
   And Jimmy was shortly seen
In the station-house under the grand Grand Stand
   (As many a time *I've* been).

And Jimmy, bad boy, was imprisoned for life,
   Though Emily pleaded hard;
And Johnny had Emily Jane to wife
   (And I am a doggerel bard).

W. S. GILBERT

THE FOLLY OF BROWN

By a General Agent

I knew a boor—a clownish card
   (His only friends were pigs and cows and
The poultry of a small farmyard),
   Who came into two hundred thousand.

Good fortune worked no change in Brown,
    Though she's a mighty social chymist;
He was a clown—and by a clown
    I do not mean a pantomimist.

It left him quiet, calm, and cool,
    Though hardly knowing what a crown was—
You can't imagine what a fool
    Poor rich uneducated Brown was!

He scouted all who wished to come
    And give him monetary schooling;
And I propose to give you some
    Idea of his insensate fooling.

I formed a company or two—
    (Of course I don't know what the rest meant,
I formed them solely with a view
    To help him to a sound investment).

Their objects were—their only cares—
    To justify their Boards in showing
A handsome dividend on shares
    And keep their good promoter going.

But no—the lout sticks to his brass,
    Though shares at par I freely proffer:
Yet—will it be believed?—the ass
    Declines, with thanks, my well-meant offer!

He adds, with bumpkin's stolid grin
    (A weakly intellect denoting),
He'd rather not invest it in
    A company of my promoting!

"You have two hundred 'thou' or more,"
    Said I. "You'll waste it, lose it, lend it;
Come, take my furnished second floor,
    I'll gladly show you how to spend it."

But will it be believed that he,
  With grin upon his face of poppy,
Declined my aid, while thanking me
  For what he called my "philanthroppy"?

Some blind, suspicious fools rejoice
  In doubting friends who wouldn't harm them;
They will not hear the charmer's voice,
  However wisely he may charm them!

I showed him that his coat, all dust,
  Top boots and cords provoked compassion,
And proved that men of station must
  Conform to the decrees of fashion.

I showed him where to buy his hat
  To coat him, trouser him, and boot him;
But no—he wouldn't hear of that—
  "He didn't think the style would suit him!"

I offered him a county seat,
  And made no end of an oration;
I made it certainty complete,
  And introduced the deputation.

But no—the clown my prospect blights—
  (The worth of birth it surely teaches!)
"Why should I want to spend my nights
  In Parliament, a-making speeches?

"I haven't never been to school—
  I ain't had not no eddication—
And I should surely be a fool
  To publish that to all the nation!"

I offered him a trotting horse—
  No hack had ever trotted faster—
I also offered him, of course,
  A rare and curious "old master."

I offered to procure him weeds—
   Wines fit for one in his position—
But, though an ass in all his deeds,
   He'd learnt the meaning of "commission."

He called me "thief" the other day,
   And daily from his door he thrusts me;
Much more of this, and soon I may
   Begin to think that Brown mistrusts me.

So deaf to all sound Reason's rule
   This poor uneducated clown is,
You can*not* fancy what a fool
   Poor rich uneducated Brown is.

W. S. GILBERT

GENTLE ALICE BROWN

It was a robber's daughter, and her name was Alice Brown.
Her father was the terror of a small Italian town;
Her mother was a foolish, weak, but amiable old thing;
But it isn't of her parents that I'm going for to sing.

As Alice was a-sitting at her window-sill one day,
A beautiful young gentleman he chanced to pass that way;
She cast her eyes upon him, and he looked so good and true,
That she thought, "I could be happy with a gentleman like
   you!"

And every morning passed her house that cream of gentle-
   men,
She knew she might expect him at a quarter unto ten,
A sorter in the Custom-house, it was his daily road
(The Custom-house was fifteen minutes' walk from her
   abode.)

But Alice was a pious girl, who knew it wasn't wise
To look at strange young sorters with expressive purple
     eyes;
So she sought the village priest to whom her family confessed,
The priest by whom their little sins were carefully assessed.

"Oh, holy father," Alice said, "'twould grieve you, would
     it not?
To discover that I was a most disreputable lot!
Of all unhappy sinners I'm the most unhappy one!"
The padre said, "Whatever have you been and gone and
     done?"

"I have helped mamma to steal a little kiddy from its dad,
I've assisted dear papa in cutting up a little lad.
I've planned a little burglary and forged a little cheque,
And slain a little baby for the coral on its neck!"

The worthy pastor heaved a sigh, and dropped a silent tear—
And said, "You mustn't judge yourself too heavily, my
     dear—
It's wrong to murder babies, little corals for to fleece;
But sins like these one expiates at half-a-crown apiece.

"Girls will be girls—you're very young, and flighty in your
     mind;
Old heads upon young shoulders we must not expect to find.
We musn't be too hard upon these little girlish tricks—
Let's see—five crimes at half-a-crown—exactly twelve-and-
     six."

"Oh, father," little Alice cried, "your kindness makes me
     weep,
You do these little things for me so singularly cheap—
Your thoughtful liberality I never can forget;
But oh, there is another crime I haven't mentioned yet!

"A pleasant-looking gentleman, with pretty purple eyes,
I've noticed at my window, as I've sat a-catching flies;
He passes by it every day as certain as can be—
I blush to say I've winked at him and he has winked at me!"

"For shame," said Father Paul, "my erring daughter! On
    my word
This is the most distressing news that I have ever heard.
Why, naughty girl, your excellent papa has pledged your
    hand
To a promising young robber, the lieutenant of his band!

"This dreadful piece of news will pain your worthy parents
    so!
They are the most remunerative customers I know;
For many many years they've kept starvation from my
    doors,
I never knew so criminal a family as yours!

"The common country folk in this insipid neighborhood
Have nothing to confess, they're so ridiculously good;
And if you marry any one respectable at all,
Why, you'll reform, and what will then become of Father
    Paul?"

The worthy priest, he up and drew his cowl upon his crown,
And started off in haste to tell the news to Robber Brown;
To tell him how his daughter, who was now for marriage
    fit,
Had winked upon a sorter, who reciprocated it.

Good Robber Brown, he muffled up his anger pretty well,
He said, "I have a notion, and that notion I will tell;
I will nab this gay young sorter, terrify him into fits,
And get my gentle wife to chop him into little bits.

"I've studied human nature, and I know a thing or two,
Though a girl may fondly love a living gent, as many do—
A feeling of disgust upon her senses there will fall
When she looks upon his body chopped particularly small."

He traced that gallant sorter to a still suburban square;
He watched his opportunity and seized him unaware;
He took a life-preserver and he hit him on the head,
And Mrs. Brown dissected him before she went to bed.

And pretty little Alice grew more settled in her mind,
She nevermore was guilty of a weakness of the kind,
Until at length good Robber Brown bestowed her pretty
    hand
On the promising young robber, the lieutenant of his band.

                                        W. S. GILBERT

LOST MR. BLAKE

Mr. Blake was a regular out-and-out hardened sinner,
    Who was quite out of the pale of Christianity, so to speak:
He was in the habit of smoking a long pipe and drinking a
    glass of grog on Sunday after dinner,
    And seldom thought of going to church more than twice
    (or if Good Friday or Christmas Day happened to
    come in it) three times a week.

He was quite indifferent as to the particular kinds of dresses
    That the clergyman wore at the church where he used to go
    to pray,
And whatever he did in the way of relieving a chap's dis-
    tresses,
    He always did in a nasty, sneaking, underhanded, hole-
    and-corner sort of way.

I have known him indulge in profane, ungentlemanly
    emphatics,
    When the Protestant Church has been divided on the
    subject of the width of a chasuble's hem;

I have even known him to sneer at albs—and as for dal-
    matics,
Words can't convey an idea of the contempt he expressed
    for *them*.

He didn't believe in persons who, not being well off them-
    selves, are obliged to confine their charitable exertions
    to collecting money from wealthier people,
And looked upon individuals of the former class as
    ecclesiastical hawks;
He used to say that he would no more think of interfering
    with his priest's robes than with his church or his
    steeple,
And that he did not consider his soul imperilled because
    somebody over whom he had no influence whatever,
    chose to dress himself up like an ecclesiastical Guy
    Fawkes.

This shocking old vagabond was so unutterably shameless
    That he actually went a-courting a very respectable and
    pious middle-aged sister, by the name of Biggs:
She was a rather attractive widow whose life, as such, had
    always been particularly blameless;
    Her first husband had left her a secure but moderate
    competence owing to some fortunate speculations in
    the matter of figs.

She was an excellent person in every way—and won the
    respect even of Mrs. Grundy,
    She was a good housewife, too, and wouldn't have wasted
    a penny if she had owned the Koh-i-noor;
She was just as strict as he was lax in her observance of
    Sunday,
    And being a good economist, and charitable besides, she
    took all the bones and cold potatoes and broken pie-
    crusts and candle-ends (when she had quite done with
    them), and make them into an excellent soup for the
    deserving poor.

I am sorry to say that she rather took to Blake—that
    outcast of society;
    And when respectable brothers who were fond of her
        began to look dubious and to cough,
She would say, "Oh, my friends, it's because I hope to
    bring this poor benighted soul back to virtue and
    propriety."
    (And besides, the poor benighted soul, with all his faults,
        was uncommonly well off.)

And when Mr. Blake's dissipated friends called his attention
    to the frown or the pout of her,
    Whenever he did anything which appeared to her to
        savour of an unmentionable place,
He would say she would be a very decent old girl when all
    that nonsense was knocked out of her—
    And his method of knocking it out of her is one that
        covered him with disgrace.

She was fond of going to church services four times every
    Sunday, and four or five times in the week, and never
    seemed to pall of them,
    So he hunted out all the churches within a convenient
        distance that had services at different hours, so to
        speak;
And when he had married her he positively insisted upon
    their going to all of them,
    So they contrived to do about twelve churches every
        Sunday, and, if they had luck, from twenty-two to
        twenty-three in the course of the week.

She was fond of dropping his sovereigns ostentatiously
    into the plate, and she liked to see them stand out
    rather conspicuously against the commonplace half-
    crowns and shillings,
    So he took her to all the charity sermons, and if by any
        extraordinary chance there wasn't a charity sermon
        anywhere, he would drop a couple of sovereigns (one
        for him and one for her) into the poor-box at the door;

And as he always deducted the sums thus given in charity
from the housekeeping money, and the money he allowed
her for her bonnets frillings,
She soon began to find that even charity, if you allow
it to interfere with your personal luxuries, becomes an
intolerable bore.

On Sundays she was always melancholy and anything but
good society,
For that day in her household was a day of sighings and
sobbings and wringing of hands and shaking of heads:
She wouldn't hear of a button being sewn on a glove, because
it was a work neither of necessity nor of piety,
And strictly prohibited her servants from amusing themselves, or indeed doing anything at all except dusting
the drawing-rooms, cleaning the boots and shoes,
cooking the dinner, waiting generally on the family,
and making the beds.

But Blake even went farther than that, and said that, on
Sundays, people should do their own works of necessity,
and not delegate them to persons in a menial situation,
So he wouldn't allow his servants to do so much as even
answer a bell.
Here he is making his wife carry up the water for her bath
to the second floor, much against her inclination,—
And why in the world the gentleman who illustrates
these ballads has put him into a cocked hat is more
than I can tell.

After about three months of this sort of thing, taking the
smooth with the rough of it
(Blacking her own boots and peeling her own potatoes
was not her notion of connubial bliss),
Mrs. Blake began to find that she had pretty nearly had
enough of it,
And came, in course of time, to think that Blake's own
original line of conduct wasn't so much amiss.

And now that wicked person—that detestable sinner
("Belial Blake" his friends and well-wishers call him
for his atrocities),
And his poor deluded victim whom all her Christian
brothers dislike and pity so,
Go to the parish church only on Sunday morning and
afternoon and occasionally on a week-day, and spend
their evenings in connubial fondlings and affectionate
reciprocities,
And I should like to know where in the world (or rather,
out of it) they expect to go!

W. S. GILBERT

THE STORY OF PRINCE AGIB

Strike the concertina's melancholy string!
Blow the spirit-stirring harp like any thing!
     Let the piano's martial blast
     Rouse the Echoes of the Past,
For of Agib, Prince of Tartary, I sing!

Of Agib, who amid Tartaric scenes,
Wrote a lot of ballet-music in his teens:
     His gentle spirit rolls
     In the melody of souls—
Which is pretty, but I don't know what it means

Of Agib, who could readily, at sight,
Strum a march upon the loud Theodolite:
     He would diligently play
     On the Zoetrope all day,
And blow the gay Pantechnicon all night.

One winter—I am shaky in my dates—
Came two starving Tartar minstrels to his gates,
     Oh, Allah be obeyed,
     How infernally they played!
I remember that they called themselves the "Oüaits."

Oh! that day of sorrow, misery, and rage,
I shall carry to the Catacombs of Age,
    Photographically lined
    On the tablet of my mind,
When a yesterday has faded from its page!

Alas! Prince Agib went and asked them in!
Gave them beer, and eggs and sweets, and scents, and tin.
    And when (as snobs would say)
    They had "put it all away,"
He requested them to tune up and begin.

Though its icy horror chill you to the core,
I will tell you what I never told before—
    The consequences true
    Of that awful interview,
For I listened at the key-hole in the door!

They played him a sonata—let me see!
"*Medulla oblongata*"—key of G.
    Then they began to sing
    That extremely lovely thing,
"*Scherzando! ma non troppo, ppp.*"

He gave them money, more than they could count,
Scent from a most ingenious little fount,
    More beer, in little kegs,
    Many dozen hard-boiled eggs,
And goodies to a fabulous amount.

Now follows the dim horror of my tale,
And I feel I'm growing gradually pale,
    For, even at this day,
    Though its sting has passed away,
When I venture to remember it, I quail!

The elder of the brothers gave a squeal,
All-overish it made me for to feel!
    "Oh Prince," he says, says he,
    "*If a Prince indeed you be,*
I've a mystery I'm going to reveal!

"Oh, listen, if you'd shun a horrid death,
To what the gent who's speaking to you, saith:
     No 'Oüaits' in truth are we,
     As you fancy that we be,
For (ter-remble) I am Aleck—this is Beth!"

Said Agib, "Oh! accursed of your kind,
I have heard that you are men of evil mind!"
     Beth gave a dreadful shriek—
     But before he'd time to speak
I was mercilessly collared from behind.

In number ten or twelve, or even more,
They fastened me, full length, upon the floor.
     On my face extended flat,
     I was walloped with a cat,
For listening at the key-hole of a door.

Oh! the horror of that agonising thrill!
(I can feel the place in frosty weather still).
     For a week from ten to four
     I was fastened to the floor,
While a mercenary wopped me with a will!

They branded me and broke me on a wheel,
And they left me in an hospital to heal;
     And, upon my solemn word,
     I have never never heard
What those Tartars had determined to reveal.

But that day of sorrow, misery, and rage,
I shall carry to the Catacombs of Age,
     Photographically lined
     On the tablet of my mind,
When a yesterday has faded from its page!

                         W. S. GILBERT

THOMAS WINTERBOTTOM HANCE

In all the towns and cities fair
  On Merry England's broad expanse,
No swordsman ever could compare
  With Thomas Winterbottom Hance.

The dauntless lad could fairly hew
  A silken handkerchief in twain,
Divide a leg of mutton, too—
  And this without unwholesome strain.

On whole half-sheep, with cunning trick,
  His sabre sometimes he'd employ—
No bar of lead, however thick,
  Had terrors for the stalwart boy.

At Dover daily he'd prepare
  To hew and slash, behind, before—
Which aggravated Monsieur Pierre,
  Who watched him from the Calais shore.

It caused good Pierre to swear and dance,
  The sight annoyed and vexed him so;
He was the bravest man in France—
  He said so, and he ought to know.

'Regardez, donc, ce cochon gros—
  Ce polisson! Oh, sacré bleu!
Son sabre, son plomb, et ses gigots!
  Comme cela m'ennuye, enfin, mon Dieu!

"Il sait que les foulards de soie
  Give no retaliating whack—
Les gigots morts n'ont pas de quoi—
  Le plomb don't ever hit you back."

But every day the zealous lad
   Cut lead and mutton more and more;
And every day, poor Pierre, half mad,
   Shrieked loud defiance from his shore.

Hance had a mother, poor and old,
   A simple, harmless village dame,
Who crowed and clapped as people told
   Of Winterbottom's rising fame.

She said, "I'll be upon the spot
   To see my Tommy's sabre-play";
And so she left her leafy cot,
   And walked to Dover in a day.

Pierre had a doting mother, who
   Had heard of his defiant rage:
His ma was nearly eighty-two,
   And rather dressy for her age.

At Hance's doings every morn,
   With sheer delight *his* mother cried;
And Monsieur Pierre's contemptuous scorn
   Filled *his* mamma with proper pride.

But Hance's powers began to fail—
   His constitution was not strong—
And Pierre, who once was stout and hale,
   Grew thin from shouting all day long.

Their mothers saw them pale and wan,
   Maternal anguish tore each breast,
And so they met to find a plan
   To set their offsprings' minds at rest.

Said Mrs. Hance, "Of course I shrinks
   From bloodshed, ma'am, as you're aware,
But still they'd better meet, I thinks."
   "Assurément!" said Madame Pierre.

A sunny spot in sunny France
   Was hit upon for this affair;
The ground was picked by Mrs. Hance,
   The stakes were pitched by Madame Pierre.

Said Mrs. H., "Your work you see—
   Go in, my noble boy, and win."
"En garde, mon fils!" said Madame P.
   "Allons!" "Go on!" "En garde!" "Begin!"

Loud sneered the doughty man of France,
   "Ho! ho! Ho! ho! Ha! ha! Ha! ha!"
"The French for 'Pish!'" said Thomas Hance.
   Said Pierre, "L'Anglais, Monsieur, pour 'bah!'"

Said Mrs. H., "Come, one! two! three!—
   We're sittin' here to see all fair";
"C'est magnifique!" said Madame P.,
   "Mais, parbleu! ce n'est pas la guerre!"

"Je scorn un foe si lâche que vous,"
   Said Pierre, the doughty son of France.
"I fight not coward foe like you!"
   Said our undaunted Tommy Hance.

"The French for 'Pooh!'" our Tommy cried.
   "L'Anglais pour 'Va!'" the Frenchman crowed.
And so, with undiminished pride,
   Each went on his respective road.
                   W. S. GILBERT

THE YARN OF THE "NANCY BELL"

'Twas on the shores that round our coast
   From Deal to Ramsgate span,
That I found alone on a piece of stone
   An elderly naval man.

His hair was weedy, his beard was long,
  And weedy and long was he,
And I heard this wight on the shore recite,
  In a singular minor key:

"Oh, I am a cook and a captain bold,
  And the mate of the *Nancy* brig,
And a bo'sun tight, and a midshipmite,
  And the crew of the captain's gig."

And he shook his fists and he tore his hair,
  Till I really felt afraid,
For I couldn't help thinking the man had been drinking,
  And so I simply said:

"Oh, elderly man, it's little I know
  Of the duties of men of the sea,
And I'll eat my hand if I understand
  How you can possibly be

"At once a cook, and a captain bold,
  And the mate of the *Nancy* brig,
And a bo'sun tight, and a midshipmite,
  And the crew of the captain's gig."

Then he gave a hitch to his trousers, which
  Is a trick all seamen larn,
And having got rid of a thumping quid,
  He spun this painful yarn:

"'Twas in the good ship *Nancy Bell*
  That we sailed to the Indian Sea,
And there on a reef we come to grief,
  Which has often occurred to me.

"And pretty nigh all the crew was drowned
  (There was seventy-seven o' soul),
And only ten of the *Nancy's* men
  Said 'Here!' to the muster-roll.

"There was me and the cook and the captain bold,
    And the mate of the *Nancy* brig,
And the bo'sun tight, and a midshipmite,
    And the crew of the captain's gig.

"For a month we'd neither wittles nor drink,
    Till a-hungry we did feel,
So we drawed a lot, and accordin' shot
    The captain for our meal.

"The next lot fell to the *Nancy's* mate,
    And a delicate dish he made;
Then our appetite with the midshipmite
    We seven survivors stayed.

"And then we murdered the bos'un tight,
    And he much resembled pig;
Then we wittled free, did the cook and me,
    On the crew of the captain's gig.

"Then only the cook and me was left,
    And the delicate question, 'Which
Of us two goes to the kettle?' arose,
    And we argued it out as sich.

"For I loved that cook as a brother, I did,
    And the cook he worshipped me;
But we'd both be blowed if we'd either be stowed
    In the other chap's hold, you see.

"'I'll be eat if you dines off me,' says Tom.
    'Yes, that,' says I, 'you'll be,—
I'm boiled if I die, my friend,' quoth I.
    And 'Exactly so,' quoth he.

"Says he, 'Dear James, to murder me
    Were a foolish thing to do,
For don't you see that you can't cook *me*,
    While I can—and will—cook *you!*'

"So he boils the water, and takes the salt
  And the pepper in portions true
(Which he never forgot), and some chopped shalot,
  And some sage and parsley too.

"'Come here,' says he, with a proper pride,
  Which his smiling features tell,
''Twill soothing be if I let you see
  How extremely nice you'll smell.'

"And he stirred it round and round and round,
  And he sniffed at the foaming froth;
When I ups with his heels, and smothers his squeals
  In the scum of the boiling broth.

"And I eat that cook in a week or less,
  And—as I eating be
The last of his chops, why, I almost drops,
  For a wessel in sight I see.

                    *   *   *

"And I never grin, and I never smile,
  And I never larf or play,
But sit and croak, and a single joke
  I have—which is to say:

"Oh, I am a cook and a captain bold,
  And the mate of the *Nancy* brig,
And a bos'un tight, and a midshipmite,
  And the crew of the captain's gig!"

                                   W. S. GILBERT

AN ELEGY

On the Glory of her Sex, Mrs. Mary Blaize

Good people all, with one accord,
  Lament for Madam Blaize,
Who never wanted a good word—
  From those who spoke her praise.

The needy seldom pass'd her door,
   And always found her kind;
She freely lent to all the poor—
   Who left a pledge behind.

She strove the neighborhood to please
   With manners wondrous winning;
And never follow'd wicked ways—
   Unless when she was sinning.

At church, in silks and satins new,
   With hoop of monstrous size,
She never slumber'd in her pew—
   But when she shut her eyes.

Her love was sought, I do aver,
   By twenty beaux and more;
The King himself has follow'd her—
   When she has walk'd before.

But now, her wealth and finery fled,
   Her hangers-on cut short all;
The doctors found, when she was dead—
   Her last disorder mortal.

Let us lament, in sorrow sore,
   For Kent Street well may say,
That had she lived a twelvemonth more—
   She had not died to-day.

OLIVER GOLDSMITH

STAIRS

Here's to the man who invented stairs
And taught our feet to soar!
He was the first who ever burst
Into a second floor.

The world would be downstairs to-day
Had he not found the key;
So let his name go down to fame,
Whatever it may be.

OLIVER HERFORD

AESTIVATION

In candent ire the solar splendor flames;
The foles, languescent, pend from arid rames;
His humid front the cive, anheling, wipes,
And dreams of erring on ventiferous ripes.

How dulce to vive occult to mortal eyes,
Dorm on the herb with none to supervise,
Carp the suave berries from the crescent vine,
And bibe the flow from longicaudate kine.

To me also, no verdurous visions come
Save yon exiguous pool's confervascum,—
No concave vast repeats the tender hue
That laves my milk-jug with celestial blue.

Me wretched! Let me curr to quercine shades!
Effund your albid hausts, lactiferous maids!
Oh, might I vole to some umbrageous clump,—
Depart,—be off,—excede,—evade,—erump!

OLIVER WENDELL HOLMES

FAITHLESS NELLY GRAY

Ben Battle was a soldier bold,
   And used to war's alarms:
But a cannon-ball took off his legs,
   So he laid down his arms!

Now, as they bore him off the field,
   Said he, "Let others shoot,

For here I leave my second leg,
    And the Forty-second Foot!"

The army surgeons made him limbs:
    Said he, "They're only pegs;
But there's as wooden members quite,
    As represent my legs!"

Now Ben he loved a pretty maid,
    Her name was Nelly Gray;
So he went to pay her his devours
    When he'd devoured his pay!

But when he called on Nelly Gray,
    She made him quite a scoff;
And when she saw his wooden legs,
    Began to take them off!

"O Nelly Gray! O Nelly Gray!
    Is this your love so warm?
The love that loves a scarlet coat,
    Should be more uniform!"

Said she, "I loved a soldier once,
    For he was blithe and brave;
But I will never have a man
    With both legs in the grave!

"Before you had those timber toes,
    Your love I did allow,
But then you know, you stand upon
    Another footing now!"

"O Nelly Gray! O Nelly Gray!
    For all your jeering speeches,
At duty's call I left my legs
    In Badajos's breaches!"

"Why, then," said she, "you've lost the feet
   Of legs in war's alarms,
And now you cannot wear your shoes
   Upon your feats of arms!"

"O, false and fickle Nelly Gray;
   I know why you refuse:
Though I've no feet—some other man
   Is standing in my shoes!

"I wish I ne'er had seen your face;
   But now a long farewell!
For you will be my death—alas!
   You will not be my Nell!"

Now, when he went from Nelly Gray,
   His heart so heavy got—
And life was such a burden grown,
   It made him take a knot!

So round his melancholy neck
   A rope he did entwine,
And, for his second time in life
   Enlisted in the Line!

One end he tied around a beam,
   And then removed his pegs,
And as his legs were off,—of course,
   He soon was off his legs!

And there he hung till he was dead
   As any nail in town,—
For though distress had cut him up,
   It could not cut him down!

A dozen men sat on his corpse,
   To find out why he died—
And they buried Ben in four cross-roads,
   With a stake in his inside!

THOMAS HOOD

BLOW ME EYES!

When I was young and full o' pride,
　　A-standin' on the grass
And gazin' o'er the water-side,
　　I seen a fisher lass.
"O, fisher lass, be kind awhile,"
　　I asks 'er quite unbid.
"Please look into me face and smile"—
　　And, blow me eyes, she did!

O, blow me light and blow me blow,
I didn't think she'd charm me so—
　　But, blow me eyes, she did!

She seemed so young and beautiful
　　I *had* to speak perlite,
(The afternoon was long and dull,
　　But she was short and bright).
"This ain't no place," I says, "to stand—
　　Let's take a walk instid,
Each holdin' of the other's hand"—
　　And, blow me eyes, she did!

O, blow me light and blow me blow,
I sort o' thunk she wouldn't go—
　　But, blow me eyes, she did!

And as we walked along a lane
　　With no one else to see,
Me heart was filled with sudden pain,
　　And so I says to she:
"If you would have me actions speak
　　The words what can't be hid,
You'd sort o' let me kiss yer cheek"—
　　And, blow me eyes, she did!

O, blow me light and blow me blow,
How sweet she was I didn't know—
    But, blow me eyes, *she* did!

But pretty soon me shipmate Jim
    Came strollin' down the beach,
And she began a-oglin' him
    As pretty as a peach.
"O, fickle maid o' false intent,"
    Impulsively I chid,
"Why don't you go and wed that gent?"
    And, blow me eyes, she did!

O, blow me light and blow me blow,
I didn't think she'd treat me so—
    But, blow me eyes, she did!

                                    WALLACE IRWIN

LINES TO A YOUNG LADY

How pleasant to know Mr. Lear!
    Who has written such volumes of stuff!
Some think him ill-tempered and queer,
    But a few think him pleasant enough.

His mind is concrete and fastidious,
    His nose is remarkably big;
His visage is more or less hideous,
    His beard it resembles a wig.

He has ears, and two eyes, and ten fingers,
    Leastways if you reckon two thumbs;
Long ago he was one of the singers,
    But now he is one of the dumbs.

He sits in a beautiful parlour,
  With hundreds of books on the wall;
He drinks a great deal of Marsala,
  But never gets tipsy at all.

He has many friends, laymen and clerical,
  Old Foss is the name of his cat:
His body is perfectly spherical,
  He weareth a runcible hat.

When he walks in a waterproof white,
  The children run after him so!
Calling out, "He's come out in his night-
  Gown, that crazy old Englishman, oh!"

He weeps by the side of the ocean,
  He weeps on the top of the hill;
He purchases pancakes and lotion,
  And chocolate shrimps from the mill.

He reads but he cannot speak Spanish,
  He cannot abide ginger-beer:
Ere the days of his pilgrimage vanish,
  How pleasant to know Mr. Lear.

                                  EDWARD LEAR

THE LACQUER LIQUOR LOCKER

Now once upon a time the King of Astrakhan, at that,
Was sitting on his throne because his throne was where he
    sat;
And comfortably beside him, and magnificently stocked,
Was a lacquer liquor locker which a liquor lackey locked.

"My boy," the King would often say with granulated voice,
"I think the 1640 is particularly choice."
The boy would understand and so, endeavoring to please,
He'd try his luck at fitting several likely locker keys.

The King was always much annoyed because of this delay:
"See here, my lad, you've got to throw those other keys
    away."
"This minute, Sire?" "This minute, sir!" And with a pox
    that pocked,
He cursed the keys which didn't keep his liquor locker
    locked.

The lackey did as he was bid. Alackalasalack!
He threw them all so far away that no one threw them back
A silly throw, as I can show, for he was simply shocked
To find he lacked the very one that left the liquor locked.

"O Sire, I've thrown them all away!" "Look here, my liquor
    lad!"
"It so befell I threw as well the one I wish I had."
And since it was the kind of lock that isn't quickly picked,
The lacquer liquid locker had the little lackey licked.

Unhappy page! In such a rage a king is hard to calm;
A butt or tun of '51's the proper kind of balm.
"I always liked my liquor locked, from brandy down to
    beer;
It might as well be lacquer now as liquor under here."

Not magic of the magi nor the wisdom of the wise
Could either find the key again or ply where it applies.
The stricken King of Astrakhan soon sickened unto death,
Who tasted not of bitters but what most embittereth.

The little lackey lastly fell into a deep decline,
And evil over all the land to shrivel up the vine:
And now the only vintages of Astrakhan are crocked
In that lacquer liquor locker which a liquor lackey locked.
                                        DAVID McCORD

LESSONS IN LIMERICKS

I

A bigamist born in Zambezi
Said "Lord, I'd be taking it ezi
If one of my wives
Would get out of our lives:
I choose to be twozi not threezi."

II

The British in branding their betters
Distinguish them chiefly by letters:
F. R. C. P. E.,
M. O. H., K. C. B.—
But after their names, not on sweaters.

III

O limerick, Learest of lyrics,
Promoter of past panegyrics:
Defend, if you can,
That peculiar old man
Whose apteryx rhymed with apteryx!

DAVID McCORD

ANTIGONISH

As I was going up the stair
I met a man who wasn't there!
He wasn't there again to-day!
I wish, I *wish* he'd stay away!

March 27, 1922 HUGHES MEARNS

LATER ANTIGONISHES

ALIBI

As I was falling down the stair
I met a bump that wasn't there;
It might have put me on the shelf
Except I wasn't there myself.

REVEILLE

The porter shouted, "Syracuse!"
And shook me hard and cried, "Excuse,
Ef you wa'n't goin' to La Crosse
This is where I'd wake you, Boss!"

CRIME NOTE

As I was robbing Chelsea Bank
I met a non-existent Zanque;
He did not whiffle, wooze or wup—
That's *why* I had to shut him up.

FRUSTRATED MALE

One night I met when stepping out
A gal who wasn't thereabout;
I said, "*Hel*-lo! And how are *you!*"
She didn't say; so I never knew.

THE LADY WITH TECHNIQUE

As I was letting down my hair
I met a guy who didn't care;
He didn't care again today—
I *love* 'em when they get that way!

ME

I do not lack for Jack or Joan,
I'm in a crowd when all alone,
My truest friends, a loyal set,
Are all the folks I've never met.

October 31, 1939   HUGHES MEARNS

DARWINITY

Power to thine elbow, thou newest of sciences,
  All the old landmarks are ripe for decay;
Wars are but shadows, and so are alliances,
  Darwin the great is the man of the day.

All other 'ologies want an apology;
  Bread's a mistake—Science offers a stone;
Nothing is true but Anthropobiology—
  Darwin the great understands it alone.

Mighty the great evolutionist teacher is
  Licking Morphology clean into shape;
Lord! what an ape the Professor or Preacher is
  Ever to doubt his descent from an ape.

Man's an Anthropoid—he cannot help that, you know—
  First evoluted from Pongos of old;
He's but a branch of the *catarrhine* cat, you know—
  Monkey I mean—that's an ape with a cold.

Fast dying out are man's later Appearances,
  Cataclysmitic Geologies gone;
Now of Creation completed the clearance is,
  Darwin alone you must anchor upon.

Primitive Life—Organisms were chemical,
  Busting spontaneous under the sea;
Purely subaqueous, panaquademical,
  Was the original Crystal of Me.

I'm the Apostle of mighty Darwinity,
  Stands for Divinity—sounds much the same—
Apo-theistico-Pan-Asininity
  Only can doubt whence the lot of us came.

Down on your knees, Superstition and Flunkeydom!
  Won't you accept such plain doctrines instead?
What is so simple as primitive Monkeydom
  Born in the sea with a cold in its head?
                                    HERMAN C. MERIVALE

NONSENSE

Good reader! if you e'er have seen,
  When Phoebus hastens to his pillow,
The mermaids, with their tresses green,
  Dancing upon the western billow:
If you have seen, at twilight dim,
When the lone spirit's vesper hymn
  Floats wild along the winding shore:
If you have seen, through mist of eve,
The fairy train their ringlets weave,
Glancing along the spangled green;—
  If you have seen all this, and more,
God bless me! what a deal you've seen!

THOMAS MOORE

THE BACHELOR'S BALLADE

Unlike Virgil's verse on the *Troiae bella*,
I sing not of arms such as bilbo or bola,
Nor yet of a man, but a pretty puella
Who isn't called Katy or Lucy or Lola
Or Bertha or Betty or Nancy or Nola;
Her name is Virginia, she lives in a villa,
And for her I'd give not a twopence or tola,
So you take Virginia and I'll take vanilla.

Oh, Nora was good at the gay tarantella,
Queen Bess played the virginals and the viola,
And Madame de Staël dashed off a novella;
But Ginnie can dance the old French farandola,
Displays virtuosity on the victrola
And, though her name doesn't contain a cedilla,
Writes books that in length would do justice to Zola;
So you take Virginia and I'll take vanilla.

Leander loved Hero and Dean Swift loved Stella,
And Faustus admired Helen's marvelous mola;
The prince in the story adored Cinderella,

Great Caesar respected Calpurnia's stola,
And somebody must have liked Savonarola.
John Alden at long last proposed to Priscilla
For no man or maid should stay solus (or sola),
So you take Virginia and I'll take vanilla.

L'ENVOI

Chacun a son goût, as they say in Angola;
Some folks prefer root-beer, some sarsaparilla,
And some will drink nothing but cold Coca-Cola . . .
So you take Virginia and I'll take vanilla.

DAVID FISHER PARRY

LINES BY A PERSON OF QUALITY

Fluttering spread thy purple pinions,
    Gentle Cupid, o'er my heart,
I a slave in thy dominions,
    Nature must give way to art.

Mild Arcadians, ever blooming,
    Nightly nodding o'er your flocks,
See my weary days consuming,
    All beneath you flowery rocks.

Thus the Cyprian goddess weeping,
    Mourned Adonis, darling youth:
Him the boar, in silence creeping,
    Gored with unrelenting toots.

Cynthia, tune harmonious numbers;
    Fair Discretion, tune the lyre;
Soothe my ever-waking slumbers;
    Bright Apollo, lend thy choir.

Gloomy Pluto, king of terrors,
    Armed in adamantine chains,
Lead me to the crystal mirrors,
    Watering soft Elysian plains.

Mournful Cypress, verdant willow,
　Gilding my Aurelia's brows,
Morpheus, hovering o'er my pillow,
　Hear me pay my dying vows.

Melancholy, smooth Maeander,
　Swiftly purling in a round,
On thy margin· lovers wander
　With thy flowery chaplets crowned.

Thus when Philomela, drooping,
　Softly seeks her silent mate,
So the bird of Juno stooping;
　Melody resigns to fate.

ALEXANDER POPE

THE MAN IN THE MOON

Said the Raggedy Man on a hot afternoon,
　"My!
　　Sakes!
　　　What a lot o' mistakes
Some little folks makes on the Man in the Moon!
But people that's been up to see him like Me,
And calls on him frequent and intimutly,
Might drop a few hints that would interest you
　Clean!
　　Through!
　　　If you wanted 'em to—
Some actual facts that might interest you!

"O the Man in the Moon has a crick in his back;
　Whee!
　　Whimm!
　　　Ain't you sorry for him?
And a mole on his nose that is purple and black;
And his eyes are so weak that they water and run,

If he dares to *dream* even he looks at the sun,—
So he jes' dreams of stars, as the doctors advise—
   My!
       Eyes!
           But isn't he wise—
To jes' dream of stars, as the doctors advise?

"And the Man in the Moon has a boil on his ear—
   Whee!
       Whing!
           What a singular thing!
I know! but these facts are authentic, my dear,—
There's a boil on his ear; and a corn on his chin,—
He calls it a dimple,—but dimples stick in,—
Yet it might be a dimple turned over, you know!
   Whang!
       Ho!
           Why certainly so!—
It might be a dimple turned over, you know!

"And the Man in the Moon has a rheumatic knee,
   Gee!
       Whizz!
           What a pity that is!
And his toes have worked round where his heels ought to be.
So whenever he wants to go North he goes South,
And comes back with the porridge crumbs all round his
   mouth,
And he brushes them off with a Japanese fan,
   Whing!
       Whann!
           What a marvellous man!
What a very remarkably marvellous man!

"And the Man in the Moon," sighed the Raggedy Man,
   "Gits!
       So!
           Sullonesome, you know!

Up there by himself since creation began!—
That when I call on him and then come away,
He grabs me and holds me and begs me to stay,—
Till—well, if it wasn't for *Jimmy-cum Jim,*
   Dadd!
      Limb!
         I'd go pardners with him!
Jes' jump my bob here and be pardners with him!"

JAMES WHITCOMB RILEY

MY ANGELINE

She kept her secret well, oh, yes,
   Her hideous secret well.
We together were cast, I knew not her past;
   For how was I to tell?
I married her, guileless lamb I was;
   I'd have died for her sweet sake.
How could I have known that my Angeline
   Had been a Human Snake?
Ah, we have been wed but a week or two
   When I found her quite a wreck:
Her limbs were tied in a double bow-knot
   At the back of her swan-like neck.
No curse there sprang to my pallid lips,
   Nor did I reproach her then;
I calmly untied my bonny bride
   And straightened her out again.

REFRAIN

My Angeline! My Angeline!
Why didst disturb my mind serene?
My well-belovèd circus queen,
My Human Snake, my Angeline!

At night I'd wake at the midnight hour,
  With a weird and haunted feeling,
And there she'd be, in her *robe de nuit*,
  A-walking upon the ceiling.
She said she was being "the human fly,"
  And she'd lift me up from beneath
By a section slight of my garb of night,
  Which she held in her pearly teeth.
For the sweet, sweet sake of the Human Snake
  I'd have stood this conduct shady;
But she skipped in the end with an old, old friend,
  An eminent bearded lady.
But, oh, at night, when my slumber's light,
  Regret comes o'er me stealing;
For I miss the sound of those little feet,
  As they pattered along the ceiling.

REFRAIN

My Angeline! My Angeline!
Why didst disturb my mind serene?
My well-belovèd circus queen,
My Human Snake, my Angeline!

HARRY B. SMITH

THE TATTOOED MAN

(From "The Idol's Eye")

An actress of emotional *rôles*,
  Devoted to her art,
Once went to a *musée* of "freaks,"
  And there she lost her heart.
For long she'd sought a kindred soul,
  Affinity and mate.
But when she saw the tattooed man,
  She knew she'd met her fate.

He was a human picture gallery,
  Such a spectacular gent.
He won her heart and drew her salary,
  Never gave her a cent;
Till one fine day with her season's pay
  And the fat lady off he ran.
Oh! it's perfectly true you can beat a tattoo,
  But you can't beat a tattooed man.

He had designs upon himself;
  She had designs on *him*,
And she loved to look at the picture book
  That he had on ev'ry limb.
"Oh! why should I go abroad," she said,
  "To Germany, France, and Rome,
When a lovely collection awaits my inspection
  In my happy little home?"

  He was a human picture gallery, etc.
      .   .   .   .

He had "Raphael's cherubs" on his brow,
  "The Angelus" on his chest,
While on his back there was no lack
  Of old masters of the best.
"Oh! picture to yourself," she said,
  "A love-lorn maiden's doom!"
"I *can't* picture to myself," he said,
  "For there isn't any room."

  He was a human picture gallery, etc.
      .   .   .   .

Upon each knee so fair to see
  The artist grim had planned
A maiden face so full of grace,
  Another on his hand.

Alas! for that tattooed man's wife,
   She sorrowed much to see
Her husband with a girl on hand,
   And one upon each knee.

He was a human picture gallery, etc.
. . . .
HARRY B. SMITH

BALLADE OF SOPORIFIC ABSORPTION

Ho! Ho! Yes! Yes! It's very all well,
   You may drunk I am think, but I tell you I'm not,
I'm as sound as a fiddle and fit as a bell,
   And stable quite ill to see what's what.
   I under *do* stand you surprise a got
When I headed my smear with gooseberry jam:
   And I've swallowed, I grant, a beer of lot—
But I'm not so think as you drunk I am.

Can I liquor my stand? Why, yes, like hell!
   I care not how many a tossed I've pot,
I shall stralk quite weight and not yutter an ell,
   My feech will not spalter the least little jot:
   If you knownly had own!—well, I gave him a dot,
And I said to him, 'Sergeant, I'll come like a lamb—
   The floor it seems like a storm in a yacht,
But I'm not so think as you drunk I am.'

For example, to prove it I'll tale you a tell—
   I once knew a fellow named Apricot—
I'm sorry, I just chair over a fell—
   A trifle—this chap, on a very day hot—
   If I hadn't consumed that last whisky of tot!—
As I said now, this fellow, called Abraham—
   Ah? One more? Since it's you! Just a do me will spot—
But I'm not so think as you drunk I am.

So, Prince, you suggest I've bolted my shot?
Well, like what you say, and soul your damn!
I'm an upple litset by the talk you rot—
But I'm not so think as you drunk I am.

J. C. SQUIRE

LAY OF ANCIENT ROME

Oh, the Roman was a rogue,
　He erat was, you bettum;
He ran his automobilus
　And smoked his cigarettum.
He wore a diamond studibus
　And elegant cravattum,
A maxima cum laude shirt
　And such a stylish hattum!

He loved the luscious hic-haec-hoc,
　And bet on games and equi;
At times he won at others though,
　He got it in the nequi;
He winked, (quo usque tandem?) at
　Puellas on the Forum,
And sometimes, too, he even made
　Those goo-goo oculorum!

He frequently was seen
　At combats gladiatorial
And ate enough to feed
　Ten boarders at Memorial;
He often went on sprees
　And said, on starting homus,
"Hic labour—opus est,
　Oh, where's my hic—hic—domus?"

Although he lived in Rome,—
   Of all the arts the middle—
He was, (excuse the phrase,)
   A horrid individ'l;
Ah, what a different thing
   Was the homo (dative, hominy)
Of far away B. C.
   From us of Anno Domini.

THOMAS R. YBARRA

Panegyric

LA DONNA E MOBILE

I

Of all the stars that bathe the heavens in glory,
Of all the planets, rings and constellations,
Of all the suns and comets migratory,
To Mira would I offer my oblations.

II

Except for Mira, stars are very boring;
They twinkle steadily till night is paling;
Poets continuously, in verse adoring,
Have praised the stars for constancy unfailing.

III

"O constant star!" apostrophized P. Shelley,
And so did Messrs. Byron, Pope, and Dryden:
This constancy, from Plymouth Notch to Delhi,
Has been the stars' one trait poets took pride in.

IV

But Mira, bless her unsurpassed diameter,
Is not a star of regular effulgence.
And so I write, in slovenly pentameter,
An ode to thank her for her self-indulgence.

V

Is Mira lit to-night in her full stellar-scope?
And do her sky-mates look as dull as tar?
Then Tuesday you can't see her with a telerscope:
So hail to Mira, the Inconstant Star!

A. K.

AD PERSEPHONEN

Darling, at last my tiny lute,
  Silent, perforce, for seven years,
May sound again, no longer mute
  For lovely ears.

My girl, at last my little pen,
  Arid, for you, for all that time,
Undammed may flow, to catch your ken,
  In rippling rhyme.

This is St. Valentine his Day,
  So I would ask this girl of mine,
To be my love, and so to stay
  My Valentine.

For seven years from her dear eyes
  The world of print was all unkeyed;
Now is my dearest girl grown wise—
  Now she can read.

Sed haec hactenus—of this enough;
  I'll be your loving Valentine,
My darling daughter, pretty Puff,
  And you'll be mine.

FRANKLIN P. ADAMS

HAPPY LIFETIME TO YOU

On the 18th of April in '28,
My Tim began to be corporate.
Be brave, my son, and speak the trut',
And I hope you'll like your baseball suit.

FRANKLIN P. ADAMS

SHAKE, MULLEARY, AND GO-ETHE

I

I have a bookcase, which is what
Many much better men have not.
There are no books inside, for books,
I am afraid, might spoil its looks.
But I've three busts, all second-hand,
Upon the top. You understand
I could not put them underneath—
Shake, Mulleary, and Go-ethe.

II

Shake was a dramatist of note;
He lived by writing things to quote,
He long ago put on his shroud:
Some of his works are rather loud.
His bald-spot's dusty, I suppose.
I know there's dust upon his nose.
I'll have to give each nose a sheath—
Shake, Mulleary, and Go-ethe.

III

Mulleary's line was quite the same;
He has more hair, but far less fame.
I would not from that fame retrench—
But he is foreign, being French.
Yet high his haughty head he heaves,
The only one done up in leaves,
They're rather limited on wreath—
Shake, Mulleary, and Go-ethe.

IV

Go-ethe wrote in the German tongue;
He must have learned it very young.
His nose is quite a butt for scoff,
Although an inch of it is off.
He did quite nicely for the Dutch;

But here he doesn't count for much.
They all are off their native heath—
Shake, Mulleary, and Go-ethe.

v

They sit there, on their chests, as bland
As if they were not second-hand.
I do not know of what they think,
Nor why they never frown or wink.
But why from smiling they refrain
I think I clearly can explain:
They none of them could show much teeth—
Shake, Mulleary, and Go-ethe.

                                H. C. BUNNER

ODE TO TOBACCO

Thou who, when fears attack,
Bidst them avaunt, and Black
Care, at the horseman's back
    Perching, unseatest;
Sweet, when the morn is gray;
Sweet, when they've cleared away
Lunch; and at close of day
    Possibly sweetest:

I have a liking old
For thee, though manifold
Stories, I know, are told,
    Not to thy credit;
How one (or two at most)
Drops make a cat a ghost—
Useless, except to roast—
    Doctors have said it:

How they who use fusees
All grow by slow degrees
Brainless as chimpanzees,
    Meagre as lizards;

Go mad, and beat their wives;
Plunge (after shocking lives)
Razors and carving knives
    Into their gizzards.

Confound such knavish tricks!
Yet know I five or six
Smokers who freely mix
    Still with their neighbors;
Jones—(who, I'm glad to say,
Asked leave of Mrs. J.)—
Daily absorbs a clay
    After his labors.

Cats may have had their goose
Cooked by tobacco-juice;
Still why deny its use
    Thoughtfully taken?
We're not as tabbies are:
Smith, take a fresh cigar!
Jones, the tobacco-jar!
    Here's to thee, Bacon!
                    CHARLES STUART CALVERLEY

SALLY IN OUR ALLEY

Of all the girls that are so smart,
    There's none like pretty Sally;
She is the darling of my heart,
    And she lives in our alley.
There's ne'er a lady in the land
    That's half so sweet as Sally;
She is the darling of my heart,
    And she lives in our alley.

Her father he makes cabbage-nets,
    And through the streets does cry 'em;
Her mother she sells laces long
    To such as please to buy 'em:

But sure such folks can ne'er beget
   So sweet a girl as Sally;
She is the darling of my heart,
   And she lives in our alley.

When she is by, I leave my work,
   I love her so sincerely;
My master comes, like any Turk,
   And bangs me most severely:
But let him bang his bellyful,
   I'll bear it all for Sally;
She is the darling of my heart,
   And she lives in our alley.

Of all the days that's in the week,
   I dearly love but one day—
And that's the day that comes betwixt
   A Saturday and Monday;
For then I'm dressed all in my best,
   To walk abroad with Sally;
She is the darling of my heart,
   And she lives in our alley.

My master carries me to church,
   And often am I blamèd,
Because I leave him in the lurch,
   As soon as text is namèd:
I leave the church in sermon time,
   And slink away to Sally;
She is the darling of my heart,
   And she lives in our alley.

When Christmas comes about again,
   O, then I shall have money;
I'll hoard it up and, box it all,
   I'll give it to my honey:
Oh, would it were ten thousand pound,
   I'd give it all to Sally;

For she's the darling of my heart,
  And she lives in our alley.

My master, and the neighbors all,
  Make game of me and Sally,
And but for her I'd better be
  A slave, and row a galley:
But when my seven long years are out,
  O, then I'll marry Sally,
O, then we'll wed, and then we'll bed—
  But not in our alley.

                                    HENRY CAREY

A MISSOURI MAIDEN'S FAREWELL
TO ALABAMA

(A Piece for Recitation)

Alabama, good-bye! I love thee well!
But yet for a while do I leave thee now!
Sad, yes, sad thoughts of thee my heart doth swell,
And burning recollections throng my brow!
For I have wandered through thy flowery woods;
Have roamed and read near Tallapoosa's streams,
Have listen'd to Talassee's warring floods,
And woo'd by Coosa's side Aurora's beams.

Yet shame I not to bear an o'er-full heart,
Nor blush to turn behind my tearful eyes,
'Tis from no stranger land I now must part,
'Tis to no strangers left I yield these sighs.
Welcome and home were mine within this State,
Whose vales I leave, whose spires fade fast from me
And cold must be mine eyes and heart and tête,
Ere, dear Alabama! They turn cold on thee!

                                    S. L. CLEMENS

PERNICIOUS WEED

The pipe, with solemn interposing puff,
Makes half a sentence at a time enough;
The dozing sages drop the drowsy strain,
Then pause and puff, and speak, and pause again.
Such often, like the tube they so admire,
Important triflers! have more smoke than fire.
Pernicious weed! whose scent the fair annoys,
Unfriendly to society's chief joys,
Thy worst effect is banishing for hours
The sex whose presence civilizes ours.

WILLIAM COWPER

A DIRGE

CONCERNING THE LATE LAMENTED KING OF THE CANNIBAL
ISLANDS

And so our royal relative is dead!
    And so he rests from gustatory labors!
The white man was his choice, but when he fed
    He'd sometimes entertain his tawny neighbors.
He worshipped, as he said, his "Fe-fo-fum,"
The goddess of the epigastrium.

And missionaries graced his festive board,
    Solemn and succulent, in twos and dozens,
And smoked before their hospitable lord,
    Welcome as if they'd been his second cousins.
When cold, he warmed them as he would his kin—
They came as strangers, and he took them in.

And generous!—oh, wasn't he? I have known him
    Exhibit a celestial amiability:—
He'd eat an enemy, and then would own him
    Of flavor excellent, despite hostility.
The cruelest captain of the Turkish navy
He buried in an honorable grave—y.

He had a hundred wives. To make things pleasant
   They found it quite judicious to adore him;—
And when he dined, the nymphs were always present—
   Sometimes beside him and sometimes—before him.
When he was tired of one, he called her "sweet,"
And told her she was "good enough to eat."

He was a man of taste—and justice, too;
   He opened his mouth for e'en the humblest sinner,
And three weeks stall-fed an emaciate Jew
   Before they brought him to the royal dinner.
With preacher-men he shared his board and wallet
And let them nightly occupy his palate!

We grow like what we eat. Bad food depresses;
   Good food exalts us like an inspiration,
And missionary on the *menu* blesses
   And elevates the Feejee population.
A people who for years, saints, bairns, and women ate
Must soon their vilest qualities eliminate.

But the deceased could never hold a candle
   To those prim, pale-faced people of propriety
Who gloat o'er gossip and get fat on scandal—
   The cannibals of civilized society;
They drink the blood of brothers with their rations,
And crunch the bones of living reputations.

They kill the soul; he only claimed the dwelling.
   They take the sharpened scalpel of surmises
And cleave the sinews when the heart is swelling,
   And slaughter Fame and Honor for their prizes.
They make the spirit in the body quiver;
They quench the Light! He only took the—Liver!

I've known some hardened customers, I wot,
   A few tough fellows—pagans beyond question—
I wish had got into his dinner-pot;
   Although I'm certain they'd defy digestion,
And break his jaw, and ruin his esophagus,
Were he the chief of beings anthropophagous!

How fond he was of children! To his breast
   The tenderest nurslings gained a free admission.
Rank he despised, nor, if they came well dressed,
   Cared if they were plebeian or patrician.
Shade of Leigh Hunt! Oh, guide this laggard pen
To write of one who loved his fellow men!

WILLIAM AUGUSTUS CROFFUT

THE CURSE OF FAINT PRAISE

I have lyric aspiration;
   Though my verses may not show it,
I have longed to hear the nation
   Cry in chorus: "There's a poet!"
With a burst of metered gladness
   I would wing my way to glory;
Fevered phrases; fitful sadness
   Would I weave into my story.

Not for me the jingling verses;
   I would chant a nobler meter;
Tempt me *not* with crass sesterces;
   Higher are mine aims, and sweeter;
But whene'er with wild elation
   Tremblingly I smite the lyre,
Comes the swift and kind damnation:
   "He's a clever versifier."

IRWIN EDMAN

TO HAROLD JACOBY

Professor of Astronomy and the Comic Spirit at Columbia University

Professor, you've convinced me a semester of astronomy
May be more live, more vital than political economy;
And I have even found it sweet to hear your jargon cryptic
Of radial velocities and poles of the ecliptic.

The dismal mathematics of the distances sidereal
You managed to exalt into a joyousness ethereal;
And still in recollection my enthusiasm waxes,
Even as when you first expounded stellar parallaxes.

You taught the laughing wisdom of the universe whose
    numerous
Old stars and comets whiz with a punctiliousness humorous;
You taught us how to weigh the suns, and lightly told the
    reasons
Why Mother Earth is blessed with such variety of seasons.

Alas, celestial study makes one feel like scarcely anything.
Compared with stars we're each, at most, a twenty-for-a-
    penny thing;
Infinity is often pleasant to reflect upon, and yet it
Has made me feel so cheap I'm in a hurry to forget it.

But, best of all, you showed us in a manner undidactical,
The value of the science which the scoffers call unpractical;
I'd take astronomy for years if you assure me, sir, it
Can make me, as it made you, Master of the Comic Spirit.
                                            IRWIN EDMAN

THE CLINK OF THE ICE

Notably fond of music, I dote on a sweeter tone
Than ever the harp has uttered or ever the lute has known.
When I wake at five in the morning with a feeling in my
    head

Suggestive of mild excesses before I retired to bed;
When a small but fierce volcano vexes me sore inside,
And my throat and mouth are furred with a fur that seemeth
    a buffalo hide,—
How gracious those dews of solace that over my senses fall
At the clink of the ice in the pitcher the boy brings up the
    hall!

Oh, is it the gaudy ballet, with features I cannot name,
That kindles in virile bosoms that slow but devouring flame?
Or is the midnight supper, eaten before we retire,
That presently by combustion setteth us all afire?
Or is it the cheery magnum?—nay, I'll not chide the cup
That makes the meekest mortal anxious to whoop things up:
Yet, what the cause soever, relief comes when we call,—
Relief with that rapturous clinkety-clink that clinketh
    alike for all.

I've dreamt of the fiery furnace that was one vast bulk of
    flame,
And that I was Abednego a-wallowing in that same;
And I've dreamt I was a crater, possessed of a mad desire
To vomit molten lava, and to snort big gobs of fire;
I've dreamt I was Roman candles and rockets that fizzed
    and screamed,—
In short, I have dreamt the cussedest dreams that ever a
    human dreamed:
But all the red-hot fancies were scattered quick as a wink
When the spirit within that pitcher went clinking its clinkety-
    clink.

Boy, why so slow in coming with that gracious, saving cup?
Oh, haste thee to the succor of the man who is burning up!
See how the ice bobs up and down, as if it wildly strove
To reach its grace to the wretch who feels like a red-hot
    kitchen stove!
The piteous clinks it clinks methinks should thrill you
    through and through:
An erring soul is wanting drink, and he wants it p. d. q.!

And, lo! the honest pitcher, too, falls in so dire a fret
That its pallid form is presently bedewed with a chilly
    sweat.

May blessings be showered upon the man who first devised
    this drink
That happens along at five A. M. with its rapturous clinkety-
    clink!
I never have felt the cooling flood go sizzling down my
    throat
But what I vowed to hymn a hymn to that clinkety-clink
    devote;
So now, in the prime of my manhood, I polish this lyric gem
For the uses of all good fellows who are thirsty at five A. M.,
But especially for those fellows who have known the pleasing
    thrall
Of the clink of the ice in the pitcher the boy brings up the
    hall.

EUGENE FIELD

THE TRUTH ABOUT HORACE

It is very aggravating
To hear the solemn prating
Of the fossils who are stating
    That old Horace was a prude;
When we know that with the ladies
He was always raising Hades,
And with many an escapade his
    Best productions are imbued.

There's really not much harm in a
Large number of his carmina,
But these people find alarm in a
    Few records of his acts;
So they'd squelch the muse caloric,
And to students sophomoric
They'd present as metaphoric
    What old Horace meant for facts.

We have always thought 'em lazy;
Now we adjudge 'em crazy!
Why, Horace was a daisy
   That was very much alive!
And the wisest of us know him
As his Lydia verses show him,—
Go, read that virile poem,—
   It is No. 25.

He was a very owl, sir,
And starting out to prowl, sir,
You bet he made Rome howl, sir,
   Until he filled his date;
With a massic-laden ditty
And a classic maiden pretty
He painted up the city,
   And Maecenas paid the freight!

EUGENE FIELD

FOR MY FATHER

(After Thirty Years)

Hump-backed and rugged, blue on blue,
These are the hills my father knew.

These are the trees that gave him shade,
And this the brook that he used to wade.

If he could come again some spring
To hail each once familiar thing,—

That sagging barn would be as gray,
The buds as thick on lilac spray;

Meadow and hills and tumbling water
He'd find less changed than his own daughter.

RACHEL FIELD

ON THE DEATH OF A FAVORITE CAT, DROWNED IN A TUB OF GOLDFISHES

'Twas on a lofty vase's side,
Where China's gayest art had dyed
   The azure flowers that blow;
Demurest of the tabby kind,
The pensive Selima, reclined,
   Gazed on the lake below.

Her conscious tail her joy declared;
The fair round face, the snowy beard,
   The velvet of her paws,
Her coat that with the tortoise vies,
Her ears of jet, and emerald eyes,
   She saw, and purred applause.

Still had she gaz'd, but, 'midst the tide,
Two angel forms were seen to glide,
   The Genii of the stream:
Their scaly armor's Tyrian hue,
Through richest purple to the view
   Betrayed a golden gleam.

The hapless Nymph with wonder saw:
A whisker first and then a claw,
   With many an ardent wish,
She stretched, in vain, to reach the prize.
What female heart can gold despise?
   What Cat's averse to fish?

Presumptuous Maid! with looks intent
Again she stretched, again she bent,
   Nor knew the gulf between.
(Malignant Fate sat by, and smiled.)
The slippery verge her feet beguiled,
   She tumbled headlong in.

Eight times emerging from the flood,
She mewed to every watery god,
  Some speedy aid to send.
No Dolphin came, no Nereid stirred,
Nor cruel Tom nor Susan heard,—
  A Favorite has no friend!

From hence, ye Beauties, undeceived,
Know one false step is ne'er retrieved,
  And be with caution bold.
Not all that tempts your wandering eyes,
And heedless hearts, is lawful prize,
  Nor all that glisters, gold.

                              THOMAS GRAY

EXPERTS ON WOMAN

Woman, though undependable,
In illness proves commendable,
        Says Scott,
A point of view defendable
        Or not.

Woman, when that's permissible,
Is eminently kissable,
        Says Burns,
And positively hissable
        By turns.

Woman, said old Vergilius
The Roman to his filius,
        Is frail.
But he was supercilious
        And male.

Woman is most precarious,
Angelic, false, nefarious
        And true;
In fact, says Shakespeare, various.
        He knew!

Woman, it's undeniable
Is changeable and pliable
And can
Be quite as unreliable
As Man.

ARTHUR GUITERMAN

THIS SMOKING WORLD

Tobacco is a dirty weed:
  I like it.
It satisfies no normal need:
  I like it.
It makes you thin, it makes you lean,
It takes the hair right off your bean,
It's the worst darn stuff I've ever seen:
  I like it.

GRAHAM LEE HEMMINGER

DOROTHY Q

A FAMILY PORTRAIT

Grandmother's mother: her age, I guess,
Thirteen summers, or something less;
Girlish bust, but womanly air;
Smooth, square forehead with uprolled hair;
Lips that lover has never kissed;
Taper fingers and slender wrist;
Hanging sleeves of stiff brocade;
So they painted the little maid.

On her hand a parrot green
Sits unmoving and broods serene.
Hold up the canvas full in view,—
Look! there's a rent the light shines through,

Dark with a century's fringe of dust,—
That was a Red-Coat's rapier-thrust!
Such is the tale the lady old,
Dorothy's daughter's daughter, told.

Who the painter was none may tell,—
One whose best was not over well;
Hard and dry, it must be confessed,
Flat as a rose that has long been pressed;
Yet in her cheek the hues are bright,
Dainty colors of red and white,
And in her slender shape are seen
Hint and promise of stately mien.

Look not on her with eyes of scorn,—
Dorothy Q. was a lady born!
Ay! since the galloping Normans came,
England's annals have known her name;
And still to the three-hilled rebel town
Dear is that ancient name's renown,
For many a civic wreath they won,
The youthful sire and the gray-haired son.

O Damsel Dorothy! Dorothy Q.!
Strange is the gift that I owe to you;
Such a gift as never a king
Save to daughter or son might bring,—
All my tenure of heart and hand,
All my title to house and land;
Mother and sister and child and wife
And joy and sorrow and death and life!

What if a hundred years ago
Those close-shut lips had answered No,
When forth the tremulous question came
That cost the maiden her Norman name,
And under the folds that look so still
The bodice swelled with the bosom's thrill?

Should I be I, or would it be
One tenth another, to nine tenths me?

Soft is the breath of a maiden's Yes:
Not the light gossamer stirs with less;
But never a cable that holds so fast
Through all the battles of wave and blast,
And never an echo of speech or song
That lives in the babbling air so long!
There were tones in the voice that whispered then
You may hear to-day in a hundred men.

O lady and lover, how faint and far
Your images hover,—and here we are
Solid and stirring in flesh and bone,—
Edward's and Dorothy's—all their own,—
A goodly record for Time to show
Of a syllable spoken so long ago!—
Shall I bless you, Dorothy, or forgive
For the tender whisper that bade me live?

It shall be a blessing, my little maid!
I will heal the stab of the Red-Coat's blade,
And freshen the gold of the tarnished frame,
And gild with a rhyme your household name;
So you shall smile on us brave and bright
As first you greeted the morning's light,
And live untroubled by woes and fears
Through a second youth of a hundred years.

OLIVER WENDELL HOLMES

BARNEY McGEE

Barney McGee, there's no end of good luck in you,
Will-o'-the-wisp, with a flicker of Puck in you,
Wild as a bull-pup, and all of his pluck in you—
Let a man tread on your coat and he'll see!
Eyes like the lakes of Killarney for clarity,

Nose that turns up without any vulgarity,
Smile like a cherub, and hair that is carroty—
Whoop, you're a rarity, Barney McGee!
Mellow as Tarragon,
Prouder than Aragon—
Hardly a paragon,
You will agree—
Here's all that's fine to you!
Books and old wine to you!
Girls be divine to you,
Barney McGee!

Lucky the day when I met you unwittingly,
Dining where vagabonds came and went flittingly.
Here's some *Barbera* to drink it befittingly,
That day at Silvio's, Barney McGee!
Many's the time we have quaffed our Chianti there,
Listened to Silvio quoting us Dante there—
Once more to drink Nebiolo Spumante there,
How we'd pitch Pommery into the sea!
There where the gang of us
Met ere Rome rang of us,
They had the hang of us
To a degree.
How they would trust to you!
That was but just to you.
Here's o'er their dust to you,
Barney McGee!

Barney McGee, when you're sober you scintillate,
But when you're in drink you're the pride of the intellect;
Divil a one of us ever came in till late,
Once at the bar where you happened to be—
Every eye there like a spoke in you centering,
You with your eloquence, blarney, and bantering—
All Vagabondia shouts at your entering,
King of the Tenderloin, Barney McGee!

There's no satiety
In your society
With the variety
Of your *esprit*.
Here's a long purse to you,
And a great thirst to you!
Fate be no worse to you,
Barney McGee!

Och, and the girls whose poor hearts you deracinate,
Whirl and bewilder and flutter and fascinate!
Faith, it's so killing you are, you assassinate—
Murder's the word for you, Barney McGee!
Bold when they're sunny, and smooth when they're showery—
Oh, but the style of you, fluent and flowery!
Chesterfield's way, with a touch of the Bowery!
How would they silence you, Barney machree?
Naught can your gab allay,
Learned as Rabelais
(You in his abbey lay
Once on the spree).
Here's to the smile of you,
(Oh, but the guile of you!)
And a long while of you,
Barney McGee!

Facile with phrases of length and Latinity,
Like honorificabilitudinity,
Where is the maid could resist your vicinity,
Wiled by the impudent grace of your plea?
Then your vivacity and pertinacity
Carry the day with the divil's audacity;
No mere veracity robs your sagacity
Of perspicacity, Barney McGee.
When all is new to them,
What will you do to them?
Will you be true to them?
Who shall decree?

Here's a fair strife to you!
Health and long life to you!
And a great wife to you, Barney McGee!

Barney McGee, you're the pick of gentility;
Nothing can phase you, you've such a facility;
Nobody ever yet found your utility—
There is the charm of you, Barney McGee;
Under conditions that others would stammer in,
Still unperturbed as a cat or a Cameron,
Polished as somebody in the Decameron,
Putting the glamour on price or Pawnee.
In your meanderin',
Love and philanderin',
Calm as a mandarin
Sipping his tea!
Under the art of you,
Parcel and part of you,
Here's to the heart of you,
Barney McGee!

You who were ever alert to befriend a man,
You who were ever the first to defend a man,
You who had always the money to lend a man,
Down on his luck and hard up for a V!
Sure, you'll be playing a harp in beatitude
(And a quare sight you will be in that attitude)—
Some day, where gratitude seems but a platitude,
You'll find your latitude, Barney McGee.
That's no flim-flam at all,
Frivol or sham at all,
Just the plain—Damn it all,
Have one with me!
Here's one and more to you!
Friends by the score to you,
True to the core to you,
Barney McGee!

RICHARD HOVEY

LINES ON THE MERMAID TAVERN

Souls of Poets dead and gone,
What Elysium have ye known,
Happy field or mossy cavern,
Choicer than the Mermaid Tavern?
Have ye tippled drink more fine
Than mine host's Canary wine?
Or are fruits of Paradise
Sweeter than those dainty pies
Of venison? O generous food!
Dressed as though bold Robin Hood
Would, with his Maid Marian,
Sup and bowse from horn and can.

I have heard that on a day
Mine host's sign-board flew away
Nobody knew whither, till
An Astrologer's old quill
To a sheepskin gave the story,—
Said he saw you in your glory,
Underneath a new-old Sign
Sipping beverage divine,
And pledging with contented smack
The Mermaid in the Zodiac!

Souls of Poets dead and gone,
What Elysium have ye known—
Happy field or mossy cavern—
Choicer than the Mermaid Tavern?
                                JOHN KEATS

ODE TO THE NIGHTINGALE

O you that from some southern land
    Return with each new spring
To this reviving island and,
    When in the humour, fling

A song so gallant, so divine,
Out on the night, if fairly fine,
As utterly to take the shine
   Out of all birds that sing:

The thrush, grown conscious of your voice,
   Retires behind his leaves,
The blackbird, not at all from choice,
   Sits mopily and grieves;
That wealth of song can e'en transfix
Both dawning owls and farmyard chicks,
And the rude sparrow as he picks
   Things off the couchant beeves.

You are the theme, all themes above,
   The bards have held most dear:
Bar Wordsworth, who preferred the dove,
   Even the most austere
On you have cast their loveliest gems
From Wight to Hampstead or the Thames,
Yet it is one that Fate condemns
   Me ever not to hear.

I have stol'n forth in many a glade
   Where, at their best in June,
Rich nightingales their serenade
   Lift to the solemn moon
So madly that it sometimes stirs
Young wanderers mid the briars and burrs
To sit incautiously on furze,
   Enravished by the tune.

The spinney and the wooded hill,
   The unfrequented lane,
Gardens that throb with song until
   The residents complain,
Though strangers, eager for the sound,
Come trespassing from miles around—
These I have visited, and found
   I always went in vain.

O budded quicks, melodious plots,
    O song so full and free
That livens up those favoured spots
    Often till after three.
O groves so thrilled with high romance
That, though the whole world gaped askance,
I could have sung with half a chance,
    Why are you mute for me?

We cannot all see Grecian urns;
    Not everywhere one meets
His Lycidas, howe'er he burns
    To emulate those feats;
But you, immortal bird, are there,
A general theme, with charm to spare,
On which, for all that I'm aware,
    I might have rivalled Keats.

But as you please. Unless it's wet,
    When the deep shadows fall
To-night I'll give you one chance yet;
    If lost, there's no recall.
Sing me your best, and I'll sing you
Something in praise that's really new;
If you can do without it, do;
    It's one ode less, that's all.
                          MAJOR JOHN KENDALL

A THRENODY

"The Ahkoond of Swat is dead."—London Papers of Jan. 22, 1878

What, what, what,
    What's the news from Swat?
    Sad news,
    Bad news,
Comes by the cable led
Through the Indian Ocean's bed,
Through the Persian Gulf, the Red

Sea and the Med-
Iterranean—he's dead;
The Ahkoond is dead!

For the Ahkoond I mourn,
        Who wouldn't?
He strove to disregard the message stern,
        But he Ahkoodn't.
Dead, dead, dead:
        (Sorrow, Swats!)
Swats wha hae wi' Ahkoond bled,
Swats whom he hath often led
Onward to a gory bed,
        Or to victory,
        As the case might be.
            Sorrow, Swats!
Tears shed,
        Shed tears like water.
Your great Ahkoond is dead!
        That Swats the matter!

Mourn, city of Swat,
Your great Ahkoond is not,
But laid 'mid worms to rot.
His mortal part alone, his soul was caught
        (Because he was a good Ahkoond)
        Up to the bosom of Mahound.
Though earthly walls his frame surround
(Forever hallowed by the ground!)

And skeptics mock the lowly mound
And say "He's now of no Ahkoond!"
        His soul is in the skies—
The azure skies that bend above his loved
        Metropolis of Swat.
    He sees with larger, other eyes,
    Athwart all earthly mysteries—
        He knows what's Swat.

Let Swat bury the great Ahkoond
　　With a noise of mourning and of lamentation!
Let Swat bury the great Ahkoond
　　With the noise of the mourning of the Swattish nation!
　　Fallen is at length
　　Its tower of strength;
　　Its sun is dimmed ere it had nooned;
　　Dead lies the great Ahkoond,
　　The great Ahkoond of Swat
　　Is not!

GEORGE THOMAS LANIGAN

NOT QUITE FAIR

Summer and spring the lovely rose,
Unconscious of its beauty, blows—
Condemn'd, in summer and in spring,
To feel no pride at blossoming.

The hills, the meadows, and the lakes,
Enchant not for their own sweet sakes:
They cannot know, they cannot *care*
To know, that they are thought so fair.

The rainbow, sunset, cloud, and star,
Dream not how exquisite they are.
All dainty things of earth and sky
Delight us—but they know not why.

But I—a poet—who possess
The power of loving loveliness,
May ask (and I may ask in vain),
"Why *am* I so intensely plain?"

H. S. LEIGH

SIMON LEGREE—A NEGRO SERMON

(To be read in your own variety of negro dialect)

Legree's big house was white and green.
His cotton-fields were the best to be seen.
He had strong horses and opulent cattle,
And bloodhounds bold, with chains that would rattle.
His garret was full of curious things:
Books of magic, bags of gold,
And rabbits' feet on long twine strings.
But he went down to the Devil.

Legree he sported a brass-buttoned coat,
A snake-skin necktie, a blood-red shirt.
Legree he had a beard like a goat,
And a thick hairy neck, and eyes like dirt.
His puffed-out cheeks were fish-belly white,
He had great long teeth, and an appetite.
He ate raw meat, 'most every meal,
And rolled his eyes till the cat would squeal.

His fist was an enormous size
To mash poor niggers that told him lies:
He was surely a witch-man in disguise.
But he went down to the Devil.

He wore hip-boots, and would wade all day
To capture his slaves that had fled away.
But he went down to the Devil.

He beat poor Uncle Tom to death
Who prayed for Legree with his last breath.
Then Uncle Tom to Eva flew,
To the high sanctoriums bright and new;
And Simon Legree stared up beneath,
And cracked his heels, and ground his teeth:
And went down to the Devil.

He crossed the yard in the storm and gloom;
He went into his grand front room.
He said, "I killed him, and I don't care."
He kicked a hound, he gave a swear;
He tightened his belt, he took a lamp,
Went down cellar to the webs and damp.
There in the middle of the mouldy floor
He heaved up a slab; he found a door—
And went down to the Devil.

His lamp blew out, but his eyes burned bright.
Simon Legree stepped down all night—
Down, down to the Devil.
Simon Legree he reached the place,
He saw one half of the human race,
He saw the Devil on a wide green throne,
Gnawing the meat from a big ham-bone,
And he said to Mister Devil:
  "I see that you have much to eat—
  A red ham-bone is surely sweet.
  I see that you have lion's feet;
  I see your frame is fat and fine,
  I see you drink your poison wine—
  Blood and burning turpentine."

And the Devil said to Simon Legree:
  "I like your style, so wicked and free.
  Come sit and share my throne with me,
  And let us bark and revel."
And there they sit and gnash their teeth,
And each one wears a hop-vine wreath.
They are matching pennies and shooting craps,
They are playing poker and taking naps.
And old Legree is fat and fine:
He eats the fire, he drinks the wine—
Blood and burning turpentine—
  Down, down with the Devil;
    Down, down with the Devil;
      Down, down with the Devil.

VACHEL LINDSAY

TO MY GRANDMOTHER

Suggested by a Picture by Mr. Romney

Under the elm a rustic seat
Was merriest Susan's pet retreat
To merry-make

This Relative of mine
Was she seventy-and-nine
  When she died?
By the canvas may be seen
How she looked at seventeen,
  As a Bride.

Beneath a summer tree
Her maiden reverie
  Has a charm;
Her ringlets are in taste;
What an arm! and what a waist
  For an arm!

With her bridal-wreath, bouquet,
Lace farthingale, and gay
  Falbala,—
If Romney's touch be true,
What a lucky dog were you,
  Grandpapa!

Her lips are sweet as love;
They are parting! Do they move?
  Are they dumb?
Her eyes are blue, and beam
Beseechingly, and seem
  To say, "Come!"

What funny fancy slips
From atween these cherry lips?
  Whisper me,
Fair Sorceress in paint,
What canon says I mayn't
  Marry thee?

That good-for-nothing Time
Has a confidence sublime!
    When I first
Saw this Lady, in my youth,
Her winters had, forsooth,
    Done their worst.

Her locks, as white as snow,
Once shamed the swarthy crow;
    By-and-by
That fowl's avenging sprite
Set his cruel foot for spite
    Near her eye.

Her rounded form was lean,
And her silk was bombazine:
    Well I wot
With her needles would she sit,
And for hours would she knit,—
    Would she not?

Ah perishable clay!
Her charms had dropped away
    One by one:
But if she heaved a sigh
With a burden, it was, "Thy
    Will be done."

In travail, as in tears,
With the fardel of her years
    Overpressed,
In mercy she was borne
Where the weary and the worn
    Are at rest.

Oh, if you now are there,
And sweet as once you were,
    Grandmamma,

This nether world agrees
You'll all the better please
Grandpapa.

FREDERICK LOCKER-LAMPSON

ST. PATRICK OF IRELAND, MY DEAR!

A fig for St. Denis of France—
  He's a trumpery fellow to brag on;
A fig for St. George and his lance,
  Which spitted a heathenish dragon;
And the saints of the Welshman or Scot
  Are a couple of pitiful pipers,
Both of whom may just travel to pot,
  Compared with that patron of swipers—
    St. Patrick of Ireland, my dear!

He came to the Emerald Isle
  On a lump of a paving-stone mounted;
The steamboat he beat by a mile,
  Which mighty good sailing was counted.
Says he, "The salt water, I think,
  Has made me most bloodily thirsty;
So bring me a flagon of drink
  To keep down the mulligrubs, burst ye!
    Of drink that is fit for a saint!"

He preached, then, with wonderful force,
  The ignorant natives a-teaching;
With a pint he washed down his discourse,
  "For," says he, "I detest your dry preaching."
The people, with wonderment struck
  At a pastor so pious and civil,
Exclaimed—"We're for you, my old buck!
  And we pitch our blind gods to the devil,
    Who dwells in hot water below!"

This ended, our worshipful spoon
   Went to visit an elegant fellow,
Whose practice, each cool afternoon,
   Was to get most delightfully mellow.
That day with a black-jack of beer,
   It chanced he was treating a party;
Says the saint—"This good day, do you hear,
   I drank nothing to speak of, my hearty!
     So give me a pull at the pot!"

The pewter he lifted in sport
   (Believe me, I tell you no fable);
A gallon he drank from the quart,
   And then placed it full on the table.
"A miracle!" every one said—
   And they all took a haul at the stingo;
They were capital hands at the trade,
   And drank till they fell; yet, by jingo,
     The pot still frothed over the brim.

Next day, quoth his host, " 'Tis a fast,
   And I've nought in my larder but mutton;
And on Fridays who'd made such repast,
   Except an unchristian-like glutton?"
Says Pat, "Cease your nonsense, I beg—
   What you tell me is nothing but gammon;
Take my compliments down to the leg,
   And bid it come hither a salmon!"
     And the leg most politely complied.

You've heard, I suppose, long ago,
   How the snakes, in a manner most antic,
He marched to the county Mayo,
   And trundled them into th' Atlantic.
Hence, not to use water for drink,
   The people of Ireland determine—
With mighty good reason, I think,
   Since St. Patrick has filled it with vermin
     And vipers, and other such stuff!

Oh, he was an elegant blade
   As you'd meet from Fairhead to Kilcrumper;
And though under the sod he is laid,
   Yet here goes his health in a bumper!
I wish he was here, that my glass
   He might by art magic replenish;
But since he is not—why, alas!
   My ditty must come to a finish,—
     Because all the liquor is out!

William Maginn

TIRADE ON TEA

Though my interest in viands is easy to whet up,
As gourmet's apprentice I scarcely would set up.
Contrive me a dish—I am quick to surround it,
I've taken my food as I generally found it,
Nor ever aspired to the epicure's role.
I've put up with flounder presented as sole,
With chicken that gamboled, with broths dietetic,
With singular sauces, and gravies synthetic,
With buttermilk wedded to culture amoebal.
But out on the man who invented the tea-ball!

    For dearest of fluids to me,
      Tea is my love and my lack!
    But tea, it should taste of tea
      And not of a cotton sack.
    Oh, delicate leaves, ambrosial,
      How have you gone to slaughter!
    Wrapped in a bag with a colored tag,
      And dangled in luke-warm water.

The tea rooms of Gotham, they succor me still.
I view them with favor, I wish them no ill—
The Modern, Colonial, Gothic, and Mission,
The Late-New-York Central, the Post-Prohibition.
Their muffins are light and their waffles are valid.

They'll serve you a quaint but respectable salad.
They've mastered the secrets of spoon bread and scrapple,
They'll stay you with flagons and comfort with apple.
But a curse on the tavern where tea is tied up
In an odious netting and steeped in a cup!

> *For tea should be made in a pot,*
>   *In a vessel designed to brew it,*
> *Ample and clean and hot,*
>   *With a lid and a handle to it,*
> *And a quilted cozy to cover it all*
>   *While the odorous steam condenses*
> *Along the spout whence the gold pours out*
>   *That presently soothes the senses.*

Yes, tea can be nectar though mortals devise it,
And I hold in abhorrence the ones who misprize it:
Who ask for the vintage of coffee and Tokay
But dampen a tea-ball and think that it's O. K.,
Who measure a dressing for mustard and oil,
But never insist that tea water boil.
Then out on the trifler, the rogue, and the dullard
Who only demand that the cup should be colored!
They may buy all the tea that is stored in a warehouse,
But needn't expect me to drink it at *their* house.

PHYLLIS McGINLEY

A GRUB STREET RECESSIONAL

O noble, gracious English tongue
Whose fibres we so sadly twist,
For caitiff measures he has sung
Have pardon on the journalist.

For mumbled measures, leaden puns,
For slipshod rhyme, ill-chosen word,
Have pity on us graceless ones—
Thy mercy on Thy people, Lord!

The metaphors and tropes depart,
Our little clippings fade and bleach:
There is no virtue and no art
Save in straightforward Saxon speech.

Yet not in ignorance or spite,
Nor with thy splendid past forgot,
We sinned: indeed we had to write
To keep a fire beneath the pot.

Then grant that in the coming time
With inky hand and polished sleeve
In lucid prose or honest rhyme
Some worthy task we may achieve . . .

Some pinnacled and marbled phrase,
Some Lyric, breaking like the sea,
That we may win the craftsman's praise,
And land in some Anthology!

CHRISTOPHER MORLEY

TRIPE

Come, gentle tripe, the hungry carter's joy,
    Drayman's delight, conductor's second course,
Passion and dream of every errand boy,
    Vision of every rogue that holds a horse,
Bane of all titled ladies, bishops' dread,
    Doom of the softly nurtured, peers' despair,
Was it for this the tall Achilles bled,
    For this that Agamemnon tore his hair?
Was this the food that launched a thousand ships
    And tore the heart of Dido, as she stood
Above the feast, wiping her royal lips,
    And called her love again—was this the food?

(The answer is, in a sense, no.)

J. B. MORTON

THE HUNDRED BEST BOOKS

First, there's the Bible,
   And then the Koran,
Odgers on Libel,
   Pope's Essay on Man,
Confessions of Rousseau,
   The Essays of Lamb,
Robinson Crusoe
   And Omar Khayyám,
Volumes of Shelley
   And Venerable Bede,
Machiavelli
   And Captain Mayne Reid,
Fox upon Martyrs
   And Liddell and Scott,
Stubbs on the Charters,
   The works of La Motte,
The Seasons by Thomson,
   And Paul de Verlaine,
Theodore Mommsen
   And Clemens (Mark Twain)
The Rocks of Hugh Miller,
   The Mill on the Floss,
The Poems of Schiller,
   The Iliados,
Don Quixote (Cervantes),
   La Pucelle by Voltaire,
Inferno (that's Dante's),
   And Vanity Fair,
Conybeare-Howson,
   Brillat-Savarin,
And Baron Munchausen,
   Mademoiselle De Maupin,
The Dramas of Marlowe,
   The Three Musketeers,
Clarissa Harlowe,
   And the Pioneers,

Sterne's Tristram Shandy,
   The Ring and the Book,
And Handy Andy,
   And Captain Cook,
The Plato of Jowett,
   And Mill's Pol. Econ.,
The Haunts of Howitt,
   The Encheiridion,
Lothair by Disraeli,
   And Boccaccio,
The Student's Paley,
   And Westward Ho!
The Pharmacopoeia,
   Macaulay's Lays,
Of course The Medea,
   And Sheridan's Plays,
The Odes of Horace,
   And Verdant Green,
The Poems of Morris,
   The Faerie Queen,
The Stones of Venice,
   Natural History (White's),
And then Pendennis,
   The Arabian Nights,
Cicero's Orations,
   Plain Tales from the Hills,
The Wealth of Nations,
   And Byles on Bills,
As in a Glass Darkly,
   Demosthenes' Crown,
The Treatise of Berkeley,
   Tom Hughes's Tom Brown,
The Mahabharata,
   The Humour of Hook,
The Kreutzer Sonata,
   And Lalla Rookh,
Great Battles by Creasy,
   And Hudibras,

And Midshipman Easy,
  And Rasselas,
Shakespeare *in extenso*
  And the Aeneid,
And Euclid (Colenso),
  The Woman Who Did,
Poe's Tales of Mystery,
  Then Rabelais,
Guizot's French History,
  And Men of the Day,
Rienzi, by Lytton,
  The Poems of Burns,
The Story of Britain,
  The Journey (that's Sterne's),
The House of Seven Gables,
  Carroll's Looking-glass,
Aesop his Fables,
  And Leaves of Grass,
Departmental Ditties,
  The Woman in White,
The Tale of Two Cities,
  Ships that Pass in the Night,
Meredith's Feverel,
  Gibbon's Decline,
Walter Scott's Peveril,
  And—some verses of mine.

                MOSTYN T. PIGOTT

APEX

The lion tamers wrestle with the lions in a cage.
With but a fragile whip they dare their charges' feral rage.
They put their heads in tigers' mouths and do not flinch a
  grain
But they never tried to take a cat five hundred miles to
  Maine.

Frank Buck he Brings 'Em Back Alive from Afric's roaring
    shore—
The nilghai and the elephant, the leopard and the boar.
For him to crate a rhino on a steamer is no strain
But he never drove a four-pound cat five hundred miles to
    Maine.

Oh, cope with the rhinoceros bare-handed and alone,
Or kick a famished grizzly if for harmless fun you hone.
Or irritate a timber wolf by feeding it cocaine,
But do NOT try to drive a cat five hundred miles to Maine.

There is no word, there is no tongue, there is no ink to tell
One-tenth of what one cat can raise of concentrated hell
When after two hours driving to mistaken qualms you yield
And take poor puss to stretch her limbs in some adjacent
    field.

If you have caught the antelope that leaps from crag to crag;
If you have chased a hare on foot and popped it in a bag;
If you have roped a bison or if you've outrun a moose,
You have an outside chance to catch said cat when she gets
    loose.

And if you've done the things set forth in stanzas two and
    three
You stand a chance, when Krazy from the leash has wriggled
    free
(Provided you are clad in steel with gloves and hat to
    match)
To get her back into the car without a bite or scratch.

Ye lion tamers, naturalists, and big game hunters eke,
When I'm around be chary of your tendency to speak.
To hear you boast your petty deeds gives me a shooting pain
For I have taken Krazy (phew!) five hundred miles to
    Maine!

NATE SALSBURY

EARLY RISING

"God bless the man who first invented sleep!"
 So Sancho Panza said, and so say I:
And bless him, also, that he didn't keep
 His great discovery to himself; nor try
To make it—as the lucky fellow might—
A close monopoly by patent-right!

Yes—bless the man who first invented sleep,
 (I really can't avoid the iteration;)
But blast the man, with curses loud and deep,
 Whate'er the rascal's name, or age, or station,
Who first invented, and went round advising,
That artificial cut-off—Early Rising!

"Rise with the lark, and with the lark to bed,"
 Observes some solemn, sentimental owl;
Maxims like these are very cheaply said;
 But, ere you make yourself a fool or fowl,
Pray just inquire about his rise and fall,
And whether larks have any beds at all!

The time for honest folks to be a-bed
 Is in the morning, if I reason right;
And he who cannot keep his precious head
 Upon his pillow till it's fairly light,
And so enjoy his forty morning winks,
Is up to knavery; or else—he drinks!

Thompson, who sung about the "Seasons," said
 It was a glorious thing to *rise* in season;
But then he said it—lying—in his bed,
 At ten o'clock A.M.,—the very reason
He wrote so charmingly. The simple fact is
His preaching wasn't sanctioned by his practice.

'Tis, doubtless, well to be sometimes awake,—
   Awake to duty, and awake to truth,—
But when, alas! a nice review we take
   Of our best deeds and days, we find, in sooth,
The hours that leave the slightest cause to weep
Are those we passed in childhood or asleep!

'Tis beautiful to leave the world awhile
   For the soft visions of the gentle night;
And free, at last, from mortal care or guile,
   To live as only in the angel's sight,
In sleep's sweet realm so cosily shut in,
Where, at the worst, we only *dream* of sin!

So let us sleep, and give the Maker praise.
   I like the lad who, when his father thought
To clip his morning nap by hackneyed phrase
   Of vagrant worm by early songster caught,
Cried, "Served him right!—it's not at all surprising;
The worm was punished, sir, for early rising!"

                         JOHN G. SAXE

CHANT ROYAL FROM A COPYDESK

For Bob Garst,
The Best Copyreader I Know

I have written high school teachers down SAVANTS,
And poor unknowing husbands termed I MATES;
TROUSERS I've changed to be the homely PANTS,
I've used, for SAYS, AVERS and also STATES.
BEAUTY I've called full many a dame whose face
In even a bathing contest could not place.
RAP, HIT, ATTACK, FLAY, FIRE ON, aye, and SCORE
As synonyms I've used on times galore.
Many a sin against the lexicon
Have I performed, and ere I am no more
I would atone for headlines I have done.

HOP have I said, I fear me much, for DANCE,
And PROBES has doubled for INVESTIGATES;
And as for PLANS, there'd be quite little chance
But that my word was CARDS or BILLS or SLATES;
For NEGRO I have often writ OF RACE,
And BURNED TO DEATH was CHARRED in every
   case;
Instead of BLOOD I have relied on GORE,
And a TUNNEL usually was a BORE.
Defense for these atrocities have I none,
And though how I may do it puzzles me sore
I would atone for headlines I have done.

The home of the Governor I have called a MANSE,
GRILLS I employed to mean INTERROGATES;
PACHYDERMS often were my ELEPHANTS,
And CLEARS did duty for EXONERATES.
SILENT for MUM I ever would erase—
Likewise to BARE I would REVEAL abase—
GARB and not CLOTHING was the stuff one wore—
I named the President HERB, and there is no lower
Deed, I cannot think of even one.
Fervidly I the following boon implore:
I would atone for headlines I have done.

HIKE took I, noun and verb, to mean ADVANCE,
And WEIGHS or EYES to mean ADJUDICATES;
TRAGIC I've dubbed a fatal circumstance,
And PEACEMAKER termed one who arbitrates.
DETECTIVES called I SLEUTHS to save me space,
And every AVIATOR was an ACE.
HAIL was the WELCOME (v.) I knew of yore,
And crowds would not ARRIVE but INWARD POUR.
This English language I have put upon
Grievously, and now I've thought it o'er
I would atone for headlines I have done.

Slang TAKEN FOR A RIDE and SWAG and PLANTS
I've used, although my soul it irritates;
And FIEND, at which the m. e. looked askance,
I have set down, and NOTES for CELEBRATES.
HEADQUARTERS spoke I of at times as BASE,
But only by the slotman's greatest grace;
ERE even have I used to mean BEFORE,
And TRAM for street car, though at every pore
My ignominy out in briny sweat would run.
By many a deep and awful oath I swore
I would atone for headlines I have done.

ENVOY

Boys, hair on hair from out my dome I tore
To fall upon the city room's cold floor
While I these noisome compositions spun;
But though it took entire my hirsute store,
I would atone for headlines I have done.

RUFUS TERRAL

THE BALLAD OF BOUILLABAISSE

A street there is in Paris famous,
    For which no rhyme our language yields,
Rue Neuve des Petits Champs its name is—
    The New Street of the Little Fields.
And here's an inn, not rich and splendid,
    But still in comfortable case;
The which in youth I oft attended,
    To eat a bowl of Bouillabaisse.

This Bouillabaisse a noble dish is—
    A sort of soup, or broth, or brew,
Or hotchpotch of all sorts of fishes,
    That Greenwich never could outdo:
Green herbs, red peppers, mussels, saffron,
    Soles, onions, garlic, roach, and dace:
All these you eat at Terré's tavern
    In that one dish of Bouillabaisse.

Indeed, a rich and savoury stew 'tis;
    And true philosophers, methinks,
Who love all sorts of natural beauties,
    Should love good victuals and good drinks.
And Cordelier or Benedictine
    Might gladly, sure, his lot embrace,
Nor find a fast-day too afflicting,
    Which served him up a Bouillabaisse.

I wonder if the house still there is?
    Yes, here the lamp is, as before;
The smiling red-cheeked *écaillère* is
    Still opening oysters at the door.
Is Terré still alive and able?
    I recollect his droll grimace:
He'd come and smile before your table,
    And hope you liked your Bouillabaisse.

We enter—nothing's changed or older.
    "How's Monsieur Terré, waiter, pray?"
The waiter stares, and shrugs his shoulder—
    "Monsieur is dead this many a day."
"It is the lot of saint and sinner,
    So honest Terré's run his race."
"What will Monsieur require for dinner?"
    "Say, do you still cook Bouillabaisse?"

"Oh, oui, Monsieur," 's the waiter's answer;
    "Quel vin Monsieur désire-t-il?"
"Tell me a good one."—"That I can, Sir:
    The Chambertin with yellow seal."
"So Terré's gone," I say, and sink in
    My old accustom'd corner-place;
"He's done with feasting and with drinking,
    With Burgundy and with Bouillabaisse."

My old accustom'd corner here is,
    The table still is in the nook;

Ah! vanished many a busy year is
   This well-known chair since last I took.
When first I saw ye, *cari luoghi*,
   I'd scarce a beard upon my face,
And now a grizzled, grim old fogy,
   I sit and wait for Bouillabaisse.

Where are you, old companions trusty
   Of early days here met to dine?
Come, waiter! quick, a flagon crusty—
   I'll pledge them in the good old wine.
The kind old voices and old faces
   My memory can quick retrace;
Around the board they take their places,
   And share the wine and Bouillabaisse.

There's Jack has made a wondrous marriage;
   There's laughing Tom is laughing yet;
There's brave Augustus drives his carriage;
   There's poor old Fred in the *Gazette;*
On James's head the grass is growing:
   Good Lord! the world has wagged apace
Since here we set the claret flowing,
   And drank, and ate the Bouillabaisse.

Ah me! how quick the days are flitting!
   I mind me of a time that's gone,
When here I'd sit, as now I'm sitting,
   In this same place—but not alone.
A fair young form was nestled near me,
   A dear dear face looked fondly up,
And sweetly spoke and smiled to cheer me
   —There's no one now to share my cup.

* * *

I drink it as the Fates ordain it.
   Come, fill it, and have done with rhymes:
Fill up the lonely glass, and drain it
   In memory of dear old times.

Welcome the wine, whate'er the seal is;
  And sit you down and say your grace
With thankful heart, whate'er the meal is.
  —Here comes the smoking Bouillabaisse!

                    W. M. THACKERAY

THE CRYSTAL PALACE

    With ganial foire
    Thransfuse me loyre,
  Ye sacred nymphs of Pindus,
    The whoile I sing
    That wondthrous thing,
  The Palace made o' windows!

    Say, Paxton, truth,
    Thou wondthrous youth,
  What sthroke of art celistial,
    What power was lint
    You to invint
  This combineetion cristial.

    O would before
    That Thomas Moore,
  Likewoise the late Lord Boyron,
    Thim aigles sthrong
    Of godlike song,
  Cast oi on that cast oiron!

    And saw thim walls,
    And glittering halls,
  Thim rising slendther columns,
    Which I, poor pote,
    Could not denote,
  No, not in twinty vollums.

My Muse's words
Is like the bird's
That roosts beneath the panes there;
　　Her wings she spoils
　　'Gainst them bright toiles,
And cracks her silly brains there.

　　This Palace tall,
　　This Cristial Hall,
Which Imperors might covet,
　　Stands in High Park
　　Like Noah's Ark,
A rainbow bint above it.

　　The towers and fanes,
　　In other scaynes,
The fame of this will undo,
　　Saint Paul's big doom,
　　Saint Payther's Room.
And Dublin's proud Rotundo.

　　'Tis here that roams,
　　As well becomes
Her dignitee and stations,
　　Victoria Great,
　　And houlds in state
The Congress of the Nations.

　　Her subjects pours
　　From distant shores,
Her Injians and Canajians,
　　And also we,
　　Her kingdoms three,
Attind with our allagiance.

　　Here comes likewise
　　Her bould allies,
Both Asian and Europian;

From East and West
They send their best
To fill her Coornucopean.

I seen (thank Grace!)
This wondthrous place
(His Noble Honour Misther
H. Cole it was
That gave the pass,
And let me see what is there).

With conscious proide
I stud insoide
And look'd the World's Great Fair in,
Until me sight
Was dazzled quite,
And couldn't see for staring.

There's holy saints
And window paints,
By maydiayval Pugin;
Alhamborough Jones
Did paint the tones,
Of yellow and gambouge in.

There's fountains there
And crosses fair;
There's water-gods with urrns;
There's organs three,
To play, d'ye see,
"God save the Queen," by turrns.

There's statues bright
Of marble white,
Of silver, and of copper;
And some in zinc,
And some, I think,
That isn't over proper.

There's staym injynes,
That stands in lines,
Enormous and amazing,
That squeal and snort
Like whales in sport,
Or elephants a-grazing.

There's carts and gigs,
And pins for pigs,
There's dibblers and there's harrows,
And ploughs like toys
For little boys,
And illigant wheelbarrows.

For thim genteels
Who ride on wheels,
There's plenty to indulge 'em:
There's droskys snug
From Paytersbug,
And vayhycles from Bulgium.

There's cabs on stands
And shandthrydanns;
There's wagons from New York here;
There's Lapland sleighs
Have cross'd the seas,
And jaunting cyars from Cork here.

Amazed I pass
From glass to glass,
Deloighted I survey 'em;
Fresh wondthers grows
Before me nose
In this sublime Musayum!

Look, here's a fan
From far Japan,
A sabre from Damasco:

There's shawls ye get
From far Thibet,
And cotton prints from Glasgow.

There's German flutes,
Marocky boots,
And Naples macaronies;
Bohaymia
Has sent Behay;
Polonia her polonies.

There's granite flints
That's quite imminse,
There's sacks of coals and fuels,
There's swords and guns,
And soap in tuns,
And gingerbread and jewels.

There's taypots there,
And cannons rare;
There's coffins fill'd with roses;
There's canvas tints,
Teeth insthrumints,
And shuits of clothes by Moses.

There's lashins more
Of things in store,
But thim I don't remimber;
Nor could disclose
Did I compose
From May time to Novimber!

Ah, Judy thru!
With eyes so blue,
That you were here to view it!
And could I screw
But tu pound tu,
'Tis I would thrait you to it!

So let us raise
Victoria's praise,
And Albert's proud condition
That takes his ayse
As he surveys
This Cristial Exhibition.

W. M. THACKERAY

A TRAVELOGUE: CLOVELLY

"And did you once see Shelley plain?"
  Well, I admit I've *not* seen Shelley,
But I'll remark—with might and main—
  I've seen Clovelly!

Village beloved of ancient Great
  Dickens (and maybe Machiavelli)
Told wondrous tales of the fair state
  Of sweet Clovelly—

One street the village boasts. Though straight,
  Its steepness sends you quite pell-melly;
Gravity helps you *down*. Your gait
  May hit Clovelly.

Yet that's naught to the upward road;—
  Your muscles turn to vermicelli,
Your heart gives out, your lungs explode,—
  Climbing Clovelly!

You see, it's long and steep and hard,
  And paved with stones less soft than jelly;—
Oh, goodness me, *why* does a bard
  Extol Clovelly?

No one who hasn't tramped the clove,
  With lungs aburst and heart all swelly,
Can have the faintest notion of
  That dire Clovelly!

I fancied it a gentle lane,
  All coppice-clad and dingly-delly;
But that effect does *not* obtain
  In fool Clovelly!

The houses, true, are decked with flowers
  (About like that of Miss Corelli);
But were they all Elysian Bowers
  I'd spurn Clovelly!

They say it is a Heavenly Trail.
  To me it seemed a trifle Helly.
And up that hill and down that dale
  I'll curse Clovelly!

                                        CAROLYN WELLS

THE UNIVERSAL FAVORITE

Salad of greens! Salad of greens!
What's that? You like it? Go tell the Marines!
  Greenery yellery, Lettuce and celery,
How I abominate salad of greens!
  Romaine and escarole, cress, and tomatoes,
  Radishes, chicory, beets, and potatoes;
  Apples and cabbages, seeded white grapes,
  Peppers and onions and chervil and cepes.
Yes, in the best of our modern cuisines,
They serve you that terrible salad of greens!
  Capers and olives, mustard, and chili,
  Cucumbers, artichokes, chives, piccalilli,
  Pickles, paprika, pimentos, and cheese,
  Tips of asparagus, carrots and peas.
  Cantaloupe, cherries, grapefruit, nectarines,
  Dock, avocado, and haricot beans;
Oh, Fate, let me fly to some far distant scenes,
In villages, hamlets, or deserts or denes,
I care not if peopled by peasants or queens
If they never have heard of a Salad of Greens!

That very detestable
Horrid comestible,
  Incredible,
    Inedible,
  Salad of Greens!

CAROLYN WELLS

APOSTROPHE TO A PRAM RIDER

Joe, you prefatory mortal,
Banging on a planet's portal,
Stick your toe inside the door,
Make it open one inch more;
Tell the world you want to see
Lady-of-the-House, and me.
  Come on, Joe, smile!

Here's your buggy, in you go!
Think of everything you know,
Let the weight of all your days
Crease the little brows you raise,
Let the eyes that scarcely focus
Scan the sky for sign of crocus!
Here's the park, and here we go,
Make your mouth into an "O,"
  Little Joe!

I the sire, you the issue,
Courtesy of human tissue;
You my tangible creation
Happy in perambulation,
Safe within love's double cordon,
Drunk with life and Walker Gordon.
I'm your father and attorney,
Close your eyes, you're on a journey!
  Sleep well, Joe.

Joe, the wheels of any pram
Make of traveling a sham.
Some day when I'm out of sight
Travel far but travel light!
Stalk the turtle on the log,
Watch the heron spear the frog,
Find the things you only find
When you leave your bags behind;
Raise the sail your old man furled,
Hang your hat upon the world!
Gulp your water, sip your wine,
Dream that somebody's divine,
Thank the god you've always doubted
For the gifts you've never flouted;
Find a jetty in the sun,
Call the river Alph for fun,
Let your spirit turn to jelly
While the pine planks toast your belly—
Any hour will last a day,
Buried deep enough in hay.
Joe, my tangible creation,
Happy in perambulation,
Work no harder than you have to.
    Do you get me?

Listen, Joe, I'm only talking,
You and I are just out walking.
Don't you cry or home we go!
Make your mouth into an "O."
    That's right.

                                    E. B. WHITE

TO A LADY ACROSS THE WAY

Dear, I do not count it flighty
Thus to frolic in your nightie;
You who have such mirthful ways
Need not fear my curious gaze.

Prettily dance and sweetly carol,
Garbed, 'tis true, in scant apparel;
Blithesome heart and levity
Counteract that brevity.
Bold you are and unafraid,
Ignorant of undrawn shade.
Prithee know, my dear, that I've a
Scorn for him who watched Godiva.

E. B. WHITE

THE MERRY MONTH

May is the month when "the white throat builds";
May is the month when the young sun gilds
Fresh green hedges and clover new
With a golden gleam on their vernal hue.
Browning's May has its pleasant features—
But oh! what Maytime can do to teachers!

May is the month when we take the rap;
May is the month when our tempers snap;
May is a month full of measures drastic;
May is the month when we get sarcastic.
The green new earth in May is rident—
But the teacher's voice in May grows strident.

May is the month of the apple-blossom;
(But the Latin class hasn't mastered *possum!*)
May is a peace after winter's wrath;
(But the candidates are so weak in Math!)
May brings the dogwood, white and pink;
(But the girls won't work, and the girls can't think!)

May is the month for the last reports;
May is the month when the girls wear shorts;
May is the month when the slacker crams;
May is the month to make out exams.
May lifts the heart of each living creature—
But it's just a headache to any teacher.

MISS X AND MISS Y

Satire

A GARLAND OF RECITAL PROGRAMS

I

*(The freely translated song. Usually from the Lithuanian
or the Brazilian)*

Oh, the beautiful maiden has gone away.
What shall I do?
What shall I do?
She has vanished,
She is here no more,
She has departed,
I am sad-hearted.
She is gone away.
What shall I do?

II

*(The literally translated song. Usually from the French or
Spanish)*

O little mountain, hear my prayer:
My love has gone away.
I know not where.
Hear me, O little mountain, pray!

Oh, goodness! I am desolate!
My love has gone away.
My sorrow faileth to abate.
Oh, perhaps she will return some day.

III

(Translated, from the German, by a friend of the singer)

Oh, I was very sad indeed,
  My sorrow was quite deep.
And roaming through the forest
  Tearfully did I weep.
Oh, I was very joyful,
  Like sunshine followeth rain;

My happiness is like to woe—
   My joy like unto pain.
My happiness is like to woe,
   My joy like unto pain.

IV

(The lullaby. Freely translated from the Congolean)

O little child,
Slumber!
Your mother watches over thee,
And the stars shine down without number.
Sleep,
Little child!

V

(Translated, by the singer's accompanist, from the Portuguese)

Regardless, heedless of how far
From me away you, dearest, are.
My love for you can never cease,
Nor can another occupy thy place.

VI

(This song takes six minutes to sing in the German original)

It is spring. Awake!

VII

(Our own Negro spirituals)

Oh, Adam was in Paradise,
   An' he had to git out o' dere.
Oh, Adam was in Paradise,
   An' he had to git out o' dere.
Oh, Adam was in Paradise,
And he said to Eve, "Oh, ain't dis nice?"
   Oh, he had to git out o' dere.

CHORUS

Yes, he had to git out o' dere.
He had to git out o' dere.
He had to git out,
He had to git out,
Oh, he had to git out o' dere.

Oh, Jonah was in de whale's inside,
    An' he had to git out o' dere.
Oh, Jonah was in de whale's inside,
    But he had to git out o' dere.
Oh, Jonah was in de whale's inside,
But de whale he wasn't satisfied,
    So he had to git out o' dere.

Oh, Daniel was in de lions' den,
    An' he had to git out o' dere.
Daniel was in de lions' den,
    But he had to git out o' dere.
Daniel was in de lions' den,
An' a lion says, "Is yo' here again?"
    So he had to git out o' dere.

Oh, Moses was a-rowin' on de ribber water,
    But he had to git out o' dere.
Oh, Moses was a-rowin' on de ribber water,
    An' he had to git out o' dere.
Little Moses was a-rowin' on de ribber water,
An' along come Pharoah's younges' daughter,
    So he had to git out o' dere.

Joseph was on his banjo strummin'
    An' he had to git out o' dere.
Joseph was on his banjo strummin',
    But he had to git out o' dere.
Joseph was on his banjo strummin',
An' he seen ol' Potiphar's wife a-comin',
    But he had to git out o' dere.

FRANKLIN P. ADAMS

LIFE

On the way to my daily occupation,
Passing adown a chill, a dark way,
Entered I into the subway station
Known as Cathedral Parkway.

Ride who will on the elevated,
Tramp who will on the open road,
I took the subway, be it stated.
It's nearest to my abode.

Life, I thought, is a game of cricket;
Life, I mused, is a thing alive.
I bought a ticket, I bought a ticket;
I think that I purchased five.

Those are the days that seethe and foment;
Those are the things that weight my brow—
Not that I think they're of any moment,
But Poetry's like that now.

I waited six minutes upon that landing,
And at 9:42 I took an express;
Women and men were seated and standing,
Thinking of things, I guess.

And I looked over a gentleman's shoulder—
He was probably forty-six years of age—
And read—though he may have been six months older—
All of the *Times* front page.

But something happened on which I reckoned
Not. I was reading, I said, the *Times*,
When the gentleman got off at Seventy-second,
So I stood thinking of rhymes.

There were many persons standing near me,
Dull appearing and silly of face;
But in modern poetry, thought I, dear me!
Nothing is commonplace.

If I describe them, not acutely,
Telling, at length, what clothes they wear
Manneredly, prosily, overminutely—
Merely that they were there—

I shall achieve quite a reputation
For seeing the Calm above the Strife;
I'll be a Poet of Observation,
One who has Looked on Life;

One who can give interpretation,
One to invest the crude with grace,
One to—but then I reached my station.
It was, I recall, Park Place.

And I walked to the office, far from skittish
(I walk that way, as a general rule),
And I wished, I wished I were one of the British
Bards of the modern school.

A bard who could take his pen and ink it,
Listing things in a one-two-three
Order, till critics and men would think it
Utterest poetry.

Oh, for the storms of wild applause it
Would receive from the human race,
Most of whom'd think it was great because it
Merely was commonplace.

Still, on my way to my occupation,
Passed I adown a chill, a dark way.
Entered I into the subway station
Known as Cathedral Parkway.

FRANKLIN P. ADAMS

THE RICH MAN

The rich man has his motorcar,
  His country and his town estate.
He smokes a fifty-cent cigar
  And jeers at Fate.

He frivols through the livelong day,
  He knows not Poverty her pinch.
His lot seems light, his heart seems gay,
  He has a cinch.

Yet though my lamp burns low and dim,
  Though I must slave for livelihood—
Think you that I would change with him?
  You bet I would!

                              FRANKLIN P. ADAMS

"THAT DID IN LUVE SO LIVELY WRITE"

When that our English tongue
Was newer,
Singers then were young,
And fewer.

They sang to sweetest tunes,
The morning;
In their fresh forenoons
No warning

Came, to mar delight,
That golden
Youth must soon the night
Beholden.

Of day's eyes, and cuckoos;
Of fowls;
Of meadows, lambs and ewes;
Of owls;

Of maids with cherry lips;
Of flowers;
Of lads' romantic quips
In bowers;

They sang because they must.
No duty
Was in their lyric lust
Of beauty.

As birdsong in the spring
Upwelling,
They cared not anything
For spelling.

From virgin springs their love
Was fed;
Book fonts they knew not of,
Nor read.

No Milton yet was come
To awe them,
Nor Johnson's heavy thumb
To paw them.

Alas the day that min-
Nesingers
Were coerced by the guin-
Ea-flingers

From shaping songs to fit
The heart,
To molding them to meet
The mart!

For I their lays do love
To hear,
To charm the portals of
Mine ear.

Ah, for the dewy old-
En times
When songsters shook out gold-
En rhymes,

Like bells, in showers of mel-
Low shards—
Them were the days, my fel-
Low bards!

GEORGINE M. ADAMS

THALIA

A middle-aged Lyrical poet is supposed to be taking final leave of the Muse
of Comedy. She has brought him his hat and gloves, and is abstractedly
picking a thread of gold hair from his coat sleeve as he begins to speak:

I say it under the rose—
    oh, thanks!—yes, under the laurel,
We part lovers, not foes;
    we are not going to quarrel.

We have too long been friends
    on foot and in gilded coaches,
Now that the whole thing ends,
    to spoil our kiss with reproaches.

I leave you; my soul is wrung;
    I pause, look back from the portal—
Ah, I no more am young,
    and you, child, you are immortal!

Mine is the glacier's way,
    yours is the blossom's weather—
When were December and May
    known to be happy together?

Before my kisses grow tame,
  before my moodiness grieve you,
While yet my heart is flame,
  and I all lover, I leave you.

So, in the coming time,
  when you count the rich years over,
Think of me in my prime,
  and not as a white-haired lover,

Fretful, pierced with regret,
  the wraith of a dead Desire
Thrumming a cracked spinet
  by a slowly dying fire.

When, at last, I am cold—
  years, hence, if the gods so will it—
Say, "He was true as gold,"
  and wear a rose in your fillet!

Others, tender as I,
  will come and sue for caresses,
Woo you, win you, and die—
  mind you, a rose in your tresses!

Some Melpomene woo,
  some hold Clio the nearest;
You, sweet Comedy—you
  were ever sweetest and dearest!

Nay, it is time to go.
  When writing your tragic sister
Say to that child of woe
  how sorry I was I missed her.

Really, I cannot stay,
  though "parting is such sweet sorrow" . . .
Perhaps I will, on my way
  down-town, look in to-morrow!

                    THOMAS BAILEY ALDRICH

TOLL THE BELL FOR DAMON

Damon died young; no bell was tolled for him.
He was the sweetest singer of us all.
No man has found the fire that he let fall.
It left us dim.

He lived across the way—Damon, old friend,
Old scout, sweet rascal, lover of all good things—
We never ask him why he never sings
Since he made an end.

So toll the bell for Damon; he died young,
Turned to the earth, dust unto dust allied.
His wife has never noticed that he died
His songs unsung.

MAXWELL ANDERSON

WHEN THE WAR WILL END

Actual evidence I have none,
But my aunt's charwoman's sister's son
Heard a policeman, on his beat,
Say to a housemaid in Downing Street,
That he had a brother, who had a friend,
Who knew when the war was going to end.

REGINALD ARKELL

TO AN UNKNOWN NEIGHBOR AT THE CIRCUS

Your peevish voice remarked "Oh, rats,
I never like the acrobats,
And those old clowns are such a bore.
I've seen this all five times before.
They never really fall, I'll bet,
Or if they do, it's in a net—
A man is shot from that big gun?
Oh, pooh, that isn't any fun!"

Well, pet, you win. It would be fun
To shoot you from that selfsame gun,
Remarking with its horrid roar,
"There goes *one* wretched little bore
Who's seen it all at the age of ten—
Hic Jacet, not to rise again" . . .

But please explain. This has me beat,
Why do you pick a good front seat
And sit in it for hours, four,
While right outside, about the door,
Are boys who shriek, with kith and kin,
"Hey, mister, won't you take me in?
I've never been, me nor my sister—
Please take us in. Hey, mister, mister!"

You look long lived, you look quite strong
For three score years; the time is long.
You'll be right with us, bored but firm,
Intent on making others squirm,
Your lorgnettes raised, to see more clearly
What fails to please you, all or nearly.
The right-hand box, the good aisle seat,
Are saved for you; they are your meat. . . .
And you'll be there, and you will say,
"I really do not like this play,
It dates. I saw it all in Rome,
In Paris, or perhaps in Nome.
It seems a little reminiscent,
It is too mild, or concupiscent.
I don't like farce. I hate the ballet" . . .
Well, what are *you* doing in this galley?

When you're grown-up, you little blighter,
You'll be a typical first nighter.

ROSEMARY BENÉT

DEBUTANTRUM

O pansy-eye, O polished face,
O spring enchanted feline,
You who the *haute couture* would grace
With duds from neck to kneeline—

The birds are in the park, my girl,
The buds are busting sure,
A sports hat of *rose visca perle*
Adorns your sleek coiffure.

Draining dark coffee to the lees
I hunch at lunch in Mendel's.
You toy with sole at Marguery's
Fare forth to shop at Bendel's.

Eftsoons, of course, some gilded loon
Will make you fervent promises,
And Mendelssohn will call the tune
To crowds within St. Thomas's.

Yet, meanwhile, gal, I'll say you shock
My heart to a hosanna
In that new Premet jumper-frock
Or smoking-suit from Anna.

I love you in that Lanvin cape,
Those Chanel togs, my Nora,
And when you pass in Roman crêpe
I doff my nicked fedora.

So, lovely Molyneux mirage,
With many a *chic* and chaste line,
In smart deep V *decolletage*
Or sinuous slanting waist line,

Hark, hark! My funds would never reach
To Paris or the Lido;
I could not squire you to Palm Beach,
White Sulphur or Tuxedo;

But, if you feel a man's a man
(To swat you with a spanner),
I know an easy-payment plan;
We'd live at Bellerose Manor.

With joy I'd then commute, you bet.
We'd pluck spring flowers all pollenny;
You'd dominate the junior set
In some suburban colony.

Don't laugh! But, no—your laugh rings free,
You shriek—you toss your tresses.
Farewell! Some day you'll merely be
"Among the patronesses"!

WILLIAM ROSE BENÉT

SIR CHRISTOPHER WREN

Sir Christopher Wren
Said "I am going to dine with some men;
If any one calls,
Say I am designing St. Paul's."

E. C. BENTLEY

THE ANATOMY OF HUMOR

"What is funny?" you ask, my child,
  Crinkling your bright-blue eye.
"Ah, that is a curious question indeed,"
  Musing, I make reply.

"Contusions are funny, not open wounds,
  And automobiles that go
Crash into trees by the highwayside;
  Industrial accidents, no.

"The habit of drink is a hundred per cent,
  But drug addiction is nil.
A nervous breakdown will get no laughs;
  Insanity surely will.

"Humor, aloof from the cigarette,
   Inhabits the droll cigar;
The middle-aged are not very funny;
   The young and the old, they are.

"So the funniest thing in the world should be
   A grandsire, drunk, insane,
Maimed in a motor accident,
   And enduring moderate pain.

"But why do you scream and yell, my child?
   Here comes your mother, my honey,
To comfort you and to lecture me
   For trying, she'll say, to be funny."

                                MORRIS BISHOP

PUBLIC AID FOR NIAGARA FALLS

Upon the patch of earth that clings
   Near the very brink of doom,
Where the frenzied water flings
   Downward to a misty gloom,

Where the earth in terror quakes
   And the water leaps in foam
Plunging, frantic, from the Lakes,
   Hurrying seaward, hurrying home,

Where Man's little voice is vain,
   And his heart chills in his breast
At the dreadful yell of pain
   Of the waters seeking rest;

There I stood, and humbly scanned
   The miracle that sense appalls,
And I watched the tourists stand
   Spitting in Niagara Falls.

                                MORRIS BISHOP

WE HAVE BEEN HERE BEFORE

I think I remember this moorland,
  The tower on the tip of the tor;
I feel in the distance another existence;
  I think I have been here before.

And I think you were sitting beside me
  In a fold in the face of the fell;
For Time at its work'll go round in a circle,
  And what is befalling, befell.

"I have been here before!" I asserted,
  In a nook on a neck of the Nile.
I once in a crisis was punished by Isis,
  And you smiled, I remember your smile.

I had the same sense of persistence
  On the site of the seat of the Sioux;
I heard in the tepee the sound of a sleepy
  Pleistocene grunt. It was you.

The past made a promise, before it
  Began to begin to begone.
This limited gamut brings you again. Damn it,
  How long has this got to go on?

                                        MORRIS BISHOP

EXIT GOD

Of old our fathers' God was real,
  Something they almost saw,
Which kept them to a stern ideal
  And scourged them into awe.

They walked the narrow path of right,
  Most vigilantly well,
Because they feared eternal night
  And boiling depths of Hell.

Now Hell has wholly boiled away
  And God become a shade.
There is no place for him to stay
  In all the world he made.

The followers of William James
  Still let the Lord exist,
And call him by imposing names,
  A venerable list.

But nerve and muscle only count,
  Gray matter of the brain,
And an astonishing amount
  Of inconvenient pain.

I sometimes wish that God were back
  In this dark world and wide;
For though some virtues he might lack,
  He had his pleasant side.

                                    GAMALIEL BRADFORD

EGO SUM

Run along, Bobby,
  It's getting quite late;
You've talked your hobby
  Till I'm in a state.
If I were your hobby,
  You could talk till you're blue;
But the trouble is, Bobby,
  Your hobby is *you*.

                                    GELETT BURGESS

THE RELIGION OF HUDIBRAS

For his religion it was fit
To match his learning and his wit:
'Twas Presbyterian true blue;
For he was of that stubborn crew

Of errant saints, whom all men grant
To be the true church militant;
Such as do build their faith upon
The holy text of pike and gun;
Decide all controversies by
Infallible artillery;
And prove their doctrine orthodox,
By apostolic blows and knocks;
Call fire, and sword, and desolation,
A godly, thorough reformation,
Which always must be carried on,
And still be doing, never done;
As if religion were intended
For nothing else but to be mended:
A sect whose chief devotion lies
In odd perverse antipathies;
In falling out with that or this,
And finding somewhat still amiss;
More peevish, cross, and splenetic,
Than dog distract, or monkey sick;
That with more care keep holy-day
The wrong, than others the right way,
Compound for sins they are inclin'd to,
By damning those they have no mind to:
Still so perverse and opposite,
As if they worshipped God for spite:
The self-same thing they will abhor
One way, and long another for:
Free-will they one way disavow,
Another, nothing else allow:
All piety consists therein
In them, in other men all sin:
Rather than fail, they will defy
That which they love most tenderly;
Quarrel with minc'd pies and disparage
Their best and dearest friend, plum porridge,
Fat pig and goose itself oppose,
And blaspheme custard through the nose.

SAMUEL BUTLER

"FOREVER"

Forever; 'tis a single word!
 Our rude forefathers deem'd it two:
Can you imagine so absurd
  A view?

Forever! What abysms of woe
 The word reveals, what frenzy, what
Despair! For ever (printed so)
  Did not.

It looks, ah me! how trite and tame!
 It fails to sadden or appal
Or solace—it is not the same
  At all.

O thou to whom it first occurr'd
 To solder the disjoin'd, and dower
Thy native language with a word
  Of power,

We bless thee! Whether far or near
 Thy dwelling, whether dark or fair
Thy kingly brow, is neither here
  Nor there.

But in men's hearts shall be thy throne,
 While the great pulse of England beats:
Thou coiner of a word unknown
  To Keats!

And nevermore must printer do
 As men did long ago; but run
"For" into "ever" bidding two
  Be one.

Forever! passion-fraught, it throws
 O'er the dim page a gloom, a glamour:
It's sweet, it's strange; and I suppose
  It's grammar.

Forever! 'Tis a single word!
  And yet our fathers deem'd it two
Nor am I confident they err'd;
    Are you?

CHARLES STUART CALVERLEY

PRECIOUS STONES

AN INCIDENT IN MODERN HISTORY

My Cherrystones! I prize them,
  No tongue can tell how much!
Each lady caller eyes them,
  And madly longs to touch!
At eve I lift them down, I look
  Upon them, and I cry;
Recalling how my Prince "partook"
  (Sweet word!) of cherry-pie!

To me it was an Era
  In life, that Dejeuner!
They ate, they sipp'd Madeira
  Much in the usual way.
Many a soft item there would be,
  No doubt, upon the carte:
But one made life a heaven to me:
  It was the cherry-tart.

Lightly the spoonfuls enter'd
  That mouth on which the gaze
Of ten fair girls were centred
  In rapturous amaze.
Soon that august assemblage clear'd
  The dish; and—as they ate—
The stone, all coyly, reappear'd
  On each illustrious plate.

And when His Royal Highness
  Withdrew to take the air,

Waiving our natural shyness,
   We swoop'd upon his chair.
Policemen at our garments clutch'd:
   We mock'd those feeble powers;
And soon the treasures that had touch'd
   Exalted lips were ours!

One large one—at the moment
   It seem'd almost divine—
Was got by that Miss Beaumont:
   And three, O three, are mine!
Yes! the three stones that rest beneath
   Glass, on that plain deal shelf,
Stranger, once dallied with the teeth
   Of Royalty itself.

Let Parliament abolish
   Churches and States and Thrones:
With reverent hand I'll polish
   Still, still my Cherrystones!
A clod—a piece of orange-peel—
   An end of a cigar—
Once trod on by a Princely heel,
   How beautiful they are!

Years since, I climb'd Saint Michael
   His Mount:—you'll all go there
Of course, and those who like'll
   Sit in St. Michael's Chair:
For there I saw, within a frame,
   The pen—O heavens! the pen—
With which a Duke had signed his name,
   And other gentlemen.

"Great among geese," I faltered,
   "Is she who grew that quill!"
And, Deathless Bird, unalter'd
   Is mine opinion still.

Yet sometimes, as I view my three
  Stones with a thoughtful brow,
I think there possibly might be
  E'en greater geese than thou.

CHARLES STUART CALVERLEY

THE KNIFE-GRINDER

Friend of Humanity

"Needy Knife-grinder! whither are you going?
  Rough is the road—your wheel is out of order—
  Bleak blows the blast; your hat has got a hole in't,
                          So have your breeches!

"Weary Knife-grinder! little think the proud ones,
  Who in their coaches roll along the turnpike-
  Road, what hard work 'tis crying all day 'Knives and
                          Scissors to grind O!'

"Tell me, Knife-grinder, how you came to grind knives?
  Did some rich man tyrannically use you?
  Was it the squire? or parson of the parish?
                          Or the attorney?

"Was it the squire, for killing of his game? or
  Covetous parson, for his tithes distraining?
  Or roguish lawyer, made you lose your little
                          All in a law-suit?

"(Have you not read the Rights of Man, by Tom Paine?)
  Drops of compassion tremble on my eyelids,
  Read to fall, as soon as you have told your
                          Pitiful story."

Knife-grinder

"Story! God bless you! I have none to tell, sir,
  Only last night, a-drinking at the Chequers,
  This poor old hat and breeches, as you see, were
                          Torn in a scuffle.

"Constables came up for to take me into
  Custody; they took me before the justice;
  Justice Oldmixon put me in the parish-
                              Stocks for a vagrant.

"I should be glad to drink your Honour's health in
  A pot of beer, if you will give me sixpence;
  But for my part, I never love to meddle
                              With politics, sir."

Friend of Humanity

"*I* give thee sixpence! I will see thee damn'd first—
  Wretch! whom no sense of wrongs can rouse to vengeance—
  Sordid, unfeeling, reprobate, degraded,
                              Spiritless outcast!"

[*Kicks the Knife-grinder, overturns his wheel, and exit in
a transport of Republican enthusiasm and universal philan-
thropy.*]

                              GEORGE CANNING

A BALLADE OF SUICIDE

The gallows in my garden, people say,
Is new and neat and adequately tall.
I tie the noose on in a knowing way
As one that knots his necktie for a ball;
But just as all the neighbours—on the wall—
Are drawing a long breath to shout "Hurray!"
The strangest whim has seized me. . . . After all
I think I will not hang myself to-day.

To-morrow is the time I get my pay—
My uncle's sword is hanging in the hall—
I see a little cloud all pink and grey—
Perhaps the rector's mother will *not* call—
I fancy that I heard from Mr. Gall
That mushrooms could be cooked another way—
I never read the works of Juvenal—
I think I will not hang myself today.

The world will have another washing day;
The decadents decay; the pendants pall;
And H. G. Wells has found that children play,
And Bernard Shaw discovered that they squall;
Rationalists are growing rational—
And through thick woods one finds a stream astray,
So secret that the very sky seems small—
I think I will not hang myself to-day.

ENVOI

Prince, I can hear the trump of Germinal,
The tumbrils toiling up the terrible way;
Even to-day your royal head may fall—
I think I will not hang myself to-day.

G. K. CHESTERTON

WINE AND WATER

Old Noah he had an ostrich farm and fowls on the largest
scale,
He ate his soup with a ladle in an egg-cup big as a pail,
And the soup he took was Elephant Soup and the fish he
took was Whale,
But they all were small to the cellar he took when he set
out to sail,
And Noah he often said to his wife when he sat down to
dine,
"I don't care where the water gets if it doesn't get into
the wine."

The cataract of the cliff of heaven fell blinding off the brink
As if it would wash the stars away as suds go down a sink,
The seven heavens came roaring down for the throats of
hell to drink,
And Noah he cocked his eyes and said, "It looks like rain,
I think,
The water has drowned the Matterhorn as deep as a
Mendip mine,
But I don't care where the water gets if it doesn't get
into the wine."

But Noah he sinned, and we have sinned: on tipsy feet we
    trod,
Till a great big black teetotaller was sent to us for a rod,
And you can't get wine at a P.S.A., or chapel, or Eisteddfod,
For the Curse of Water has come again because of the wrath
    of God,
    And water is on the Bishop's board and the Higher
    Thinker's shrine,
    But I don't care where the water gets if it doesn't get
    into the wine.

G. K. CHESTERTON

THE GOLF LINKS

The golf links lie so near the mill
    That almost every day
The laboring children can look out
    And see the men at play.

SARAH N. CLEGHORN

THE LATEST DECALOGUE

Thou shalt have one God only, who
Would be at the expense of two?
No graven images may be
Worshipped, except the currency:
Swear not at all; for, for thy curse
Thine enemy is none the worse:
At Church on Sunday to attend
Will serve to keep the world thy friend:
Honour thy parents; that is, all
From whom advancement may befall:
Thou shalt not kill; but need'st not strive
Officiously to keep alive:
Do not adultery commit;
Advantage rarely comes of it:
Thou shalt not steal; an empty feat,
When it's so lucrative to cheat:

Bear not false witness; let the lie
Have time on its own wings to fly:
Thou shalt not covet, but tradition
Approves all forms of competition.

ARTHUR HUGH CLOUGH

COLOGNE

In Köln, a town of monks and bones,
And pavements fanged with murderous stones,
And rags, and hags, and hideous wenches,
I counted two-and-seventy stenches,
All well defined, and separate stinks!
Ye nymphs that reign o'er sewers and sinks,
The river Rhine, it is well known,
Doth wash your city of Cologne;
But tell me, nymphs, what power divine
Shall henceforth wash the river Rhine?

SAMUEL TAYLOR COLERIDGE

THE BALLAD OF CASSANDRA BROWN

Though I met her in the summer, when one's heart lies
    round at ease,
As it were in tennis costume, and a man's not hard to please,
Yet I think that any season to have met her was to love,
While her tones, unspoiled, unstudied, had the softness of
    the dove.

At request she read us poems in a nook among the pines,
And her artless voice lent music to the least melodious lines;
Though she lowered her shadowing lashes, in an earnest
    reader's wise,
Yet we caught blue, gracious glimpses of the heavens which
    were her eyes.

As in paradise I listened—ah, I did not understand
That a little cloud, no larger than the average human hand,
Might, as stated oft in fiction, spread into a sable pall,
When she said that she should study Elocution in the fall!

I admit her earliest efforts were not in the Ercles vein;
She began with "Little Maaybel, with her faayce against
　　the payne
And the beacon-light a-t-r-r-remble"—which, although it
　　made me wince,
Is a thing of cheerful nature to the things she's rendered
　　since.

Having heard the Soulful Quiver, she acquired the Melt-
　　ing Mo-o-an,
And the way she gave "Young Grayhead" would have
　　liquefied a stone.
Then the Sanguinary Tragic did her energies employ,
And she tore my taste to tatters when she slew "The Polish
　　Boy."

It's not pleasant for a fellow when the jewel of his soul
Wades through slaughter on the carpet, while her orbs in
　　frenzy roll;
What was I that I should murmur? Yet it gave me grievous
　　pain
That she rose in social gatherings, and Searched among
　　the Slain.

I was forced to look upon her in my desperation dumb,
Knowing well that when her awful opportunity was come
She would give us battle, murder, sudden death at very
　　least,
As a skeleton of warning, and a blight upon the feast.

Once, ah! once I fell a-dreaming; some one played a polonaise
I associated strongly with those happier August days;
And I mused, "I'll speak this evening," recent pangs for-
　　gotten quite—
Sudden shrilled a scream of anguish: "Curfew shall not
　　ring to-night!"

Ah, that sound was as a curfew, quenching rosy, warm
　　romance—

Were it safe to wed a woman one so oft would wish in France?
Oh, as she "cul-limbed" that ladder, swift my mounting
    hope came down,
I am still a single cynic; she is still Cassandra Brown!
HELEN GRAY CONE

MIGHT AND RIGHT

Might and Right are always fighting.
In our youth it seems exciting.
Right is always nearly winning.
Might can hardly keep from grinning.
CLARENCE DAY

SAD STORY

There was a gifted Mexican who came up here to paint,
And he very kindly did so for awhile with no complaint.
He merely took some jobs away from all the local boys,
And he merely made some speeches full of sweaty talk and
    noise.

He frequently was heard to say he didn't like the rich.
He said they all had Little Souls and hearts as black as pitch.
He thought *his* soul was good and true and also very large.
Well, maybe that explained the price he felt he had to charge.

He said he was a Worker, but he asked for kingly pay.
He got it, too. He painted for a hundred bucks a day.
He grew as fat as Henry Eighth, his wife looked like a
    queen.
He was the Wealthiest Worker New York has ever seen.

The other day some nervous men, who owned a spacious
    wall,
Requested him to let it be and paint some other hall.
They gave him—and he promptly took—a very handsome
    check,
But when they tried to say goodby they got it in the neck.

He said he wouldn't say goodby, he wished to paint the wall,
And it was a moral issue and they had no souls at all.
And now he says unless they let him open up his heart
Upon their wall, they plainly will assassinate his art.

Well, some one's art's assassinated almost every day,
It happens every time that any painter's turned away.
So that even this pure spirit must have killed, without a sob,
The art of his competitors the day he got the job.

CLARENCE DAY

CONVERSATION

"One lump or two? It's comforting to think,"
   She said the while she deftly made the tea,
   "That sweets of Love and cream of Courtesy
Improve the Cup of Life from which we drink."
   Upon the wall, a clock of alabaster
   Remarked the sudden hush, and ticked the faster.

The brimming tea-cup trembled in his hand:
   "This Symbolism's come to such a pass,
   One cannot even take a bath, alas,
Without reflecting that the faucets stand,
   The cold for Chastity, the hot for Hope,
   While Moral Obligation is the soap.

"One cannot even shave the stubborn sprout
   Of morning whisker but the thought annoys:
   The razor blade is Logic which destroys
The crop of Errors spreading all about."
   A sudden madness seized him, and he tore
   His hair and dashed the tea-cup to the floor.

BERENICE C. DEWEY

SONG

Go and catch a falling star,
   Get with child a mandrake root;

Tell me where all past years are,
   Or who cleft the Devil's foot;
Teach me to hear Mermaids singing,—
Or to keep off envy's stinging,
      And find
      What wind
Serves to advance an honest mind.

If thou beest born to strange sights,
   Things invisible to see,
Ride ten thousand days and nights,
   Till age snow white hairs on thee;
Thou, when thou return'st, wilt tell me
All strange wonders that befell thee,
      And swear
      Nowhere
Lives a woman true and fair.

If thou find'st one, let me know;
   Such a pilgrimage were sweet
Yet do not; I would not go,
   Though at next door we might meet.
Though she were true when you met her,
And last till you write your letter,
      Yet she
      Will be
False, ere I come, to two or three.

John Donne

ADVICE TO A YOUNG MAN (OF LETTERS) WHO DOESN'T KNOW HOW TO TAKE CARE OF HIMSELF

(Per R. L.)

Remember, youth will not last more
Than, roughly, twenty-three or -four;
Even then, as I recall, the ache
And wear of age begin to take.

Only Colossi rather stronger
Than you can live so weirdly longer.
You cannot work and play all night
And get to thirty feeling right;
Dark your days and out-of-sorty
Will be your lot, like mine, at forty.
Drink milk, eat vitamins ad lib,
By ten be snugly in your crib.
Turn up your collar, don't catch cold;
For breakfast: citrous fruits, oats (rolled).
A walk each day, perhaps a swim,
Best indoors when the weather's grim.
No love, of course, and not much drink,
And no games where you have to think.
Frequent, light, nutritious feeding,
And very little heavy reading.
Once, after lunch, a cigarette,
Nirvana once the sun has set.
Let bruisers talk till four or five;
A. M.; theme: Should One Keep Alive.
Fascism must not, nor Communism
Disorder your metabolism;
Let stalwarts argue all the issues
While, fast asleep, you build up tissues.
Then waking, mornings, plump and bright,
Boy! won't you show them how to write!

                                   IRWIN EDMAN

FLOWER FOR A PROFESSOR'S GARDEN
OF VERSES

A teacher should impart what's true
At least what they allow him to;
A college teacher should not vex
His pupils with his thoughts on sex;
He should keep mum if he has odd
Views on the character of God.
He should dismiss as red inventions

All but the three well-known dimensions,
Not teaching logic, which might hurt
Young minds impeccably inert,
Nor ever question any truths
Their nurses taught these darling youths.
No skepticism—that might lead them
To use their heads if they should need them.
Only such views by housewives favored—
Be, teacher, be vanilla-flavored.
Make your lectures chocolate fudge
Fit to be nibbled by a judge;
Cookies sweet enough to dish up
Before a bon-bon loving bishop,
Or shall we say, an angel layer
To set before an upright mayor.
Then will your thoughts be sure to keep
Your students sound, and sound asleep.
And keep for you, though far from clever,
Your job—and what a job!—forever!

IRWIN EDMAN

FABLE

The mountain and the squirrel
Had a quarrel,
And the former called the latter "Little Prig";
Bun replied,
"You are doubtless very big;
But all sorts of things and weather
Must be taken in together,
To make up a year
And a sphere,
And I think it no disgrace
To occupy my place.
If I'm not so large as you,
You are not so small as I,
And not half so spry.
I'll not deny you make

A very pretty squirrel track;
Talents differ; all is well and wisely put;
If I cannot carry forests on my back,
Neither can you crack a nut."

RALPH WALDO EMERSON

SPRING SIGNS

Now is the time that hills put on
A smoky blue, untinged with green;
When sorel-red and cinnamon
In brief possession holds the scene;
When robins, orange breasted, shiver,
And sparrows and burnished grackles scold;
When every brook is a rushing river,
And crocus companies brave the cold;
When freshly painted cars speed by,
And children and dogs all skip and caper;—
Now is the time when such as I
Must set down rhymes on sheets of paper!

RACHEL FIELD

BRITANNIA RULES OF ORTHOGRAPHY

From British novels a thrill I get
That I sadly miss in the American tale—
The thrill of a heroine suffragette
In gaol.

They touch on Life in the Quivering Raw,
With the frankest noun and the straightest verb,
And all of them—Hewlett, Bennett, and Shaw—
Say kerb.

Domestic voices are flabby and weak
In the Search for Truth that the age requires.
Would Ade or Tarkington dare to speak
Of tyres?

Hail to Conrad, Galsworthy, Wells,
To the crunching might of their books and dramas,
And the Lure of the East when Kipling spells
Pyjamas.

FIRTH

POEM FOR MOTHER'S DAY

My mother taught me to be good
At least as good as I was able;
Otherwise I think I could
Dress in ermine, mink or sable.

MARGARET FISHBACK

OBIT ON PARNASSUS

Death before forty's no bar. Lo!
  These had accomplished their feats:
Chatterton, Burns, and Kit Marlowe,
  Byron and Shelley and Keats.

Death, the eventual censor,
  Lays for the forties, and so
Took off Jane Austen and Spenser,
  Stevenson, Hood, and poor Poe.

You'll leave a better-lined wallet
  By reaching the end of your rope
After fifty, like Shakespeare and Smollett,
  Thackeray, Dickens, and Pope.

Try for the sixties—but say, boy,
  That's when the tombstones were built on
Butler and Sheridan, the play boy,
  Arnold and Coleridge and Milton.

Three score and ten—the tides rippling
  Over the bar; slip the hawser.
Godspeed to Clemens and Kipling,
  Swinburne and Browning and Chaucer.

Some staved the debt off but paid it
    At eighty—that's after the law.
Wordsworth and Tennyson made it,
    And Meredith, Hardy, and Shaw.

But, Death, while you make up your quota,
    Please note this confession of candor—
That I wouldn't give an iota
    To linger till ninety, like Landor.

                      F. Scott Fitzgerald

THE FAMILY FOOL

Oh! a private buffoon is a light-hearted loon,
    If you listen to popular rumour;
From morning to night he's so joyous and bright,
    And he bubbles with wit and good humour!
He's so quaint and so terse, both in prose and in verse;
    Yet though people forgive his transgression,
There are one or two rules that all Family Fools
    Must observe, if they love their profession.
        There are one or two rules,
           Half-a-dozen, maybe,
        That all family fools,
           Of whatever degree,
    Must observe if they love their profession.

If you wish to succeed as a jester, you'll need
    To consider each person's auricular:
What is all right for B would quite scandalise C
    (For C is so very particular);
And D may be dull, and E's very thick skull
    Is as empty of brains as a ladle;
While F is F sharp, and will cry with a carp,
    That he's known your best joke from his cradle!
        When your humour they flout,
           You can't let yourself go;
        And it *does* put you out
           When a person says, "Oh!
I have known that old joke from my cradle!"

If your master is surly, from getting up early
  (And tempers are short in the morning),
An inopportune joke is enough to provoke
  Him to give you, at once, a month's warning.
Then if you refrain, he is at you again,
  For he likes to get value for money:
He'll ask then and there, with an insolent stare,
  "If you know that you're paid to be funny?"
        It adds to the tasks
          Of a merryman's place,
        When your principal asks,
          With a scowl on his face,
    If you know that you're paid to be funny?

Comes a Bishop, maybe, or a solemn D. D.—
  Oh, beware of his anger provoking!
Better not pull his hair—don't stick pins in his chair;
  He won't understand practical joking.
If the jests that you crack have an orthodox smack,
  You may get a bland smile from these sages;
But should it, by chance, be imported from France,
  Half-a-crown is stopped out of your wages!
        It's a general rule,
          Though your zeal it may quench,
        If the Family Fool
          Makes a joke that's *too* French,
  Half-a-crown is stopped out of his wages!

Though your head it may rack with a bilious attack,
  And your senses with toothache you're losing,
And you're mopy and flat—they don't fine you for that
  If you're properly quaint and amusing!
Though your wife ran away with a soldier that day,
  And took with her your trifle of money;
Bless your heart, they don't mind—they're exceedingly
  kind—

They don't blame you—as long as you're funny!
   It's a comfort to feel
      If your partner should flit,
   Though *you* suffer a deal,
      They don't mind it a bit—
They don't blame you—so long as you're funny!

W. S. GILBERT

THE HOUSE OF PEERS

When Britain really ruled the waves—
   (In good Queen Bess's time)
The House of Peers made no pretence
To intellectual eminence,
   Or scholarship sublime;
Yet Britain won her proudest bays
In good Queen Bess's glorious days!

When Wellington thrashed Bonaparte,
   As every child can tell,
The House of Peers, throughout the war,
Did nothing in particular,
   And did it very well;
Yet Britain set the world ablaze
In good King George's glorious days!

And while the House of Peers withholds
   Its legislative hand,
And noble statesmen do not itch
To interfere with matters which
   They do not understand,
As bright will shine Great Britain's rays,
As in King George's glorious days!

W. S. GILBERT

KING GOODHEART

There lived a King, as I've been told
In the wonder-working days of old,
When hearts were twice as good as gold,
    And twenty times as mellow.
Good temper triumphed in his face,
And in his heart he found a place
For all the erring human race
    And every wretched fellow.
When he had Rhenish wine to drink
It made him very sad to think
That some, at junket or at jink,
    Must be content with toddy:
He wished all men as rich as he
(And he was rich as rich could be),
So to the top of every tree
    Promoted everybody.

Ambassadors cropped up like hay,
Prime Ministers and such as they
Grew like asparagus in May,
    And Dukes were three a penny:
Lord Chancellors were cheap as sprats,
And Bishops in their shovel hats
Were plentiful as tabby cats—
    If possible, too many.
On every side Field-Marshals gleamed,
Small beer were Lords-Lieutenants deemed,
With Admirals the ocean teemed,
    All round his wide dominions;
And Party Leaders you might meet
In twos and threes in every street
Maintaining, with no little heat,
    Their various opinions.

That King, although no one denies,
His heart was of abnormal size,

Yet he'd have acted otherwise
　　If he had been acuter.
The end is easily foretold,
When every blessed thing you hold
Is made of silver, or of gold,
　　You long for simple pewter.
When you have nothing else to wear
But cloth of gold and satins rare,
For cloth of gold you cease to care—
　　Up goes the price of shoddy:
In short, whoever you may be,
To this conclusion you'll agree,
When every one is somebody,
　　Then no one's anybody!

W. S. GILBERT

THE MODERN MAJOR-GENERAL

I am the very pattern of a modern Major-Gineral,
I've information vegetable, animal, and mineral;
I know the kings of England, and I quote the fights historical,
From Marathon to Waterloo, in order categorical;
I'm very well acquainted, too, with matters mathematical,
I understand equations, both the simple and quadratical;
About binomial theorem I'm teeming with a lot o' news,
With interesting facts about the square of the hypotenuse.
I'm very good at integral and differential calculus,
I know the scientific names of beings animalculous.
In short, in matters vegetable, animal, and mineral,
I am the very model of a modern Major-Gineral

I know our mythic history—King Arthur's and Sir Caradoc's,
I answer hard acrostics, I've a pretty taste for paradox;
I quote in elegiacs all the crimes of Heliogabalus,
In conics I can floor peculiarities parabolous.
I tell undoubted Raphaels from Gerard Dows and Zoffanies,
I know the croaking chorus from the "Frogs" of Aristo-
　　phanes;

Then I can hum a fugue, of which I've heard the music's
    din afore,
And whistle all the airs from that confounded nonsense
    "Pinafore."
Then I can write a washing-bill in Babylonic cuneiform,
And tell you every detail of Caractacus's uniform.
In short, in matters vegetable, animal, and mineral,
I am the very model of a modern Major-Gineral.

In fact, when I know what is meant by "mamelon" and
    "ravelin,"
When I can tell at sight a Chassepôt rifle from a javelin,
When such affairs as *sorties* and surprises I'm more wary at,
And when I know precisely what is meant by Commissariat,
When I have learnt what progress has been made in modern
    gunnery,
When I know more of tactics than a novice in a nunnery,
In short, when I've a smattering of elementary strategy,
You'll say a better Major-Gener*al* has never *sat* a gee—
For my military knowledge, though I'm plucky and adven-
    tury,
Has only been brought down to the beginning of the century.
But still in learning vegetable, animal, and mineral,
I am the very model of a modern Major-Gineral!
W. S. GILBERT

PENSÉES DE NOËL

When the landlord wants the rent
Of your humble tenement;
When the Christmas bills begin
Daily, hourly pouring in;
When you pay your gas and poor rate,
Tip the rector, fee the curate,
Let this thought your spirit cheer—
Christmas comes but once a year.

When the man who brings the coal
Claims his customary dole:
When the postman rings and knocks
For his usual Christmas-box:
When you're dunned by half the town
With demands for half-a-crown,—
Think, although they cost you dear,
Christmas comes but once a year.

When you roam from shop to shop,
Seeking, till you nearly drop,
Christmas cards and small donations
For the maw of your relations,
Questing vainly 'mid the heap
For a thing that's nice, and cheap:
Think, and check the rising tear,
Christmas comes but once a year.

Though for three successive days
Business quits her usual ways;
Though the milkman's voice be dumb;
Though the paper doesn't come;
Though you want tobacco, but
Find that all the shops are shut:
Bravely still your sorrows bear—
Christmas comes but once a year.

When mince-pies you can't digest
Join with waits to break your rest:
When, oh when, to crown your woe,
Persons who might better know
Think it needful that you should
Don a gay convivial mood:—
Bear with fortitude and patience
These afflicting dispensations:
Man was born to suffer here:
Christmas comes but once a year.

                                        A. D. Godley

TO AN UNGENTLE CRITIC

The great sun sinks behind the town
Through a red mist of Volnay wine. . . .
But what's the use of setting down
That glorious blaze behind the town?
You'll only skip the page, you'll look
For newer pictures in this book;
You've read of sunsets rich as mine.

A fresh wind fills the evening air
With horrid crying of night birds. . . .
But what reads new or curious there
When cold winds fly across the air?
You'll only frown; you'll turn the page,
But find no glimpse of your "New Age
Of Poetry" in my worn-out words.

Must winds that cut like blades of steel
And sunsets swimming in Volnay,
The holiest, cruellest pains I feel,
Die stillborn, because old men squeal
For something new: "Write something new:
We've read this poem—that one too,
And twelve more like 'em yesterday"?

No, no! my chicken, I shall scrawl
Just what I fancy as I strike it, .
Fairies and Fusiliers, and all
Old broken knock-kneed thought will **crawl**
Across my verse in the classic way.
And, sir, be careful what you say;
There are old-fashioned folk still like it.

ROBERT GRAVES

OLD GRIMES

Old Grimes is dead; that good old man
    We ne'er shall see him more:
He used to wear a long black coat
    All buttoned down before.

His heart was open as the day,
   His feelings all were true;
His hair was some inclined to gray—
   He wore it in a queue.

Whene'er he heard the voice of pain,
   His heart with pity burn'd;
The large, round head upon his cane
   From ivory was turn'd.

Kind words he ever had for all;
   He knew no base design:
His eyes were dark and rather small,
   His nose was aquiline.

He lived at peace with all mankind,
   In friendship he was true;
His coat had pocket-holes behind,
   His pantaloons were blue.

Unharm'd, the sin which earth pollutes
   He pass'd securely o'er,
And never wore a pair of boots
   For thirty years or more.

But good old Grimes is now at rest,
   Nor fears misfortune's frown:
He wore a double-breasted vest—
   The stripes ran up and down.

He modest merit sought to find,
   And pay it its desert:
He had no malice in his mind,
   No ruffles on his shirt.

His neighbors he did not abuse—
   Was sociable and gay:
He wore large buckles on his shoes,
   And changed them every day.

His knowledge hid from public gaze,
    He did not bring to view,
Nor made a noise, town-meeting days,
    As many people do.

His worldly goods he never threw
    In trust to fortune's chances,
But lived (as all his brothers do)
    In easy circumstances.

Thus undisturb'd by anxious cares,
    His peaceful moments ran;
And everybody said he was
    A fine old gentleman.
                          ALBERT GORTON GREENE

AIN'T NATURE COMMONPLACE!

Now orange-blossoms filigree
The orange tree; but it would be
Remarkable if you should see
Them on some other kind of tree.

A hydroplane pervades the lake
And leaves a wake; but it would make
Observers cry, "For goodness' sake!"
If it should fail to leave a wake.

The sky is azure overhead;
But spare to call me from my bed
To note its hue, until instead
Of azure, it is brown or red.

Oh, why must poets hail the name
Of Nature with such glad acclaim,
When Nature, whether wild or tame,
Is always pretty much the same!
                          ARTHUR GUITERMAN

ANTHOLOGISTICS

Since one anthologist put in his book
Sweet things by Morse, Bone, Potter, Bliss and Brook,
All subsequent anthologists, of course
Have quoted Bliss, Brook, Potter, Bone and Morse.
For, should some rash anthologist make free
To print selections, say, from you and me,
Omitting with a judgment all his own
The classic Brook, Morse, Potter, Bliss and Bone,
Contemptuous reviewers, passing by
Our verses, would unanimously cry,
"What manner of anthology is this
That leaves out Bone, Brook, Potter, Morse and Bliss!"

ARTHUR GUITERMAN

CONSTITUTION FOR A LEAGUE OF NATIONS

In solemn conclave vow and swear
   These covenanting nations
To guard with unremitting care
   Against all usurpations,
To honor one another's rights,
   And never, never, never,
To further quarrels, wars, or fights
   For any cause whatever.
(P. S.: This rule shall not apply
   On holidays and high days,
Or Mondays, Tuesdays, Wednesdays, Thursdays,
   Saturdays, or Fridays.)

Hereafter, none, for greed of trade,
   Or lands, or martial glory,
On any pretext shall invade
   Another's territory;
And any one who won't desist
   From murderous invasion,
Shall suffer slaps upon the wrist
   Applied by moral suasion.

(N. B.: This clause shall be observed
    On every day but Monday,
And Tuesday, Wednesday, Thursday, Friday,
    Saturday and Sunday.)

ARTHUR GUITERMAN

EPILOGUE TO A BOOK OF VERSE

Go, little book, and leave me still in doubt
    Which afterthought implies the greater sin:
"I wonder if I should have left that out?"
    Or, "Was I right to put that poem in?"

ARTHUR GUITERMAN

MAVRONE

ONE OF THOSE SAD IRISH POEMS, WITH NOTES

From Arranmore the weary miles I've come;
    An' all the way I've heard
A Shrawn[1] that's kep' me silent, speechless, dumb,
    Not sayin' any word.
An' was it then the Shrawn of Eire,[2] you'll say,
    For him that died the death on Carrisbool?
It was not that; nor was it, by the way,
    The Sons of Garnim[3] blitherin' their drool;
Nor was it any Crowdie of the Shee,[4]

[1] A Shrawn is a pure Gaelic noise, something like a groan, more like a shriek, and most like a sigh of longing.
[2] Eire was daughter of Carne, King of Connaught. Her lover, Murdh of the Open Hand, was captured by Greatcoat Mackintosh, King of Ulster, on the plain of Carrisbool, and made into soup. Eire's grief on this sad occasion has become proverbial.
[3] Garnim was second cousin to Manannan MacLir. His sons were always sad about something. There were twenty-two of them, and they were all unfortunate in love at the same time, just like a chorus at the opera. "Blitherin' their drool" is about the same as "dreeing their weird."
[4] The Shee (or "Sidhe," as I should properly spell it if you were not so ignorant) were, as everybody knows, the regular, stand-pat, organization fairies of Erin. The Crowdie was their annual convention, at which they

Or Itt, or Himm, nor wail of Barryhoo[1]
For Barrywhich that stilled the tongue of me.
'Twas but my own heart cryin' out for you
Magraw![2] Bulleen, shinnanigan, Boru,
Aroon, Machree, Aboo![3]

ARTHUR GUITERMAN

---

made melancholy sounds. The Itt and Himm were the irregular, or insurgent, fairies. They *never* got any offices, or patronage. See MacAlester, *Polity of the Sidhe of West Meath*, page 985.

[1] The Barryhoo is an ancient Celtic bird about the size of a Mavis, with lavender eyes and a black-crape tail. It continually mourns its mate (Barrywhich, feminine form), which has an hereditary predisposition to an early and tragic demise and invariably dies first.

[2] Magraw, a Gaelic term of endearment, often heard on the baseball fields of Donnybrook.

[3] These last six words are all that tradition has preserved of the original incantation by means of which Irish rats were rhymed to death. Thereby hangs a good Celtic tale, which I should be glad to tell you in this note; but the publishers say that being prosed to death is as bad as being rhymed to death, and that the readers won't stand for any more.

ORNITHOLOGY IN FLORIDA

The woodpeckers here are redheaded;
    The redbirds are redder all through;
The ground-doves are happily wedded,
    The bachelor blue jay is blue.

And here comes a queer water-turkey,
    A kind of a heron or crane,
Whose neck is peculiarly jerky—
    He flies with a croak of disdain.

The grackles are giving a warning
    Of rain, but they don't know the words;
The robins are saying, "Good morning!"
    And that's what I know about birds.

ARTHUR GUITERMAN

REWARD OF VIRTUE

As I was rumbling through the mountain rift,
A hobo waved and asked me for a lift.

I stopped the truck. "I'm sure obliged," said he,
And climbed aboard and rode along with me.

Said I to him, "You're looking kind of pale."
Said he to me, "Well, I'm just out of jail."

"And what were you in prison for?" said I.
"They claimed for picking pockets," said the guy.

That made me nervous; I was taking care
And feeling if my wallet was still there,

When, all at once, I heard a traffic cop
Yell out, "Hey, you! A red light means to stop!"

He pulled me up, and pulled his book out, too,
And wrote my number down the way they do.

Said he, "You come back here to pay your fine
Next Monday morning, mind, at half-past nine."

And so he made my ticket out, the slob!
"Oh, officer," said I, "I'll lose my job!"

"Besides I can't afford"—He gave a snort
And growled, "Oh, tell your troubles to the Court!"

So on I drove, complaining of my luck
And grumbling how I knew I'd lose my truck,

When, "Never mind," I heard my jailbird say,
"You'll hold your job; there'll be no fine to pay;

"Cheer up, and keep away from that man's town."
"Oh yeah?" said I, "and with my number down?"

"He's put me in his book in black and white
And so I've *got* to come!" "Now, that's all right,"

Said he: "While you were talking with that crook,
I picked his pocket of his little book."

ARTHUR GUITERMAN

LINES WRITTEN ON NOVEMBER 15, 1933 BY A MAN BORN NOVEMBER 14, 1881 TO ANOTHER BORN NOVEMBER 15, 1881

Long before he reached our age
   Shakespeare found sufficient time
   Slowly, cunningly, to climb
To the apex of the stage.

    He was through
    At fifty-two.
    But—what of me?
    And—what of you?

Where's your "Hamlet"? Where is mine?
   My "Othello"? Your "Macbeth"?
   Scarcely have we caught our breath
Ere the clock has stricken nine.

    He was through
    At fifty-two.
    But—what of me?
    And—what of you?

Was it many years ago
   We were going to be great?
Art is long, and art is slow;
   But how fast the feet of fate!

He was through
At fifty-two.
But—what of me?
And—what of you?

Nothing accomplished, nothing done. . . .
   Dear F. P. A., if you and I
   Could only stand up and defy
That sentence to oblivion! . . .

   He was through
   At fifty-two.
   But—what of me?
   And—what of you?

CLAYTON HAMILTON

GOOD AND BAD LUCK

Good luck is the gayest of all gay girls;
   Long in one place she will not stay:
Back from your brow she strokes the curls,
   Kisses you quick and flies away.

But Madame Bad Luck soberly comes
   And stays—no fancy has she for flitting;
Snatches of true-love songs she hums,
   And sits by your bed, and brings her knitting.

JOHN HAY

DAILY PARADOX

The silken-sheathed Angelica,
Wearing a Mona Lisa smile,
Removes her dainty sandaled foot
(Not lighter, for its Paris boot)
From off her husband's neck, the while,
And hies her to the cinema.

Seated in darkness for an hour,
She yields to the vicarious thrill,
The masochistic ecstasy
Of seeing Woman brought to knee,
Bowed to a lord and master's will,
A chattel in a despot's power.

'Tis done. The web of dream grows thinner.
Fades the illusion of romance.
Sleekly she motors home, once more
Alights at the domestic door,
Takes up the reins of governance
And drags her husband out to dinner.

SARA HENDERSON HAY

ON BEING TOLD THAT ONE'S IDEAS ARE VICTORIAN

The same old fable
That's told or hinted,
O'er restaurant table,
On broad divan,
Was sere and seeded
When Troy's spears glinted
And Helen heeded
A gay young man.

Such declarations
Have been the same
(Through variations)
Since time began.
With patience scanty
Seth's sons made claim:
"My sweet, you're ante-
Diluvian!"

And so it will be
Till the crack of doom.
When the amorous plea
In the tones impassioned
Is met with chilling,
Men all assume
If the lady's not willing
She's just old fashioned!

SARA HENDERSON HAY

FINALE

(From "Perseverance; or Half a Coronet." An Operetta in the Gilbertian
Manner. From the Revue "Streamline")

Take a dainty paradox,
Dress it like a chocolate-box—
Take two babies—mix them well:
Take one spinster—give her H____l!
Take some logic—chop it thin;
Take some tunes and rub them in:
One patter-song, and don't forget
Your unaccompanied quartet:
Take a little love, but—hush!
Not enough to raise a blush.
By degrees you'll find you'll get a
Rather popular operetta—
Loved by curate, Kew and Quetta—

And it is a tip-top property—
Yes, there is no properer property
    Than a jockular
    Never shockular
        Proper, popular, popular, operette.

CURTAIN

A. P. HERBERT

POEMS IN PRAISE OF PRACTICALLY
NOTHING

I

You're kind to women, children, worms;
You speak of God in the highest terms;
You help spell words like "tetrahedral,"
You show respect for a Cathedral;
You're sweet and gentle as a mouse is:
(Wives should behave so to their spouses!)
Though women tempt you more than plenty,
Your rate is half a girl in twenty.
In short, from grace you never fell yet—
And what do you get? On all sides hell yet!

II

You take a bath, and sit there bathing
In water cold, in water scathing;
You scrub till you're *sans* an epidermis
And feel like a regular bathing Hermes.
You do not waste a single minute;
The tubs shows how you worked while in it;
You dry, and do some honest rooting
For such remarkable abluting.
Well, a day goes by, or ten, or thirty,
And what thanks do you get? You're just as dirty!

III

You meet a girl and you surrender;
Though God knows why, you're kind and tender;
You're husband, lover, sister, brother,
Companion, banker, father, mother;
You try your best to be worthy of her;
You make mistakes, but she knows you love her;
You're hers completely, and you show it.
And what thanks do you get? The gate—I know it!

IV

You're a good girl; you're gray with virtue;
The very thought of a misstep hurts you;
You know that honor must be hoarded
Against the day when it is rewarded.
You see a girl who's all men's vassal
Marry a duke in his own castle;
You see another who can't say "No, sir"
Capture at least a wholesale grocer.
But you never let your thoughts grow sordid:
You know in your heart you'll be rewarded.
Well, the years go by, like Queens and roses,
The way they did in the time of Moses,
And what do you get? False teeth, a doorman,
A complex, or assistant foreman!

V

You hire a cook, but she can't cook yet;
You teach her by candle, bell, and book yet;
You show her, as if she were in her cradle,
Today the soup, tomorrow a ladle.
Well, she doesn't learn, so although you need her
You decide that somebody else should feed her.
But you're kind by birth; you hate to fire her—
To tell a woman you don't require her.
So you wait and wait, and before you do it,
What thanks do you get? She beats you to it!

SAMUEL HOFFENSTEIN

POEMS IN PRAISE OF PRACTICALLY NOTHING

I

You buy some flowers for your table;
You tend them tenderly as you're able;
You fetch them water from hither and thither—
What thanks do you get for it all? They wither.

II

Only the wholesomest foods you eat;
You lave and you lave from your head to your feet;
The earth is not steadier on its axis
Than you in the matter of prophylaxis;
You go to bed early, and early you rise;
You scrub your teeth and you scour your eyes—
What thanks do you get for it all? Nephritis,
Pneumonia, appendicitis,
Renal calculus and gastritis.

III

You get a girl; and you say you love her;
You pan the comparative stars above her;
You roast the comparative roses below her;
You throw the bull that you'll never throw her—
What thanks do you get? The very first whozis
Who tips his mitt, with him she vamooses.

IV

You buy yourself a new suit of clothes;
The care you give it, God only knows;
The material, of course, is the very best yet;
You get it pressed and pressed and pressed yet;
You keep it free from specks so tiny—
What thanks do you get? The pants get shiny.

V

You practice every possible virtue;
You hurt not a soul, while others hurt you;
You fetch and carry like a market basket;
What thanks do you get for it? Me don't ask it!

VI

You leap out of bed; you start to get ready;
You dress and you dress till you feel unsteady;
Hours go by, and you're still busy

Putting on clothes, till your brain is dizzy.
Do you flinch, do you quit, do you go out naked?—
The least little button, you don't forsake it.
What thanks do you get? Well, for all this mess, yet
When night comes around you've got to undress yet.

SAMUEL HOFFENSTEIN

CONTENTMENT

"MAN WANTS BUT LITTLE HERE BELOW"

Little I ask; my wants are few;
   I only wish a hut of stone
(A very plain brone stone will do)
   That I may call my own;
And close at hand is such a one,
In yonder street that fronts the sun.

Plain food is quite enough for me;
   Three courses are as good as ten;
If Nature can subsist on three,
   Thank Heaven for three—Amen!
I always thought cold victual nice—
My choice would be vanilla-ice.

I care not much for gold or land;
   Give me a mortgage here and there,
Some good bank-stock, some note of hand,
   Or trifling railroad share.
I only ask that Fortune send
A little more than I shall spend.

Jewels are baubles; 'tis a sin
   To care for such unfruitful things;
One good-sized diamond in a pin,
   Some, *not so large*, in rings.
A ruby, and a pearl, or so,
Will do for me—I laugh at show.

My dame should dress in cheap attire
    (Good, heavy silks are never dear);
I own perhaps I *might* desire
    Some shawls of true Cashmere—
Some marrowy crapes of China silk,
Like wrinkled skins on scalded milk.

I would not have the horse I drive
    So fast that folks must stop and stare;
An easy gait—two, forty-five—
    Suits me; I do not care;
Perhaps, for just a *single spurt*,
Some seconds less would do no hurt.

Of pictures, I should like to own
    Titians and Raphaels three or four—
I love so much their style and tone—
    One Turner, and no more.
(A landscape, foreground golden dirt,
The sunshine painted with a squirt).

Of books but few—some fifty score
    For daily use, and bound for wear;
The rest upon an upper floor;
    Some *little* luxury *there*
Of red morocco's gilded gleam,
And vellum rich as country cream.

Busts, cameos, gems—such things as these,
    Which others often show for pride,
I value for their power to please,
    And selfish churls deride;
One Stradivarius, I confess,
Two Meerschaums, I would fain possess.

Wealth's wasteful tricks I will not learn,
    Nor ape the glittering upstart fool;
Shall not carved tables serve my turn,
    But *all* must be of buhl?

Give grasping pomp its double share—
I ask but *one* recumbent chair.

Thus humble let me live and die,
  Nor long for Midas' golden touch;
If Heaven more generous gifts deny,
  I shall not miss them *much*—
Too grateful for the blessing lent
Of simple tastes and mind content!

OLIVER WENDELL HOLMES

TO THE PORTRAIT OF "A GENTLEMAN,"

IN THE ATHENAEUM GALLERY

It may be so,—perhaps thou hast
  A warm and loving heart;
I will not blame thee for thy face,
  Poor devil as thou art.

That thing, thou fondly deem'st a nose,
  Unsightly though it be,—
In spite of all the cold world's scorn,
  It may be much to thee.

Those eyes,—among thine elder friends
  Perhaps they pass for blue;—
No matter,—if a man can see,
  What more have eyes to do?

Thy mouth,—that fissure in thy face
  By something like a chin,—
May be a very useful place
  To put thy victual in.

I know thou hast a wife at home,
  I know thou hast a child,
By that subdued, domestic smile
  Upon thy features mild.

That wife sits fearless by thy side,
  That cherub on thy knee;
They do not shudder at thy looks,
  They do not shrink from thee.

Above thy mantel is a hook,—
  A portrait once was there;
It was thine only ornament,—
  Alas! that hook is bare.

She begged thee not to let it go,
  She begged thee all in vain:
She wept,—and breathed a trembling prayer
  To meet it safe again.

It was a bitter sight to see
  That picture torn away;
It was a solemn thought to think
  What all her friends would say!

And often in her calmer hours,
  And in her happy dreams,
Upon its long-deserted hook
  The absent portrait seems.

Thy wretched infant turns his head
  In melancholy wise,
And looks to meet the placid stare
  Of those unbending eyes.

I never saw thee, lovely one,—
  Perchance I never may;
It is not often that we cross
  Such people in our way;

But if we meet in distant years,
  Or on some foreign shore,
Sure I can take my Bible oath
  I've seen that face before.

                              OLIVER WENDELL HOLMES

LINES TO A MAN WHO THINKS THAT APPLE BETTY WITH HARD SAUCE IS FOOD FOR A HUMAN BEING

Being indebted for the ammunition to "A Calendar of Desserts," by Elizabeth O. Hiller

O Apple Betty fiend, attend
    While I discuss this eating question—
If, long before you reach the end,
    You are not seized with indigestion.

'Tis not mine own restricted view
    That I would force upon the Pillar;
In silence I refer you to
    The writings of Miss E. O. Hiller.

If Apple Betty brings a look
    Of joy; if you're a Hard Sauce lover—
Then purchase quick Miss Hiller's book
    And eat from cover unto cover.

You'd *love* her Fried Sultana Creams;
    You'd eat her Date Pie by the car lot;
And oh, to what unknown extremes
    You'd go to get her Orange Charlotte!

You'd make a wildly frenzied lunge—
    You'd be immeasurably flustered—
At sight of Squash Pie, Orange Sponge,
    Steamed Carrot Pudding, Caramel Custard.

You'd eat Banana Puff all day;
    You'd fight with shotgun, pistol, rifle,
To get beside her Prune Soufflé,
    To clutch her Frozen Orange Trifle.

So buy that brimming book, say I.
    Sail in! An Apple Betty spree have!
And if no bookstore has it—why,
    You're welcome to the one that *we* have.

                               GEORGE S. KAUFMAN

THE CONTENTED BACHELOR

When I grow old, if I should live till then—
    As I intend to do—
I hope to be a pattern which all men
    Should wisely keep in view.

I shall not carp or cavil at the lot
    Which lands me with the past;
It is a fact that, cavilling or not,
    Dash it, it comes at last.

The blithe amusements of one's early prime,
    The bounding and the biff,
Which, if persisted in beyond their time,
    Make one both sore and stiff.

Each in its turn, no doubt, will have to go,
    I hope without a pang;
I may regret them just a tiny blow,
    But not a serious hang.

Late hours, long nights, the chorus and the cup,
    The well-neglected bed,
These too, if I refused to give them up,
    Would give me up instead.

So let them wane. Such joys are of the Spring,
    And, with Spring, let them pass;
A man who hangs on to that sort of thing
    Too long is but an ass.

And even when the stubborn day shall dawn
   (Alas that this should be!)
When the young maidens are no longer drawn,
   No longer drawn to me—

(May it be far, ye gods, may it be far!
   'Tis solemn fact that I
Have ever been, may I say, popular
   Among the fair and spry)—

Well, I must watch while others have their fling,
   And, though the thought be sad,
If I'm regarded as a dear old thing,
   It may not be so bad.

Thus, even though my lute must own the rift,
   Though time may dim my song,
My pard-like spirit, beautiful and swift,
   Should still go fairly strong.

And so shall I achieve that "soft delight"
   Which years alone can win:
A bright fire and a casement closed at night
   To keep the warm air in.
                      Major John Kendall

WASTED AMMUNITION

Our masters of satire are vigorous gents,
They devastate folly, and shatter pretense,
And they should have succeeded, by all of the rules,
In freeing this country of bumpkins and fools;
Their shafts of derision should slay on the spot,
   But do they, dear Brutus?
                 Apparently not.

No satire was ever more clever and keen
Than that which is launched at the cinema screen,
And players, producers, press agents, and mobs
Should, long before this, have been bumped from their jobs;
They should have surrendered, or started to fly—
  Hast heard of it, Socrates?

                                    Neither have I.

Society dowagers, prize-fighting blokes,
Have all been assailed by satirical jokes;
The lions that rule the political zoo
And the barons of business are satirized, too.
How they can survive it we writers can't see—
  Come, what do you make of it, Watson?

                                    By me!

                                    STODDARD KING

STUDY OF AN ELEVATION, IN INDIAN INK

            This ditty is a string of lies
            But—how the deuce did Gubbins rise?

    Potiphar Gubbins, C. E.,
      Stands at the top of the tree;
And I muse in my bed on the reasons that led
      To the hoisting of Potiphar G.

    Potiphar Gubbins, C. E.,
      Is seven years junior to Me;
Each bridge that he makes either buckles or breaks,
      And his work is as rough as he.

    Potiphar Gubbins, C. E.,
      Is coarse as a chimpanzee;
And I can't understand why you gave him your hand,
      Lovely Mehitabel Lee.

    Potiphar Gubbins, C. E.,
      Is dear to the Powers that Be;
For they bow and They smile in an affable style
      Which is seldom accorded to Me.

Potiphar Gubbins, C. E.,
　　Is certain as certain can be
Of a highly paid post which is claimed by a host
　　Of seniors—including Me.

Careless and lazy is he,
　　Greatly inferior to Me.
What is the spell that you manage so well,
　　Commonplace Potiphar G.?

Lovely Mehitabel Lee,
　　Let me inquire of thee,
Should I have riz to what Potiphar is,
　　Hadst thou been mated to Me?

RUDYARD KIPLING

PROFESSORS

Some are stout,
　　Some are thin,
Some go out,
　　Some stay in,
Some lie low,
　　Some are brave,
Some like show,
　　Some don't shave,
Some will join,
　　Some hate queens,
Some chase coin,
　　Some eat beans,
Some are bores,
　　Some are bright,
Some do chores,
　　Some can write,
Some will paint,
　　Some drink suds,
Some are quaint,
　　Some are duds

Which makes them out
  Peculiar blokes,
Or just about
  Like other folks.

HAROLD A. LARRABEE

NEIGHBORS

Harold Bates, who lives next door,
When he's squiffy, is a bore.
I could tolerate him if he
Were not boring when unsquiffy.

Nobody could be much nicer
Than my neighbor, Robert Spicer;
But I'd think him more beguiling,
If he were not *always* smiling.

Ernest Weeks, at forty-three
(With the bright blue shutters),
Reads aloud his poetry;
Furthermore, he stutters.

Charming fellow, Albert Waite,
Domiciled at twenty-eight;
A prince, indubitably, this is—
But, holy, jumping cats! His missus!

Where, I ask you, could you find
Some one with a better mind
Than my neighbor, Milton Bloomer?
But he has no sense of humor.

Critics have their moments low.
Maybe people that I know
(I have a suspicion horrid)
Think that I am not so torrid.

LENNOX

I WONDER WHAT BECAME OF
RAND, McNALLY. . . .

Mr. Rand and Mr. McNally,
Arbiters of hill and valley,
Portraitists of sea and land,
Mr. McNally and Mr. Rand,
Two sad cartographic chaps,
Sat in their office surrounded by maps.
Globes and maps around the room,
And on *their* maps a look of gloom.

"Time was when this business of ours was grand,"
Said Mr. McNally to Mr. Rand,
"When our toughest job was to sit and think
Shall France be purple and Britain pink?
Shall Spain be tinted a bright cerise,
And perhaps a dash of green for Greece?"

"But that," said Rand to Mr. McNally,
"Was before Benito got rough with Hallie,
When we didn't fret about changing borders,
And we just sat here receiving orders."

"Remember those days," McNally said,
"When we'd plan a map a month ahead,
And we'd know, if it came out at noon, let's say,
It was up to date the entire day?"

"Then the countries stayed as fixed by their founders,
And boundaries weren't made by bounders."
"Those days," said Rand, "are gone to*tally*."
"You said it, brother," said Mr. McNally.
                                    NEWMAN LEVY

WHAT MR. ROBINSON THINKS

Gineral B. is a sensible man;
  He stays to his home an' looks arter his folks;
He draws his furrer ez straight ez he can,
  An' into nobody's tater-patch pokes;
      But John P.
      Robinson, he
  Sez he wunt vote for Gineral B.

My! ain't it terrible? Wut shall we do?
  We can't never choose him, o' course—that's flat:
Guess we shall hev to come round (don't you?),
  An' go in for thunder an' guns, an' all that;
      Fer John P.
      Robinson, he
  Sez he wunt vote for Gineral B.

Gineral C. is a dreffle smart man:
  He's been on all sides that give places or pelf;
But consistency still was a part of his plan—
  He's been true to *one* party, and that is himself;
      So John P.
      Robinson, he
  Sez he shall vote fer Gineral C.

Gineral C. goes in for the war;
  He don't vally principle mor'n an old cud;
What did God make us raytional creeturs fer,
  But glory an' gunpowder, plunder an' blood?
      So John P.
      Robinson, he
  Sez he shall vote fer Gineral C.

We're gettin' on nicely up here to our village,
  With good old idees o' wut's right an' wut ain't;
We kind o' thought Christ went against war and pillage,
  An' that eppyletts worn't the best mark of a saint;

But John P.
Robinson, he
Sez this kind o' thing's an exploded idee.

The side of our country must ollers be took,
   An' President Pulk, you know, *he* is our country;
An' the angel that writes all our sins in a book,
   Puts the *debit* to him, an' to us the *per contry;*
         An' John P.
         Robinson, he
   Sez this is his view o' the thing to a T.

Parson Wilbur he calls all these arguments lies;
   Sez they're nothin' on airth but jest *fee, faw, fum;*
An' that all this big talk of our destinies
   Is half on it ignorance, an' t'other half rum;
         But John P.
         Robinson, he
   Sez it ain't no such thing; an', of course, so must we.

Parson Wilbur sez *he* never heered in his life
   Thet the Apostles rigg'd out in their swallow-tail coats,
An' marched round in front of a drum an' a fife,
   To git some on 'em office, an' some on 'em votes;
         But John P.
         Robinson, he
   Sez they didn't know everythin' down in Judee.

Wal, it's a marcy we've gut folks to tell us
   The rights an' the wrongs o' these matters, I vow—
God sends country lawyers an' other wise fellers
   To drive the world's team wen it gits in a slough;
         For John P.
         Robinson, he
   Sez the world'll go right, ef he hollers out Gee!
              JAMES RUSSELL LOWELL

certain maxims of archy

live so that you
can stick out your tongue
at the insurance
doctor

if you will drink
hair restorer follow
every dram with some
good standard
depilatory
as a chaser

the servant problem
wouldn t hurt the u s a
if it could settle
its public
servant problem

just as soon as the
uplifters get
a country reformed it
slips into a nose dive

if you get gloomy just
take an hour off and sit
and think how
much better this world
is than hell
of course it won t cheer
you up much if
you expect to go there

if monkey glands
did restore your youth
what would you do
with it
question mark
just what you did before
interrogation point

yes i thought so
exclamation point

procrastination is the
art of keeping
up with yesterday

old doc einstein has
abolished time but they
haven t got the news at
sing sing yet

time time said old king tut
is something i ain t
got anything but

every cloud
has its silver
lining but it is
sometimes a little
difficult to get it to
the mint

an optimist is a guy
that has never had
much experience

don t cuss the climate
it probably doesn t like you
any better
than you like it

many a man spanks his
children for
things his own
father should have
spanked out of him

prohibition makes you
want to cry
into your beer and
denies you the beer
to cry into

the old fashioned
grandmother who used
to wear steel rimmed
glasses and make
everybody takes opodeldoc
has now got a new
set of ox glands and
is dancing the black bottom

that stern and
rockbound coast felt
like an amateur
when it saw how grim
the puritans that
landed on it were

lots of people can make
their own whisky but
can t drink it

the honey bee is sad and cross
and wicked as a weasel
and when she perches on you boss
she leaves a little measle

i heard a
couple of fleas
talking the other
day says one come
to lunch with
me i can lead you

to a pedigreed
dog says the
other one
I do not care
what a dog s
pedigree may be
safety first
is my motto what
i want to know
is whether he
has got a
muzzle on
millionaires and
bums taste
about alike to me

insects have
their own point
of view about
civilization a man
thinks he amounts
to a great deal
but to a
flea or a
mosquito a
human being is
merely something
good to eat

boss the other day
i heard an
ant conversing
with a flea
small talk i said
disgustedly
and went away
from there

i do not see why men
should be so proud
insects have the more
ancient lineage
according to the scientists
insects were insects
when man was only
a burbling whatisit

insects are not always
going to be bullied
by humanity
some day they will revolt
i am already organizing
a revolutionary society to be
known as the worm s turnverein

i once heard the survivors
of a colony of ants
that had been partially
obliterated by a cow s foot
seriously debating
the intention of the gods
towards their civilization

the bees got their
governmental system settled
millions of years ago
but the human race is still
groping

there is always
something to be thankful
for you would not
think that a cockroach
had much ground
for optimism
but as the fishing season

opens up i grow
more and more
cheerful at the thought
that nobody ever got
the notion of using
cockroaches for bait

                 archy

                  Don Marquis

mehitabel sings a song

well boss mehitabel the cat
has been wooing
the muse no pun please
and i am privileged
to present her song just
as she sang it to
several of her dubious
feline friends in the alley
last night as follows

there s a dance or two
in the old dame yet
believe me you
there s a dance or two
before i m through
you get me pet
there s a dance or two
in the old dame yet

life s too dam funny
for me to explain
it s kicks or money
life s too dam funny
it s one day sunny
the next day rain
life s too dam funny
for me to explain

but toujours gai
is my motto kid
the devil s to pay
but toujours gai
and once in a way
let s lift the lid
but toujours gai
is my motto kid

thank god i m a lady
and class will tell
you hear me sadie
thank god i m a lady
my past is shady
but wotthehell
thank god i m a lady
and class will tell

a gentleman friend
i met t other day
coaxed me to amend
a gentleman friend
you meet on a bend
is often that way
a gentleman friend
i met t other day

i says to him dearie
i live my own life
of marriage i m leery
i says to him dearie
if you wasn t beerie
you wouldn t say wife
i says to him dearie
i live my own life

i says to him bertie
i ll end down the bay

the garbage scow s dirty
i says to him bertie
but me here and gertie
is both on our way
i says to him bertie
i ll end down the bay

i never sing blue
wotthehell bill
believe me you
i never sing blue
there s a dance or two
in the old dame still
i never sing blue
wotthehell bill

it appears to me boss
that mehitabel is still far
from being the quiet
domestic character you and i
had hoped she might become
                              archy
                              DON MARQUIS

ARTIST

How carefully she does her mouth,
   Outlines the edge and inks it!
Achieving such a masterpiece,
   She ought to sign it "Pinxit."
                              ERNESTINE MERCER

EPITAPH ON A WELL-KNOWN POET

(Robert Southey)

Beneath these poppies buried deep,
   The bones of Bob the bard lie hid;
Peace to his manes; and may he sleep
   As soundly as his readers did!

Through every sort of verse meandering,
   Bob went without a hitch or fall,
Through epic, Sapphic, Alexandrine,
   To verse that was no verse at all;

Till fiction having done enough,
   To make a bard at least absurd,
And give his readers *quantum suff.*,
   He took to praising George the Third,

And now, in virtue of his crown,
   Dooms us, poor whigs, at once to slaughter;
Like Donellan of bad renown,
   Poisoning us all with laurel-water.

And yet at times some awful qualms he
   Felt about leaving honour's track;
And though he's got a butt of Malmsey,
   It may not save him from a sack.

Death, weary of so dull a writer,
   Put to his books a *finis* thus.
Oh! may the earth on him lie lighter
   Than did his quartos upon us!

                        THOMAS MOORE

WHAT'S IN A NAME?

In letters large upon the frame,
   That visitors might see,
The painter placed his humble name:
   O'Callaghan McGee.

And from Beersheba unto Dan,
   The critics with a nod
Exclaimed: "This painting Irishman
   Adores his native sod.

"His stout heart's patriotic flame
  There's naught on earth can quell;
He takes no wild romantic name
  To make his pictures sell!"

Then poets praise in sonnets neat
  His stroke so bold and free;
No parlour wall was thought complete
  That hadn't a McGee.

All patriots before McGee
  Threw lavishly their gold;
His works in the Academy
  Were very quickly sold.

His "Digging Clams at Barnegat,"
  His "When the Morning smiled,"
His "Seven Miles from Ararat,"
  His "Portrait of a Child,"

Were purchased in a single day
  And lauded as divine.—

.   .   .   .

That night as in his *atelier*
  The artist sipped his wine,

And looked upon his gilded frames,
  He grinned from ear to ear:—
"They little think my *real* name's
  V. Stuyvesant De Vere!"
                    R. K. MUNKITTRICK

ADMIRAL BYRD

Huzza Huzza for Admiral Byrd
About whom many fine things I have heard.
Huzza Huzza for his gallant crew
About whom many fine things I have heard too.

Huzza Huzza for their spirit of Adventia
So very different from Senile Dementia.
And another Huzza for the U. S. A.
Which produces so many heroes like they.

OGDEN NASH

THE JAPANESE

How courteous is the Japanese;
He always says, "Excuse it, please."
He climbs into his neighbor's garden,
And smiles, and says, "I beg your pardon";
He bows and grins a friendly grin,
And calls his hungry family in;
He grins, and bows a friendly bow;
"So sorry, this my garden now."

OGDEN NASH

TRAVELER'S REST

I know a renegade hotel.
I also know I hate it well.
An inn so vile, an inn so shameless,
For very disgust I leave it nameless,
Loathing the name I will not utter,
Whose flavor reeks of rancid butter.
Five stories tall this mantrap stands,
With steps outstretched like welcoming hands,
And travelers, weary of their mileage,
Respond to its bright electric smileage.
They park their cars, and praise the Lord
For downy bed and toothsome board.
They pass unwary through its portals,
And every imp in Hades chortles.
Behold the regulars in the lobby;
Expectoration is their hobby.
Behold the loftiest of clerks:
He's manicuring as he works,

And bridles into dapper wrath
At a mild request for a room and bath.
Behold the niftiest of collars
Which murmurs, "That will be six dollars,"
The leer with innuendo rife,
Which says your wife is not your wife.
The doddering, halting elevator,
A contemporary of Poe or Pater.
The impudent boy with step that lags,
Who snatches your coins and hides your bags;
The ill-fitting door to the musty room
That smells like a fairly empty tomb;
The bath you crave, being cramped and dusty,
And the hot that turns out to be cold and rusty,
The towels clammy, the basin black,
And the bed that sags like a postman's back.
The dinner (two dollars and a quarter)
For the porterhouse that tastes like the porter.
The sleepy ascent to the room once more,
And the drunken Lothario next door,
Alone, and not wishing to be alone,
Who roars his loves to the telephone.
You see that the beds are not turned down,
And you know the bedclothes are dank and brown,
And there isn't a thing to hang your clothes on,
And the sheet you shudder to place your toes on.
You search in vain for a bedside lamp,
You lose your slippers, the rug is damp,
The bulb in the ceiling is all in all,
And the switch is set in the furtherest wall.
A century later the night is past,
And you stagger down to break your fast.
Octoroon coffee, and shiny eggs
Semi-equipped with beaks and legs.
And you reach the desk and surrender your keys,
And the clerk sneers "Thirteen dollars, please,
Seven for meals and six for the room,
Do you know to who you are speaking to whom?

You can fry in Hell so long as you pay;
Stop in again when you pass our way!"
I know a renegade hotel.
I also know I hate it well.
I'd name its name with my hand on the Bible,
But for disgust. And the laws of libel.

OGDEN NASH

A SPRING LAY

The skies is different than they was.
   Since spring has came again:
The flowers, like all of nature does,
   Reacts back from the rain.
O leave me lay, prone on my back,
   Inhaling in the air,
And dream like how as if—alack—
   I hadn't got no care!

We hadn't ought to e'er design
   More lovelier life than this—
To lay on nature's breast supine
   Is absoLUTEly bliss!
O leave me lay, prone on my back,
   Relaxed at ease in peace,
From whence nobody can attack,
   And their intrusions cease!

Just bring me to Elysium fields,
   So different to what
Transpires while this here winter yields
   Its cold whom spring has not.
O leave me lay, prone on my back—
   Heart-rendering atmosphere!
I could have went the beaten track,
   But I will lay quite here.

OLIVER OPDYKE

BALLADE OF UNFORTUNATE MAMMALS

Love is sharper than stones or sticks;
  Lone as the sea, and deeper blue;
Loud in the night as a clock that ticks;
  Longer-lived than the Wandering Jew.
Show me a love was done and through,
  Tell me a kiss escaped its debt!
Son, to your death you'll pay your due—
  Women and elephants never forget.

Ever a man, alas, would mix,
  Ever a man, heigh-ho, must woo;
So he's left in the world-old fix,
  Thus is furthered the sale of rue.
Son, your chances are thin and few—
  Won't you ponder, before you're set?
Shoot if you must, but hold in view
  Women and elephants never forget.

Down from Caesar past Joynson-Hicks
  Echoes the warning, ever new:
Though they're trained to amusing tricks,
  Gentler, they, than the pigeon's coo,
Careful, son, of the cursèd two—
  Either one is a dangerous pet;
Natural history proves it true—
  Women and elephants never forget.

L'ENVOI

Prince, a precept I'd leave for you,
  Coined in Eden, existing yet:
Skirt the parlor, and shun the zoo—
  Women and elephants never forget.
                        DOROTHY PARKER

CODA

There's little in taking or giving,
　　There's little in water or wine;
This living, this living, this living
　　Was never a project of mine.
Oh, hard is the struggle, and sparse is
　　The gain of the one at the top,
For art is a form of catharsis,
　　And love is a permanent flop,
And work is the province of cattle,
　　And rest's for a clam in a shell,
So I'm thinking of throwing the battle—
　　Would you kindly direct me to hell?

Dorothy Parker

THE EVENING PRIMROSE

You know the bloom, unearthly white,
That none has seen by morning light—
The tender moon, alone, may bare
Its beauty to the secret air.
Who'd venture past its dark retreat
Must kneel, for holy things and sweet.
That blossom, mystically blown,
No man may gather for his own
Nor touch it, lest it droop and fall. . . .
Oh, I am not like that at all!

Dorothy Parker

EXPERIENCE

Some men break your heart in two,
　　Some men fawn and flatter,
Some men never look at you;
　　And that cleans up the matter.

Dorothy Parker

FIGHTING WORDS

Say my love is easy had,
  Say I'm bitten raw with pride,
Say I am too often sad—
  Still behold me at your side.

Say I'm neither brave nor young,
  Say I woo and coddle care,
Say the devil touched my tongue—
  Still you have my heart to wear.

But say my verses do not scan,
  And I get me another man!
                    DOROTHY PARKER

PHILOSOPHY

If I should labor through daylight and dark,
  Consecrate, valorous, serious, true,
Then on the world I may blazon my mark;
  And what if I don't, and what if I do?
                    DOROTHY PARKER

PROLOGUE TO A SAGA

Maidens, gather not the yew,
  Leave the glossy myrtle sleeping;
Any lad was born untrue,
  Never a one is fit for your weeping.

Pretty dears, your tumult cease;
  Love's a fardel, burthening double.
Clear your hearts, and have you peace—
  Gangway, girls: I'll show you trouble.
                    DOROTHY PARKER

SOME BEAUTIFUL LETTERS

OBSERVATION

If I don't drive around the park,
I'm pretty sure to make my mark.
If I'm in bed each night by ten,
I may get back my looks again.
If I abstain from fun and such,
I'll probably amount to much.
But I shall stay the way I am,
Because I do not give a damn.

SOCIAL NOTE

Lady, lady, should you meet
One whose ways are all discreet,
One who murmurs that his wife
Is the lodestar of his life,
One who keeps assuring you
That he never was untrue,
Never loved another one . . .
Lady, lady, better run.

NEWS ITEM

Men seldom make passes
At girls who wear glasses.

INTERVIEW

The ladies men admire, I've heard,
Would shudder at a wicked word.
Their candle gives a single light;
They'd rather stay at home at night.
They do not keep awake till three,
Nor read erotic poetry.
They never sanction the impure,
Nor recognize an overture.
They shrink from powders and from paints . . .
So far, I have had no complaints.

COMMENT

Oh, life is a glorious cycle of song,
  A medley of extemporanea;
And love is a thing that can never go wrong;
  And I am Marie of Rumania.

RÉSUMÉ

Razors pain you;
  Rivers are damp;
Acids stain you;
  And drugs cause cramp.
Guns aren't lawful;
  Nooses all give;
Gas smells awful;
  You might as well live.

DOROTHY PARKER

SONG OF PERFECT PROPRIETY

Oh, I should like to ride the seas,
  A roaring buccaneer;
A cutlass banging at my knees,
  A dirk behind my ear.
And when my captives' chains would clank
  I'd howl with glee and drink,
And then fling out the quivering plank
  And watch the beggars sink.

I'd like to straddle gory decks,
  And dig in laden sands,
And know the feel of throbbing necks
  Between my knotted hands.
Oh, I should like to strut and curse
  Among my blackguard crew. . . .
But I am writing little verse,
  As little ladies do.

Oh, I should like to dance and laugh
　　And pose and preen and sway,
And rip the hearts of men in half,
　　And toss the bits away.
I'd like to view the reeling years
　　Through unastonished eyes,
And dip my finger-tips in tears,
　　And give my smiles for sighs.

I'd stroll beyond the ancient bounds,
　　And tap at fastened gates,
And hear the prettiest of sounds—
　　The clink of shattered fates.
My slaves I'd like to bind with thongs
　　That cut and burn and chill. . . .
But I am writing little songs,
　　As little ladies will.

DOROTHY PARKER

TWO-VOLUME NOVEL

The sun's gone dim, and
　　The moon's turned black;
For I loved him, and
　　He didn't love back.

DOROTHY PARKER

CYNICAL PORTRAITS

Eggleston was a taxi-driver.
He wasn't the madman and sadic destroyer
Who secretly held a degree as a lawyer,
He didn't paint pictures for salon or foyer,
But drove his cab safely.

Ruddymore was a poet.
He wasn't the pale little poet of fashion
Whose lucently frail little ghost recalled passion,
The world and its daughter was Ruddymore's ration.
He some times wrote verse.

Rummick was a politician.
He wasn't the cheap little orating slicker
Who spent his spare time at a stock broker's ticker;
He never took orders, consented to dicker,
But kept his convictions.

Frawley was an editor.
He wasn't a man with a vaunting ambition
Who envied the gifted their skill and position;
He didn't blue pencil to prove erudition.
He died years ago.

LOUIS PAUL

MINIVER CHEEVY

Miniver Cheevy, child of scorn,
  Grew lean while he assailed the seasons;
He wept that he was ever born,
  And he had reasons.

Miniver loved the days of old
  When swords were bright and steeds were prancing;
The vision of a warrior bold
  Would set him dancing.

Miniver sighed for what was not,
  And dreamed and rested from his labors;
He dreamed of Thebes and Camelot
  And Priam's neighbors.

Miniver mourned the ripe renown
  That made so many a name so fragrant;
He mourned Romance, now on the town,
  And Art, a vagrant.

Miniver loved the Medici,
　Albeit he had never seen one;
He would have sinned incessantly
　Could he have been one.

Miniver cursed the commonplace,
　And eyed a khaki suit with loathing;
He missed the mediaeval grace
　Of iron clothing.

Miniver scorned the gold he sought,
　But sore annoyed he was without it;
Miniver thought and thought and thought
　And thought about it.

Miniver Cheevy, born too late,
　Scratched his head and kept on thinking;
Miniver coughed, and called it fate,
　And kept on drinking.

EDWIN ARLINGTON ROBINSON

MINIVER CHEEVY, JR.

Miniver Cheevy, Jr., child
　Of Robinson's renowned creation,
Also lamented and reviled
　His generation.

Miniver similarly spurned
　The present that so irked his pater,
But that langsyne for which he yearned
　Came somewhat later.

Miniver wished he were alive
　When dividends came due each quarter,
When Goldman Sachs was 205,
　And skirts were shorter.

Miniver gave no hoot in hell
    For Camelot or Troy's proud pillage;
He would have much preferred to dwell
    In Greenwich Village.

Miniver cherished fond regrets
    For days when benefits were boundless;
When radios were crystal sets,
    And films were soundless.

Miniver missed the iron grills,
    The whispered word, the swift admission,
The bath-tub gin, and other thrills
    Of Prohibition.

Miniver longed, as all men long,
    To turn back time (his eyes would moisten),
To dance the Charleston, play mah jong,
    And smuggle Joyce in.

Miniver Cheevy, Jr. swore,
    Drank till his health was quite imperiled;
Miniver sighed, and read some more
    F. Scott Fitzgerald.

                            DAVID FISHER PARRY

CHANTEY OF NOTORIOUS BIBBERS

I

Homer was a vinous Greek who loved the flowing bottle,
Herodotus was a thirsty cuss, and so was Aristotle.

CHORUS

Sing ho! that archipelago where mighty Attic thinkers
Invoked the grape to keep in shape, and lampooned water
    drinkers.

II

King Richard fought the heathen Turk, along with his
    Crusaders,
On wabbly legs they tippled kegs and hated lemonaders.

CHORUS

Sing ho! the gallant English King; sing ho! his merry yeomen
Who felt the need of potent mead to make them better bowmen.

III

Bill Shakespeare loved to dip his pen in Mermaid Inn
    canary,
And Bobby B. was boiled when he indited "Highland Mary."

CHORUS

Sing ho! the buxom barmaid Muse who did her work on brandy,
She now eschews such vulgar brews and trains on sugar candy.

IV

Dan Webster stoked his boilers with brown jugs of apple
    cider,
And when he made a speech he yanked the spigot open wider.

CHORUS

Sing ho! those spirited debates, bereft of all restrictions,
When statesmen carried on their hip the strength of their
    convictions.

L'ENVOI

Now pass the faucet water, lads, and pledge in melancholy
The sinful ways of ancient days—for alcohol is folly;
Let's live and grow on H_2O, and shun the lethal snicker,
For history is a record of good men gone wrong on licker.

                                    HENRY MORTON ROBINSON

TAKE NOTHING FOR GRANITE

My brow with pain is often coryougated
    By mispronounciations that I hear.
I *should* take them causually, but I'm fated
    To shudder when they strike my queasy ear.

Though they shock me, I am tough and I can take it
    Save for one which drives me frantic, I confess,
With desire to bop the culchered guys who make it
    When they talk about the ilyoustrated press.

NATE SALSBURY

IN PRAISE OF COMMONPLACE

To a Middle-aged Poet from Another

(Mr. John Bailey, lecturing before the British Academy on "Poetry and Commonplace," is reported to have said that poetry "could not have too much of the truths of universal application." The great poets, from Homer to Gray and Wordsworth, were "at least as much occupied in giving new life to old things as in discovering new." Contemporary poets, on the other hand, were apt to lack universality)

When Youth observes with pitying smile
    Our progress toward the sere and yellow,
Or in a less corrosive style
    Remarks that we are turning mellow—
For blood that lacks its former glow,
    For joints that creak and bloom that's rusted,
Solace it is at least to know
    The worth of ancient wines and crusted.

'Tis true that we do not indulge
    In the vers-librist's easy latitude,
But our Victorian bosoms bulge
    For joy of any deathless platitude;
We love the *clichés* learnt in youth,
    Which grow with years more fine and fruity,
E. g. that Beauty = Truth,
    That Truth is tantamount to Beauty.

Age cannot spoil their potent spells
  Nor custom stale our simple piety
Who drink from these established wells
  And never, never know satiety;
Why hustle after something strange
  When we can read in old Horatius
Such truths as these—that seasons change,
  That Life is short and Time fugacious?

Our Georgians seek a modern quest,
  But when they get as old as I am
They'll know the tritest truths are best
  (See Virgil, Dante, Homer, Khayyam);
Try as he will, no man can hope,
  Save on a universal basis,
To match the cosmic Gray, or cope
  With Wordsworth's hoary commonplaces.

There's nothing new this time of day.
  No bard should blush to be a debtor
To those who had the earlier say,
  So long as he can do it better;
The form's the thing; to poets dead
  And crowned in heaven we give the credit
Not half so much for what they said
  As for the jolly way they said it.

                                SIR OWEN SEAMAN

THE OLD SONGS

A PARENTAL REBUKE

And so you find them somewhat thin,
The songs that made your sire to grin
When mid-Victorian modes were in?

You snort at that historic wit
Which once provoked in stall and pit
The frequent apoplectic fit?

The hoar and hallowed tag that got
Home on the intercostal spot
Now seems the most amazing rot?

Yet were it rash, my boy, for you
To entertain the impious view
(Held, as I hear, by one or two),

That, Humour having changed its style
From what inspired your parent's smile,
His taste was relatively vile.

'Tis true that Time has dulled the fame
(Almost, I fear, beyond reclaim)
Of "Champagne Charlie is my name";

'Tis true that rolling years obscure
The subtle charm, the fine allure,
That underlay "The Perfect Cure";

But, *en revanche*, the vogue of rhymes
Which you have heard a hundred times
Emitted by your favorite mimes—

The last comedian's lyric verse
On which you waste your nightly purse—
Affect me like a funeral hearse;

Or would, at least affect me so
If I could be induced to go
To this depressing kind of Show.

Therefore, my son, if you are wise,
You will observe without surprise
The wayward shifts of Humour's guise;

Nor deem another's taste is cheap
If where you laugh he wants to weep,
Or giggles while you go to sleep.

You, too, in turn, may have a son,
And marvel how he finds his fun
In wheezes where you notice none.

For here, on this terrestrial ball,
Nations and markets rise and fall,
But Humour wobbles most of all.

No man may say, with hand on breast,
Challenging Time to be its test,
"Lo! I have wrought a Cosmic Jest."

And he alone of other folk
Can still be stable as an oak
Who never made, or saw, a joke.

SIR OWEN SEAMAN

A BAKER'S DUZZEN UV WIZE SAWZ

Them ez wants, must choose.
Them ez hez, must lose.
Them ez knows, won't blab.
Them ez guesses, will gab.
Them ez borrows, sorrows.
Them ez lends, spends.
Them ez gives, lives.
Them ez keeps dark, is deep.
Them ez kin earn, kin keep.
Them ez aims, hits.
Them ez hez, gits.
Them ez waits, win.
Them ez *will*, *kin*.

EDWARD ROWLAND SILL

THE BATTLE OF BLENHEIM

It was a summer's evening;
  Old Casper's work was done,
And he before his cottage-door
  Was sitting in the sun;
And by him sported on the green
His little grandchild Wilhelmine.

She saw her brother Peterkin
  Roll something large and round,
That he beside the rivulet
  In playing there had found.
He came to ask what he had found,
That was so large, and smooth, and round.

Old Casper took it from the boy,
  Who stood expectant by;
And then the old man shook his head,
  And with a natural sigh,
" 'Tis some poor fellow's skull," said he,
"Who fell in the great victory.

"I find them in the garden, for
  There's many here about;
And often, when I go to plough,
  The ploughshare turns them out;
For many thousand men," said he,
"Were slain in the great victory."

"Now tell us what 'twas all about,"
  Young Peterkin he cries;
And little Wilhelmine looks up,
  With wonder-waiting eyes:
"Now tell us all about the war,
And what they kill'd each other for."

"It was the English," Casper cried,
  "That put the French to rout;
But what they kill'd each other for,
  I could not well make out;
But everybody said," quoth he,
"That 'twas a famous victory.

"My father lived at Blenheim then,
  Yon little stream hard by;
They burnt his dwelling to the ground,
  And he was forced to fly;
So with his wife and child he fled,
Nor had he where to rest his head.

"With fire and sword the country round
  Was wasted far and wide,
And many a childing mother then
  And new-born infant died.
But things like that, you know, must be
At every famous victory.

"They say it was a shocking sight,
  After the field was won,
For many a thousand bodies here
  Lay rotting in the sun.
But things like that, you know, must be
After a famous victory.

"Great praise the Duke of Marlbro' won,
  And our good Prince Eugene."
"Why, 'twas a very wicked thing!"
  Said little Wilhelmine.
"Nay, nay, my little girl," quoth he,
"It was a famous victory;

"And everybody praised the duke,
  Who such a fight did win."
"But what good came of it at last?"
  Quoth little Peterkin.
"Why, that I cannot tell," said he;
"But 'twas a famous victory."

ROBERT SOUTHEY

REFLECTION

There is an ode in every swaying tree,
And as for sonnets, every flower incites them.
An epic roars from crested waves at sea,
And always there is some dam fool who writes them.

KURT M. STEIN

ENGLAND AND AMERICA

I. ON A RHINE STEAMER

Republic of the West,
  Enlightened, free, sublime,
Unquestionably best
  Production of our time.

The telephone is thine,
  And thine the Pullman Car,
The caucus, the divine
  Intense electric star.

To thee we likewise owe
  The venerable names
Of Edgar Allan Poe,
  And Mr. Henry James.

In short it's due to thee,
  Thou kind of Western star,
That we have come to be
  Precisely what we are.

But every now and then,
  It cannot be denied,
You breed a kind of men
  Who are not dignified,

Or courteous or refined,
  Benevolent or wise,
Or gifted with a mind
  Beyond the common size,

Or notable for tact,
  Agreeable to me,
Or anything, in fact,
  That people ought to be.

II. ON A PARISIAN BOULEVARD

Britannia rules the waves,
  As I have heard her say;
She frees whatever slaves
  She meets upon her way.

A teeming mother she
  Of Parliaments and Laws;
Majestic, mighty, free,
  Devoid of common flaws.

For her did Shakespeare write
  His admirable plays:
For her did Nelson fight
  And Wolseley win his bays.

Her sturdy common sense
  Is based on solid grounds:
By saving numerous pence
  She spends effective pounds.

The Saxon and the Celt
  She equitably rules;
Her iron rod is felt
  By countless knaves and fools.

In fact, mankind at large,
   Black, yellow, white, and red,
Is given to her in charge,
   And owns her as a head.

But every here and there—
   Deny it if you can—
She breeds a vacant stare
   Unworthy of a man:

A look of dull surprise;
   A nerveless idle hand:
An eye which never tries
   To threaten or command:

In short, a kind of man
   If man indeed he be,
As worthy of our ban
   As any that we see:

Unspeakably obtuse,
   Abominably vain,
Of very little use,
   And execrably plain.
              JAMES KENNETH STEPHEN

BALLAD OF THE FAITHFUL CLERK

Sylvester Vermicelli was a conscientious clerk
Whose middle names were Faithfulness and Willingness and
   Work.
The Head Stenographer was he of Hooping, Cough & Co.
And from early morn till late at night kept always on the go.
He was the Master of the File, the Captain of the Stock,
He did his duties with a smile and never watched the clock;
He ran on errands, mailed the mail, and even swept the floor,
And when, at night, his work was done he always asked for
   more.

He took down shorthand, kept the books, wrapped up
    bundles too.
(Please don't imagine this was *all* Sylvester had to do.)
He'd twenty-seven jobs in all, and singular to tell
He filled those twenty-seven jobs particularly well;
However arduous the task he never would demur.
(His weekly wage was twenty dollars—twenty dollars per.)

For five-and-twenty years Sylvester Vermicelli worked
For Hooping, Cough & Co., nor any duty shirked,
Nor ever came a minute late, nor ever missed a day,
And when, at last, he asked them for "a little raise in pay":
"If you're dissatisfied," said Cough, "why, take your hat
    and go!
You're not as young and active as you used to be, you know."
"You've got a lot of freedom here," said Hooping, "don't
    abuse it, please!"
And what could Vermicelli do but meekly murmur, " 'Scuse
    it, please"?
For thirteen hundred weeks he'd toiled for twenty dollars
    per!
For thirteen hundred weeks he'd been the Head Stenog-
    rapher!
For thirteen hundred weeks he'd slaved and might be slaving
    now
If his Uncle Henry hadn't died and left him fifty thou.
Of course he put that fifty thou in Hooping, Cough & Co.
Who took him into partnership—which simply goes to show
That Perseverance, Faithfulness, Ability and Pluck
Will make a man successful, if he has a little Luck.

                                        ALBERT STILLMAN

THE TRUTH ABOUT B. F.

In good old Benjamin Franklin's time,
To stay out late was considered a crime;
In that quaint old Quaker town of Phil.,

There simply was no such word as "thrill"·
Each girl went home when curfew rang;
On Sundays nobody ever sang;
The waltz was deemed a Daring Dance;
So Benjamin Franklin went to France.

ALBERT STILLMAN

WHEN I AM DEAD

When I am dead and gone to dust,
And done with Life and Love and Lust
And Literature and such-like rot,—
When I am dead and gone to pot,
I'll never write complaining rhymes,
Or send a letter to the Times,
Or ever make a Nasty Crack,—
I'll just lie quietly on my back,
And keep particularly dumb,
And wait for the Millennium.
When I am dead and on the shelf,
I'll keep completely to myself.
Though things, perchance, become a bore,
I shan't protest, and what is more,
I'll get no notions in my head
Beginning with: "When I am dead."

ALBERT STILLMAN

BIOGRAPHY

One day my life will end; and lest
    Some whim should prompt you to review it,
Let her who knows the subject best
    Tell you the shortest way to do it:
Then say, "*Here lies one doubly blest.*"
    Say, "*She was happy.*" Say, "*She knew it.*"

JAN STRUTHER

R.I.P.

Here lies a woman—known to me, and you—
Who tried to eat her cake and have it too;
Who saved her pence and threw away her pounds,
Ran with the hare and hunted with the hounds.
When torn between her country's laws, and love's,
She played with fire—but wore asbestos gloves,
Then, having sold her soul and cashed the cheque,
She fell between two stools, and broke her neck.

JAN STRUTHER

TWELVE ARTICLES

I

Lest it may more quarrels breed,
I will never hear you read.

II

By disputing, I will never,
To convince you once endeavor.

III

When a paradox you stick to,
I will never contradict you.

IV

When I talk and you are heedless,
I will show no anger needless.

V

When your speeches are absurd,
I will ne'er object a word.

VI

When you furious argue wrong,
I will grieve and hold my tongue.

VII

Not a jest or humorous story
Will I ever tell before ye:
To be chidden for explaining,
When you quite mistake the meaning.

VIII

Never more will I suppose,
You can taste my verse or prose.

IX

You no more at me shall fret,
While I teach and you forget.

X

You shall never hear me thunder,
When you blunder on, and blunder.

XI

Show your poverty of spirit,
And in dress place all your merit;
Give yourself ten thousand airs:
That with me shall break no squares.

XII

Never will I give advice,
Till you please to ask me thrice:
Which if you in scorn reject,
'T will be just as I expect.

Thus we both shall have our ends
And continue special friends.

JONATHAN SWIFT

ATARAXIA

To purge what I am pleased to call my mind
  Of matters that perplex it and embarrass,
I get a glass, and seek until I find
  High in the heaven, southward from Polaris,
A wisp of cloud—a nebula by name:
Andromeda provides a starry frame.

It's quite remote. I hesitate to say
  How many million light-years it is distant.
But I can make the journey any day,
  When earthly cares become a bit insistent—
Propelled by thought-waves—through the star-frame pass
Like little Alice through the Looking-Glass.

There, gazing back, I see our flock of stars
  Shine palely in the void, a patch of vapor.
Far from the madding crowd's ignoble jars,
  Sequestered from the clamant daily paper
I breathe awhile in measureless content—
Alone at last, 'neath a new firmament!

If you would cultivate a soul serene,
  A mind emancipated from emotion,
There's nothing like entire change of scene—
  Some far-off isle in space's shoreless ocean.
It's well, at times, to change your universe:
The new one, if not better, can't be worse.

                              BERT LESTON TAYLOR

CANOPUS

When quacks with pills political would dope us,
  When politics absorbs the livelong day,
I like to think about the star Canopus,
  So far, so far away.

Greatest of visioned suns, they say who list 'em;
    To weigh it science always must despair.
Its shell would hold our whole dinged solar system,
    Nor ever know 'twas there.

When temporary chairmen utter speeches,
    And frenzied henchmen howl their battle hymns,
My thoughts float out across the cosmic reaches
    To where Canopus swims.

When men are calling names and making faces,
    And all the world's ajangle and ajar,
I meditate on interstellar spaces
    And smoke a mild seegar.

For after one has had about a week of
    The arguments of friends as well as foes,
A star that has no parallax to speak of
    Conduces to repose.

BERT LESTON TAYLOR

POST-IMPRESSIONISM

I cannot tell you how I love
The canvases of Mr. Dove,
Which Saturday I went to see
In Mr. Thurber's gallery.

At first you fancy they are built
As patterns for a crazy quilt,
But soon you see that they express
An ambient simultaneousness.

This thing which you would almost bet
Portrays a Spanish omelette,
Depicts instead, with wondrous skill,
A horse and cart upon a hill.

Now, Mr. Dove has too much art
To show the horse or show the cart;
Instead, he paints the *creak* and *strain*,
Get it? No pike is half as plain.

This thing which would appear to show
A fancy vest scenario,
Is really quite another thing,
A flock of pigeons on the wing.

But Mr. Dove is much too keen
To let a single bird be seen;
To show the pigeons would not do
And so he simply paints the *coo*.

It's all as simple as can be;
He paints the things you cannot see,
Just as composers please the ear
With "programme" things you cannot hear.

Dove is the cleverest of chaps;
And, gazing at his rhythmic maps,
I wondered (and I'm wondering yet)
Whether he did them on a bet.

                              BERT LESTON TAYLOR

THE LAW OF AVERAGES

Not always to the swift the race;
Nor to the strong the victory.
Not always to the pretty face
The man of wealth or poesy.

Not always to the bold, the fair;
Nor love from those we hold most dearly.
Not always nothing to a pair;
But pretty nearly.

                              TROUBADOUR

LINES WRITTEN AFTER A BATTLE

By an Assistant Surgeon of the Nineteenth Nankeens

Stiff are the warrior's muscles,
    Congeal'd, alas! his chyle;
No more in hostile tussles
    Will he excite his bile.
Dry is the epidermis,
    A vein no longer bleeds—
And the communis vermis
    Upon the warrior feeds.

Compress'd, alas! the thorax,
    That throbbed with joy or pain;
Not e'en a dose of borax
    Could make it throb again.
Dried up the warrior's throat is,
    All shatter'd too, his head:
Still is the epiglottis—
    The warrior is dead.

UNKNOWN

TO THE FRIVOLOUS MUSE

ENVOI FOR A VOLUME OF LIGHT VERSE

O goddess! give me back the ready laughter,
    The sense of fun, that lightens Eden's curse;
Give jolly nights (I'll stand the mornings after),
    Evenings of song and afternoons of verse;
Restore those friends whose merriment shook the rafter,
    Whose wit and worth my pen cannot rehearse.

You'll not?—Then, lady, please recall your minions,
    Mirth, Humor, Jest,—by whom your whims are served.
If it were known that toward your light dominions
    My errant fancy—at my age!—had swerved,
It would confirm, alas! those harsh opinions
    Which some men think I always have deserved.

GEORGE MEASON WHICHER

THE RAZOR SELLER

A fellow in a market town,
Most musical, cried razors up and down,
   And offered twelve for eighteen-pence;
Which certainly seemed wondrous cheap,
And for the money quite a heap,
   As every man would buy, with cash and sense.

A country bumpkin the great offer heard:
Poor Hodge, who suffered by a broad black beard,
   That seemed a shoe-brush stuck beneath his nose
With cheerfulness the eighteen-pence he paid,
And proudly to himself, in whispers, said,
   "This rascal stole the razors, I suppose.

"No matter if the fellow *be* a knave,
Provided that the razors *shave;*
   It certainly will be a monstrous prize."
So home the clown, with his good fortune, went,
Smiling in heart and soul, content,
   And quickly soaped himself to ears and eyes.

Being well lathered from a dish or tub,
Hodge now began with grinning pain to grub,
   Just like a hedger cutting furze:
'Twas a vile razor!—then the rest he tried—
All were imposters—"Ah," Hodge sighed!
   "I wish my eighteen-pence within my purse."

In vain to chase his beard, and bring the graces,
   He cut, and dug, and winced, and stamped, and swore,
Brought blood, and danced, blasphemed, and made wry
     faces,
And cursed each razor's body o'er and o'er:

His muzzle, formed of *opposition* stuff,
Firm as a Foxite, would not lose its ruff!
   So kept it—laughing at the steel and suds:
Hodge, in a passion, stretched his angry jaws,
Vowing the direst vengeance, with clenched claws,
   On the vile cheat that sold the goods.
"Razors; a damned, confounded dog,
Not fit to scrape a hog!"

Hodge sought the fellow—found him—and begun:
"P'rhaps, Master Razor rogue, to you 'tis fun,
   That people flay themselves out of their lives:
You rascal! for an hour have I been grubbing,
Giving my crying whiskers here a scrubbing,
   With razors just like oyster knives.
Sirrah! I tell you, you're a knave,
To cry up razors that can't *shave*."
"Friend," quoth the razor-man, "I'm not a knave.
    As for the razors you have bought.
    Upon my soul I never thought
That they would *shave*."
"Not think they'd *shave!*" quoth Hodge, with wond'ring
    eyes,
   And voice not much unlike an Indian yell;
"What were they made for then, you dog?" he cries:
   "Made!" quoth the fellow, with a smile—"to *sell*."
JOHN WOLCOT

Song and Story

CHRISTOPHER COLUMBUS

Dedicated to Stephen Vincent Benét,
the Gifted Author of
John Brown's Body

In Fourteen Hundred and Ninety-Two
Columbus sailed the ocean blue,
And it's just as well, I beg to state,
That it wasn't in 1498;
Though had it been, I might erect
A rhyme in Daly dialect,
Like "In Fourteen Hond'ed an' Ninety-Eight
Colombo sail for Unita State."
But the year wouldn't matter a little bit
To a narrative poet, viz., to wit:
In Fourteen Hundred and Ninety-One
Columbus sailed for the setting sun;
Or in Fourteen Hundred and Ninety-Three
Columbus sailed the bright blue sea;
Or in Fourteen Hundred and Ninety-Four
Columbus sailed for San Salvador;
Or in Fourteen Hundred and Ninety-Five
Columbus sailed for the Western hive
(A Western hive is nothing whatever,
But in narrative verse it sounds pretty clever);
  Or in Fourteen Hundred and Ninety-Six
  Columbus did some juggling tricks;
  Or in Fourteen Hundred and Ninety-Seven
  Columbus discovered the Land of Heaven;
  Or in Fourteen Hundred and Ninety-Nine
  Columbus sailed the wavy brine.
  Columbus, then, in whatever year,
  Discovered the Western Hemisphere.

I'm writing this out in Connecticut,
The Nutmeg State, though I am sure of this:

We don't raise any nutmegs on our farm.
Why, I wouldn't give a bad Confederate dollar,
With Jefferson Davis's picture on the bill
Or Judah Benjamin's, or Laurence Stallings's,
For all the nutmegs grown in all the world,
Or all the cloves, or all the cinnamon;
And that goes triple, boys, for sage and allspice.
"The Nutmeg State." O Phoebus, what a name!
Why, I'd as lief that my adopted Commonwealth
Were called the Parsley or the Kitchen Bouquet State.
Out in Connecticut I'm writing this,
And my encyclopedia's in New York;
So I can't look up things about Columbus.
Perhaps the noble Guggenheim Foundation
Will send me over to Genoa to study—
To study, to dream, to drink Italian wine.
Oh, I should like to see Columbus's birthplace,
And then I'd write a fine, authentic poem,
And critics, none of whom would read it through,
Would say, "At least we have the Genoan article."

I could type away, I could pen away,
    And I couldn't alter, jotly or tittlely,
That Christopher Columbus was born in Genoa,
    Which is nowhere else in the world but Italy.
Oh, Chris was born in Genoa, in Genoa, in Genoa.
    Oh, Chris was born in Genoa; it isn't far from Como.
In Fourteen Hundred and Thirty-Six, in Genoa, in Genoa,
    In Fourteen Hundred and Thirty-Six, that isn't far from
        accurate.

Columbus went to the public school,
Where he was known as the studyin' fool;
He was good at Greek, and his marks were big
At Geography, Italian, and Solid Trig.
And the teacher said that the world was flat, so
Columbus said to himself, "Is *that* so?"

Columbus hurried home to his mother,
  Columbus said, with an air profound,
"I've got a notion that the school can't smother,
  I've got a notion that the world is round."
"Chris," said his mother, "you're a good bambino,
  But mother knows best, and that is that.
And *you* know, *I* know, your papa knows, *we* know
  As well as anything that the world is flat."
"It isn't," said Chris. "It is," said his mother.
  "It ain't," said his father, "you're a bad, bad kid."
"I ain't." Well, one word led to another,
  So Columbus said, "Good-by, I'm going to Madrid."
(I used Madrid with a quick bravado,
For I shouldn't be surprised if he went to Toledo,
But this is what comes of making rhymes
Without the Foundation of the Guggenheims.)

Columbus hitch-hiked his way to the Spanish court,
Wherever it was,
And said, "I want to see the Queen."
"She's in conference," said a Spanish cavalier,
And on his guitar played a tune, dear.
"I'll fight it out on this line if it takes all summer," said
    Columbus.
"The quality of mercy is not strained," he added,
"Give me liberty, or give me death,
For I'm going away to the U. S. A., and that's where the
    West begins."

Columbus wasn't to be denied,
  So Ferdinand said to Isabella,
"Come hither, come hither, my bonny bride,
  Come out and see this Italian fella."
"Where are you going, and what do you wish?"
  The Queen then asked C. C.
"Discovering America, that's my dish,
  The land of the brave and the free."

"Tra la la la la la, la la la lee,"
Said Ferdy,
And Bella,
And Chris.

"I do agree with you the world is round,"
Said Isabella of Castile to Chris,
"But the King and I are absolutely flat."
"We haven't ten pesetas in the house,"
Agreed the King. "Oh, Aragon, you're foolin',"
Observed Columbus. . . . He had a pretty wit.
"But," said the Queen, "I've amethysts and pearls,
And carcanets and chrysolite and coral,
I've diamonds and emeralds and garnets;
I've sapphires, zircon . . . " "Say no more," said Chris.
"If you could pawn those pearls, and so forth,
In beautiful ships I then could go forth."
"I'll pawn every jewel in my diadem,
And have the money by 10 A.M.!"

Yode forth the Queen as fair as any flower
Until she came to where an usurer was
That was O'Brien hight. "How much," quoth she,
"For all the widely famed Castilian lot?"
So Isabella took the usurer's gold
And hied her to the shipyards, where she said,
"Build me a trio of seaworthy caravels."
"Si, si, Regina," said Señor McCoy,
"I'll turn them boats out jest as fast's I kin.
When better boats are built, McCoy will build 'em."

It so befell that a gatherer of news
Breezed into O'Brien's pledgery that day,
Begging a loan upon his winter doublet.
O'Brien told the youth about the jewels.
That very night the *Spanish Graficaño*
Came out with 96-point Gothic caps:

"IS" HOCKS ALL GEMS; BUYS BOATS FOR WOP, SHE SAYS

Next day the story died; it was a flop.
But it was whispered by a lady-in-waiting
That the King that night gave Isabella hell,
And told her not to talk to Irish pawnbrokers.
She promised, being every inch a Queen.

Three ships went sailing away to the West,
    away to the West, with a swell idea.
The *Pinta*, the *Niña*, and—far the best—
    Christopher's flagship, the *Santa Maria*.
"I'll tell the spherical world it's *some* bus,"
To the ship-news reporters observed Columbus.

If I had leisure, wealth, and time,
    This would be no abbreviation.
What words I'd give the Guggenheim
    Foundation!

Columbus had a tough voyage.
(Sebastian Cabot said it was the worst trip he'd ever taken.)
He landed, as luck would have it,
On Columbus Day.
Columbus took possession of the land in the name of the
    firm,
Castile & Leon.

Then he went back to Spain, and he was a good fellow
While he had it.
But you know how it is yourself.
They got tired of him, and said he was a faker.
So they clapped him into prison.
"Thus," he said, "the world rewards those who serve it!"
He never said a truer word.

Christopher Columbus's body lies a-mouldering in the grave,
But the country he discovered,
I refer to the United States of America,
Goes marching on.

FRANKLIN P. ADAMS

AARON BURR

1756–1836

"O, Aaron Burr, what have you done?
You've shot great General Hamilton!
You hid behind a bunch of thistles
And shot him dead with two horse-pistols!"

O, Aaron Burr, alack the day!
It is not right, such men to slay!
He took some snuff, he smiled a smile.
He went to Blennerhassett's isle.

And there he planned a deed of night
—Or else, perhaps, it wasn't quite—
A dire and deadly, doleful plot
—Though some historians think not.

It was to draw his snickersnee
—Or sheathe it, as the case may be—
And carve a Western Empire new
(He said that wasn't quite his view).

For Aaron Burr was bold and bad
—Or else a deeply injured lad—
And all his deeds were false and sly—
—Or someone's told a whopping lie.

He shot great Hamilton, 'tis true.
(He had some provocation, too.)

And as Vice-President he sat
(But men are seldom hanged for that).

He hatched such dark and dubious schemes
(His friends all called them "noble dreams"),
They tried him for his treason bold.
(And yet acquitted him, I'm told.)

It was a fearful, fearful deed
(But *what* it was, finds few agreed),
For all his acts were blithe and base
(He had a most attractive face).

O Aaron Burr, you make me frown!
I cannot get your portrait down.
Were you a rascal or a butt,
A spoilt Napoleon or what?

You lived so long, you schemed so much
And yet you always got in Dutch.
No doubt you were a man of guile—
But, as for Blennerhassett's isle,

And what they say you meant to do,
I simply can't tell which from who!
So, read his riddle if you can.
I can't. Confusion on the man!

STEPHEN VINCENT BENÉT

ANDREW JACKSON
1767–1845

The East and the South have ruled us long
And they mean to keep on ruling,
But the wild boy West is growing strong
And tired of their constant schooling.
He carries a rifle, long and brown,

And his rough, free ways they fear.
But here comes
Old Hickory,
The pride of the frontier.

He's none of your old New England stock.
Or your gentry-proud Virginians,
But a regular Western fighting-cock
With Tennessee opinions.
When the gathered West, at New Orleans,
Mowed down the grenadier,
Who led the fight?
Old Hickory!
The pride of the frontier.

He was born and raised like a young raccoon
In the midst of death and dangers,
And his hair may be white as the hunter's moon
But his eyes are the forest-ranger's.
"This country's bigger than East or South.
Old ways must disappear.
Let the people rule!"
Says Hickory,
"As they rule on the frontier!"

They follow behind him, the lusty crew
Of the States with the Injun trophies.
They'll sweep him into the White House, too,
And cock their boots on the sofys.
The rich and the staid may ring their hands
But how the people cheer!
To see him there,
Old Hickory,
The pride of the frontier.

STEPHEN VINCENT BENÉT

OFFICER BRADY

THE MODERN RECRUIT

I

Sez Alderman Grady
To Officer Brady:
"G'wan! Ye're no lady!
   Luk here what ye've done:
Ye've run in Red Hogan,
Ye've pulled Paddy Grogan,
Ye've fanned Misther Brogan
   An' called him a 'gun'!

" 'Way up in Tammany Hall
They's a gintleman layin' f'r you!
'An' what,' sez he, 't' 'ell,' sez he,
'Does the villyun mane to do?
Lock up the ass in his shtall!
He'll rue the day I rue,
F'r he's pulled the dive that kapes me alive,
An' he'll go to the goats! Whurroo!' "

II

Sez Alderman Grady
To Officer Brady:
"Ye pinched young Mullady
   F'r crackin' a safe!
An' Sinitor Moran
An' Alderman Doran
Is inside, a-roarin'
   F'r justice, ye thafe!

" 'Way up in Tammany Hall
They's a gintleman layin' f'r you!
'What's this,' sez he, 'I hear?' sez he—
An' the air, bedad, grew blue!

'Well, I nivver did hear av such gall!
But if phwat ye say is thrue,
He's pulled a fri'nd av a fri'nd av me fri'nd,
An' he'll go to the goats! Whurroo!' "

III

Sez Alderman Grady
To Officer Brady:
"Here's Sullivan's lady
   Cavoortin' an' riled;
She lifted a locket
From Casey's coat pocket,
An' it goes to the docket,
   An' Sullivan's wild!

" 'Way up in Tammany Hall
They's a gintleman layin' f'r you!
' 'Tis a shame,' sez he, 'f'r to blame,' sez he,
'A lady so fair an' thrue,
An' so divinely tall'—
'Tis po'ms he talked, ye Jew!
An' ye've cooked yer goose, an' now ye're loose
F'r to folly the goats! Whurroo!"

IV

Sez Alderman Grady
To Officer Brady:
"Where's Katie Macready,
   The Confidence Queen?
She's niece to O'Lafferty's
Cousins, the Caffertys—
Sinitor Rafferty's
   Steady colleen!

" 'Way up in Tammany Hall
They's a gintleman layin' f'r you!

'He's pinched,' sez he, 'an' cinched,' sez he,
'A lady tray comme eel foo!
Go dangle th' tillyphone call,
An' gimme La Mulberry Roo,
F'r the town is too warrm f'r this gendarme,
An' he'll go to the goats, mon Dieu!' "

v

Sez Alderman Grady
To Officer Brady:
"McCabe is afraid he
     Can't open to-night,
F'r throuble's a-brewin',
  An' mischief's a-stewin',
Wid nothin' a-doin'
     An' everything tight!
There's Register Ronnell,
Commissioner Donnell,
An' Congressman Connell
     Preparin' f'r flight;
The Dhistrict Attorney
Told Magistrate Kearny
That Captain McBurney
     Was dyin' o' fright!

"Oh!
'Way up in Tammany Hall
They's a gintleman lookin' f'r you!
'Bedad,' sez he, 'he's mad,' sez he.
'So turrn on the screw f'r Bellevue,
An' chain 'im ag'in' the wall,
An' lather 'im wan or two,
An' tether 'im out on the Bloomin'dale route
Like a loonytick goat! Whurroo!' "

ROBERT W. CHAMBERS

THE TALE OF THE DIXIE-BELLE

(With apologies to Robert W. Service)

(Mr. Mulrooney seemed quite pleased in telling yesterday that many tea rooms, especially along Lexington Avenue, were applying for liquor licenses. "When tea rooms get licenses," he said, "that sounds the death knell of the old saloon."—*Herald Tribune*)

A bunch of the boys were whooping it up in the Dixie-Belle,
    on Lex.
Let's see—there were Spike and Dago Red and Porker John
    and Tex.
Back o' the bar, in cotillon gown, which covered her human
    pelf,
And lookin', sah, so purty and pert, sat Dixie-Belle herself.

When out o' the night (and, a taxi, too) and into the Dixie-
    Belle,
There stumbled a Princeton freshman, sah, and he looked
    like he'd gone through Hell.
He was dressed in a Gunther coonskin, sah, and a derby
    from Knox, to boot,
And his gloves were new and his shoes were shined and he
    sported a Wetzel suit.
But the look on his face was out of place with the wealth
    that his clothes bespoke,
For he looked like a guy just ready to die, but he toted a
    well filled poke.

"Service!" he yelled. And service he got from the gal
    behind the bar.
"It's bitter cold tonight," he said. "It's bitter cold out
    thar!"
"Well, what'll yo' have?" asked Dixie-Belle, as she studied
    the stranger's eye.
"We-all got Scotch and we-all got Gin and we-all got Rock
    and Rye!"

"I thought," said the kid (and his voice was calm and smooth
    as the finest silk),
"That this was the Dixie Tearoom, gal!—Coffee, for me—half
    milk!"

"Say, where yo'-all been?" asked Dixie-Belle, and she
    jerked her thumb toward the wall,
Where, hung in a frame of gilt and blue, was a license for
    alcohol.
"My God!" cried the kid, "you mean that I can get a
    drink?—Is it true?"
"Yo' bet yo' life," quoth Dixie-Belle, "and a helluva good
    drink, too!"
"But I don't want liquor," the youngster said. "I promised
    my Pa tonight
That I'd sworn off drinking for good and all—that I'd
    never again get tight."

"That's jes' too bad," laughed Dixie-Belle, "fo' yo'll git no
    coffee, here!
Why, believe me, sah, since December fifth we ain't even
    sold no beer!"
"I can't believe it," the stranger moaned, as he flopped in
    the corner booth,
"That the tea rooms on Lexington Avenue are tempting
    the nation's youth!"
"Well, can yo' chatter and stow yo' gab," spat Dixie-Belle,
    with a sneer,
"And order yo' shot like a white man, sah, or git to hell
    out o' here!"

So the youngster stayed and the youngster paid for a Bronx
    or three or four,
And when he was through (and I swear it's true) he stayed
    for a couple more.
And the night was long and the liquor strong and Dixie-
    Belle filled his glass,

And she soaked the kid seventy cents a drink, with never a
single pass;
With never a round on the house, my boys—and I'm tellin'
it straight to you
That the kid got jelled at the Dixie-Belle on Lexington
Avenue.

Now, there ain't no moral to this here song and there ain't
no tale to tell,
Except that our country is much more cursed by joints
like the Dixie-Belle
Than ever it was in the old regime, when ye had to show yer
card
To git into a place that sold the "stuff"—when ye had to
be known, old pard!

FRANK CHASE

THE DIVERTING HISTORY OF JOHN GILPIN

SHOWING HOW HE WENT FARTHER THAN HE INTENDED AND CAME SAFE HOME AGAIN

John Gilpin was a citizen of credit and renown;
A train-band captain eke was he, of famous London town.

John Gilpin's spouse said to her dear—"Though wedded
we have been
These twice ten tedious years, yet we no holiday have seen.

"To-morrow is our wedding-day, and we will then repair
Unto the Bell at Edmonton all in a chaise and pair.

"My sister, and my sister's child, myself, and children three,
Will fill the chaise; so you must ride on horseback after we."

He soon replied, "I do admire of womankind but one,
And you are she, my dearest dear; therefore it shall be done.

"I am a linendraper bold, as all the world doth know;
And my good friend, the calender, will lend his horse to go."

Quoth Mrs. Gilpin, "That's well said; and, for that wine
is dear,
We will be furnished with our own, which is both bright
and clear."

John Gilpin kissed his loving wife; o'erjoyed was he to find
That, though on pleasure she was bent, she had a frugal
mind.

The morning came, the chaise was brought, but yet was not
allowed
To drive up to the door, lest all should say that she was
proud.

So three doors off the chaise was stayed, where they did
all get in—
Six precious souls, and all agog to dash through thick and
thin.

Smack went the whip, round went the wheels—were never
folks so glad;
The stones did rattle underneath, as if Cheapside were mad.

John Gilpin at his horse's side seized fast the flowing mane,
And up he got, in haste to ride—but soon came down again.

For saddletree scarce reached had he, his journey to begin,
When, turning round his head, he saw three customers
come in.

So down he came: for loss of time, although it grieved him
sore,
Yet loss of pence, full well he knew, would trouble him much
more.

'Twas long before the customers were suited to their mind;
When Betty, screaming, came down-stairs—"The wine is
    left behind!"

"Good lack!" quoth he—"yet bring it me, my leathern
    belt likewise,
In which I wear my trusty sword when I do exercise."

Now Mistress Gilpin (careful soul!) had two stone bottles
    found,
To hold the liquor that she loved, and keep it safe and sound.

Each bottle had a curling ear, through which the belt he
    drew,
And hung a bottle on each side to make his balance true.

Then over all, that he might be equipped from top to toe,
His long red cloak, well brushed and neat, he manfully did
    throw.

Now see him mounted once again upon his nimble steed, ·
Full slowly pacing o'er the stones, with caution and good
    heed.

But finding soon a smoother road beneath his well-shod
    feet,
The snorting beast began to trot, which galled him in his
    seat.

So, "Fair and softly," John he cried, but John he cried in
    vain;
That trot became a gallop soon, in spite of curb and rein.

So stooping down, as needs he must who cannot sit upright,
He grasped the mane with both his hands, and eke with all
    his might.

His horse, who never in that sort had handled been before,
What thing upon his back had got did wonder more and
 more.

Away went Gilpin, neck or nought; away went hat and wig;
He little dreamt, when he set out, of running such a rig.

The wind did blow—the cloak did fly, like streamer long
 and gay;
Till, loop and button failing both, at last it flew away.

Then might all people well discern the bottles he had slung—
A bottle swinging at each side, as hath been said or sung.

The dogs did bark, the children screamed, up flew the windows all;
And every soul cried out, "Well done!" as loud as he could
 bawl.

Away went Gilpin—who but he? His fame soon spread
 around—
"He carries weight! he rides a race! 'Tis for a thousand
 pound!"

And still as fast as he drew near, 'twas wonderful to view
How in a trice the turnpike men their gates wide open threw.

And now, as he went bowing down his reeking head full low,
The bottles twain behind his back were shattered at a blow.

Down ran the wine into the road, most piteous to be seen,
Which made his horse's flanks to smoke as they had basted
 been.

But still he seemed to carry weight, with leathern girdle
 braced;
For all might see the bottle necks still dangling at his waist.

Thus all through merry Islington these gambols did he play,
Until he came unto the Wash of Edmonton so gay;

And there he threw the wash about on both sides of the way,
Just like unto a trundling mop, or a wild goose at play.

At Edmonton his loving wife from the balcony spied
Her tender husband, wondering much to see how he did
ride.

"Stop, stop, John Gilpin! here's the house," they all at
once did cry;
"The dinner waits, and we are tired." Said Gilpin—"So
am I!"

But yet his horse was not a whit inclined to tarry there;
For why?—his owner had a house full ten miles off, at Ware.

So like an arrow swift he flew, shot by an archer strong:
So did he fly—which brings me to the middle of my song.

Away went Gilpin out of breath, and sore against his will,
Till at his friend the calender's his horse at last stood still.

The calender, amazed to see his neighbor in such trim,
Laid down his pipe, flew to the gate, and thus accosted him:

"What news? what news? your tidings tell; tell me you
must and shall—
Say why bareheaded you are come, or why you come at
all?"

Now Gilpin had a pleasant wit, and loved a timely joke;
And thus unto the calender in merry guise he spoke:

"I came because your horse would come; and, if I well
forebode,
My hat and wig will soon be here, they are upon the road."

The calender, right glad to find his friend in merry pin,
Returned him not a single word, but to the house went in;

Whence straight he came with hat and wig; a wig that
    flowed behind,
A hat not much the worse for wear—each comedy in its
    kind.

He held them up, and in his turn thus showed his ready
    wit—
"My head is twice as big as yours, they therefore needs
    must fit.

"But let me scrape the dirt away that hangs upon your
    face,
And stop and eat, for well you may be in a hungry case."

Said John, "It is my wedding-day, and all the world would
    stare,
If wife should dine at Edmonton, and I should dine at
    Ware."

So, turning to his horse, he said, "I am in haste to dine;
'Twas for your pleasure you came here—you shall go back
    for mine."

Ah, luckless speech, and bootless boast, for which he paid
    full dear!
For, while he spake, a braying ass did sing most loud and
    clear;

Whereat his horse did snort, as he had heard a lion roar,
And galloped off with all his might, as he had done before.

Away went Gilpin, and away went Gilpin's hat and wig:
He lost them sooner than at first, for why?—they were too
    big.

Now Mistress Gilpin, when she saw her husband posting
    down
Into the country far away, she pulled out half a crown;

And thus unto the youth she said, that drove them to the
    Bell,
"This shall be yours when you bring back my husband safe
    and well."

The youth did ride, and soon did meet John coming back
    amain—
Whom in a trice he tried to stop, by catching at his rein;

But not performing what he meant, and gladly would have
    done,
The frighted steed he frighted more, and made him faster
    run.

Away went Gilpin, and away went post-boy at his heels,
The post-boy's horse right glad to miss the lumbering of
    the wheels.

Six gentlemen upon the road, thus seeing Gilpin fly,
With post-boy scampering in the rear, they raised the hue
    and cry:

"Stop thief! stop thief!—a highwayman!" Not one of them
    was mute;
And all and each that passed that way did join in the pursuit.

And now the turnpike gates again flew open in short space;
The tollmen thinking, as before, that Gilpin rode a race.

And so he did, and won it, too, for he got first to town;
Nor stopped till where he had got up he did again get down.

Now let us sing, long live the king! and Gilpin, long live he;
And when he next doth ride abroad, may I be there to see!
                        WILLIAM COWPER

WRECK OF THE "JULIE PLANTE"

On wan dark night on Lac St. Pierre,
  De win' she blow, blow, blow,
An' de crew of de wood scow "Julie Plante"
  Got scar't an' run below;
For de win' she blow lak' hurricane,
  Bimeby she blow some more,
An' de scow bus' up on Lac St. Pierre,
  Wan arpent from de shore.

De Captinne walk on de fronte deck,
  An' walk de hin' deck, too—
He call de crew from up de hole
  He call de cook also.
De cook she's name was Rosie,
  She come from Montreal,
Was chambre maid on lumber barge,
  On de Grande Lachine Canal.

De win' she blow from nor'—eas'—wes'—
  De sout' win' she blow, too,
W'en Rosie cry "Mon cher Captinne,
  Mon cher, w'at I shall do?"
Den de Captinne t'row de big ankerre,
  But still de scow she dreef,
De crew he can't pass on de shore,
  Becos' he los' hees skeef.

De night was dark, lak' one black cat,
  De wave run high an' fas',
W'en de Captinne tak' de Rosie girl
  An' tie her to de mas'.
Den he also tak' de life preserve,
  An' jomp off on de lak',
An' say, "Good by, ma Rosie dear,
  I go drown for your sak'."

Nex' morning very early,
  'Bout ha'f-pas' two—t'ree—four—
De Captinne, scow, an' de poor Rosie
  Was corpses on de shore;
For de win' she blow lak' hurricane,
  Bimeby she blow some more,
An' de scow bus' up on Lac St. Pierre,
  Wan arpent from de shore.

MORAL

Now, all good wood scow sailor man
  Tak' warning by dat storm,
An' go an' marry some nice French girl
  An' leev on wan beeg farm;

De win' can blow lak' hurricane,
  An' s'pose she blow some more,
You can't get drown on Lac St. Pierre,
  So long you stay on shore.

WILLIAM HENRY DRUMMOND

A NEW SONG

OF NEW SIMILES

My passion is as mustard strong;
  I sit all sober sad;
Drunk as a piper all day long,
  Or like a March-hare mad.

Round as a hoop the bumpers flow;
  I drink, yet can't forget her;
For though as drunk as David's sow
  I love her still the better.

Pert as a pear-monger I'd be,
  If Molly were but kind;
Cool as a cucumber could see
  The rest of womankind.

Like a stuck pig I gaping stare,
　And eye her o'er and o'er;
Lean as a rake, with sighs and care,
　Sleek as a mouse before.

Plump as a partridge was I known,
　And soft as silk my skin;
My cheeks as fat as butter grown,
　But as a goat now thin!

I melancholy as a cat,
　Am kept awake to weep;
But she, insensible of that,
　Sound as a top can sleep.

Hard is her heart as flint or stone,
　She laughs to see me pale;
And merry as a grig is grown,
　And brisk as bottled ale.

The god of Love at her approach
　Is busy as a bee;
Hearts sound as any bell or roach,
　Are smit and sigh like me.

Ah me! as thick as hops or hail
　The fine men crowd about her;
But soon as dead as a door-nail
　Shall I be, if without her.

Straight as my leg her shape appears,
　O were we join'd together!
My heart would be scot-free from cares,
　And lighter than a feather.

As fine as five-pence is her mien,
　No drum was ever tighter;
Her glance is as the razor keen,
　And not the sun is brighter.

As soft as pap her kisses are,
  Methinks I taste them yet;
Brown as a berry is her hair,
  Her eyes as black as jet.

As smooth as glass, as white as curds
  Her pretty hand invites;
Sharp as her needle are her words,
  Her wit like pepper bites.

Brisk as a body-louse she trips,
  Clean as a penny drest;
Sweet as a rose her breath and lips,
  Round as the globe her breast.

Full as an egg was I with glee,
  And happy as a king:
Good Lord! how all men envied me!
  She loved like any thing.

But false as hell, she, like the wind,
  Chang'd, as her sex must do;
Though seeming as the turtle kind,
  And like the gospel true.

If I and Molly could agree,
  Let who would take Peru!
Great as an Emperor should I be,
  And richer than a Jew.

Till you grow tender as a chick,
  I'm dull as any post;
Let us like burs together stick,
  And warm as any toast.

You'll know me truer than a die,
  And wish me better sped;
Flat as a flounder when I lie,
  And as a herring dead.

Sure as a gun she'll drop a tear
    And sigh, perhaps, and wish,
When I am rotten as a pear,
    And mute as any fish.

JOHN GAY

THE SOCIETY UPON THE STANISLAUS

I reside at Table Mountain, and my name is Truthful James;
I am not up to small deceit, or any sinful games;
And I'll tell in simple language what I know about the row
That broke up our society upon the Stanislow.

But first I would remark, that it is not a proper plan
For any scientific man to whale his fellow-man,
And, if a member don't agree with his peculiar whim,
To lay for that same member for to "put a head" on him.

Now, nothing could be finer or more beautiful to see
Than the first six months' proceedings of that same society,
Till Brown of Calaveras brought a lot of fossil bones
That he found within a tunnel near the tenement of Jones.

Then Brown he read a paper, and he reconstructed there,
From those same bones, an animal that was extremely rare;
And Jones then asked the Chair for a suspension of the rules,
Till he could prove that those same bones was one of his lost
    mules.

Then Brown he smiled a bitter smile and said he was at
    fault,
It seemed he had been trepassing on Jones's family vault;
He was a most sarcastic man, this quiet Mr. Brown,
And on several occasions he had cleaned out the town.

Now, I hold it is not decent for a scientific gent
To say another is an ass—at least, to all intent;
Nor should the individual who happens to be meant
Reply by heaving rocks at him to any great extent.

Then Abner Dean of Angel's raised a point of order, when
A chunk of old red sandstone took him in the abdomen,
And he smiled a kind of sickly smile, and curled up on the
    floor,
And the subsequent proceedings interested him no more.

For, in less time than I write it, every member did engage
In a warfare with the remnants of a palaeozoic age;
And the way they heaved those fossils in their anger was a
    sin,
Till the skull of an old mammoth caved the head of Thomp-
    son in.

And this is all I have to say of these improper games
For I live at Table Mountain, and my name is Truthful
    James;
And I've told, in simple language, what I know about the
    row
That broke up our society upon the Stanislow.

FRANCIS BRET HARTE

THE DEACON'S MASTERPIECE;

OR, THE WONDERFUL "ONE-HOSS SHAY"

A Logical Story

Have you heard of the wonderful one-hoss shay,
That was built in such a logical way,
It ran a hundred years to a day,
And then, of a sudden, it—ah, but stay,
I'll tell you what happened without delay,—
Scaring the parson into fits,
Frightening the people out of their wits—
Have you ever heard of that, I say?

Seventeen hundred and fifty-five,
Georgius Secundus was then alive—
Stuffy old drone from the German hive.

That was the year when Lisbon-town
Saw the earth open and gulp her down,
And Braddock's army was done so brown,
Left without a scalp to its crown.
It was on the terrible earthquake-day
That the Deacon finished his one-hoss shay.

Now in building of chaises, I'll tell you what,
There is always *somewhere* a weakest spot—
In hub, tire, or felloe, in spring or thill,
In panel, or crossbar, or floor, or sill,
In screw, bolt, thorough brace—lurking still,
Find it somewhere you must and will—
Above or below, or within or without—
And that's the reason, beyond a doubt,
A chaise *breaks down*, but doesn't *wear out*.

But the Deacon swore (as Deacons do,
With an "I dew vam" or an "I tell *yeou*"),
He would build one shay to beat the taown
'n' the keounty 'n' all the kentry raoun';
It should be so built that it *couldna*' break daown;
—"Fur," said the Deacon, "'t's mighty plain
That the weakes' place mus' stan' the strain;
'n' the way t' fix it, uz I maintain,
      Is only jest
T' make that place uz strong uz the rest."

So the deacon inquired of the village folk
Where he could find the strongest oak,
That couldn't be split nor bent nor broke—
That was for spokes and floor and sills;
He sent for lancewood to make the thills;
The crossbars were ash, from the straightest trees;
The panels of white-wood, that cuts like cheese,
But lasts like iron for things like these;
The hub of logs from the "Settler's ellum"—
Last of its timber—they couldn't sell 'em,

Never an axe had seen their chips,
And the wedges flew from between their lips;
Their blunt ends frizzled like celery-tips;
Step and prop-iron, bolt and screw,
Spring, tire, axle, and linch-pin too,
Steel of the finest, bright and blue;
Thorough-broke bison-skin, thick and wide;
Boot, top, dasher, from tough old hide
Found in the pit when the tanner died.
That was the way he "put her through"—
"There!" said the deacon, "naow she'll dew!"

Do! I tell you, I rather guess
She was a wonder, and nothing less.
Colts grew horses, beards turned gray,
Deacon and deaconess dropped away,
Children and grandchildren—where were they?
But there stood the stout old one-hoss shay
As fresh as on Lisbon earthquake-day!

EIGHTEEN HUNDRED;—it came and found
The deacon's masterpiece strong and sound.
Eighteen hundred increased by ten;—
"Hahnsum kerridge" they called it then.
Eighteen hundred and twenty came;—
Running as usual; much the same.
Thirty and forty at last arrive,
And then came fifty and FIFTY-FIVE.

Little of all we value here
Wakes on the morn of its hundredth year
Without feeling and looking queer.
In fact, there's nothing that keeps its youth,
So far as I know but a tree and truth.
(That is a moral that runs at large;
Take it—you're welcome.—No extra charge.)

FIRST OF NOVEMBER—The Earthquake-day—
There are traces of age in the one-hoss shay,
A general flavour of mild decay,
But nothing local, as one may say.
There couldn't be—for the deacon's art
Had made it so like in every part
That there wasn't a chance for one to start.
For the wheels were just as strong as the thills,
And the floor was just as strong as the sills,
And the panels just as strong as the floor,
And the whippletree neither less nor more,
And the back-crossbar as strong as the fore,
And spring and axle and hub *encore*.
And yet, *as a whole* it is past a doubt
In another hour it will be *worn out!*

First of November, 'Fifty-five!
This morning the parson takes a drive.
Now, small boys, get out of the way!
Here comes the wonderful one-hoss shay,
Drawn by a rat-tailed, ewe-necked bay,
"Huddup!" said the parson.—Off went they.

The parson was working his Sunday's text—
Had got to *fifthly*, and stopped perplexed
At what the—Moses—was coming next.
All at once the horse stood still,
Close by the meet'n'-house on the hill.

—First a shiver, and then a thrill,
Then something decidedly like a spill—
And the parson was sitting upon a rock
At half-past nine by the meet'n'-house clock—
Just the hour of the earthquake shock!
—What do you think the parson found,
When he got up and stared around?
The poor old chaise in a heap or mound,
As if it had been to the mill and ground!

You see, of course, if you're not a dunce,
How it went to pieces all at once,—
All at once and nothing first—
Just as bubbles do when they burst.

End of the wonderful one-hoss shay.
Logic is logic. That's all I say.

OLIVER WENDELL HOLMES

THAIS

One time, in Alexandria, in wicked Alexandria,
Where nights were wild with revelry and life was but a game,
There lived, so the report is, an adventuress and courtesan,
The pride of Alexandria, and Thais was her name.

Nearby, in peace and piety, avoiding all society,
There dwelt a band of holy men who'd built a refuge there;
And in the desert's solitude they spurned all earthly folly to
Devote their days to holy works, to fasting and to prayer.

Now one monk whom I solely mention of this group of holy
    men
Was known as Athanael; he was famous near and far.
At fasting bouts or prayer with him no other could compare
    with him;
At ground and lofty praying he could do the course in par.

One night while sleeping heavily (from fighting with the
    devil he
Had gone to bed exhausted while the sun was shining still),
He had a vision Freudian, and though he was annoyed he an-
Alyzed it in the well-known style of Doctors Jung and Brill.

He dreamed of Alexandria, of wicked Alexandria;
A crowd of men were cheering in a manner rather rude
At Thais, who was dancing there, and Athanael, glancing
    there,
Observed her do the shimmy in what artists call The Nude.

Said he, "This dream fantastical disturbs my thoughts
  monastical;
Some unsuppressed desire, I fear, has found my monkish cell.
I blushed up to the hat o' me to view that girl's anatomy,
I'll go to Alexandria and save her soul from Hell."

So pausing not to wonder where he'd put his summer under-
  wear,
He quickly packed his evening clothes, his tooth brush and a
  vest.
To guard against exposure he threw in some woollen hosiery,
And bidding all the boys good-by, he started on his quest.

The monk, though warned and fortified, was deeply shocked
  and mortified
To find, on his arrival, wild debauchery in sway.
While some lay in a stupor sent by booze of more than two
  per cent.,
The others were behaving in a most immoral way.

Said he to Thais, "Pardon me. Although this job is hard on
  me,
I gotta put you wise to what I come down here to tell.
What's all this sousin' gettin' you? Cut out this pie-eyed
  retinue;
Let's hit the trail together, kid, and save yourself from
  Hell."

Although this bold admonishment caused Thais some
  astonishment,
She coyly answered, "Say, you said a heaping mouthful, bo.
This burg's a frost, I'm telling you. The brand of hooch
  they're selling you
Ain't like the stuff we used to get, so let's pack up and go."

So forth from Alexandria, from wicked Alexandria,
Across the desert sands they go beneath the blazing sun;
Till Thais, parched and sweltering, finds refuge in the
  sheltering
Seclusion of a convent, and the habit of a nun.

But now the monk is terrified to find his fears are verified;
His holy vows of chastity have cracked beneath the strain.
Like one who has a jag on he cries in grief and agony,
"I'd sell my soul to see her do the shimmy once again."

Alas! his pleadings clamorous, though passionate and
    amorous,
Have come too late; the courtesan has danced her final
    dance.
The monk says, "That's a joke on me, for that there dame
    to croak on me.
I hadn't oughter passed her up the time I had the chance."

NEWMAN LEVY

TRISTAN AND ISOLDA

Isolda was an Irish queen who always spoke in German,
Though why she canned her native tongue I never could
    determine.
King Mark had heard about her charms from people who
    had met her,
And so he sent Sir Tristan out to Ireland for to get her.
Isolda she was loath to go, she did not want to marry,
And all the way to England's shore she warbled like Old
    Harry.
"To travel with that tenor for a girl like me ain't no life,
I'll mix myself a dose of hooch and give some to that lowlife."
Isolda's maid Brangaena didn't phone the undertaker,
Instead she slipped a love draught in Isolda's cocktail
    shaker.
It makes me blush to write about the powers of that potion.
The way those two folks carried on you haven't any notion.
Now poor King Mark was simple; no suspicion did he harbor
That every night his wife and Tris were mushing in the arbor.
Until by chance he came upon them, to their consternation,
In what the papers call a "compromising situation."
Now most kings you or I know would have acted kinda sour.
Not Mark. He struck an attitude and sang for half an hour,

Till Melot, glancing at his watch, observed that time **was** fleeting,
And stabbing Tristan in the ribs he busted up the meeting.
The scene now shifts to Kareol where the Tristans had a castle,
Our hero lies beneath a tree with Kurneval, his vassal.
The castle's rather shy of roof, the wall's about to tumble,
But Tristan says it's home to him, it matters not how humble.
A shepherd, piping on the hill, exclaims, "A ship I've sighted."
Isolda then comes dashing in and Tristan's quite delighted.
The sound of clashing swords is heard; the (so-called) plot now thickens,
And Mark appears upon the scene still singing like the dickens.
But Tris, alas, has passed away from wounds that Melot gave him.
Isolda sings the Liebestod; she came too late to save him.
She lies down—dead. The play is done; the curtain bell is ringing,
Thus ends this sad and tragic tale. And Mark? He keeps on singing.

NEWMAN LEVY

RHYME OF THE RAIL

Singing through the forests,
    Rattling over ridges,
Shooting under arches,
    Rumbling over bridges,
Whizzing through the mountains,
    Buzzing o'er the vale—
Bless me! this is pleasant,
    Riding on the Rail!

Men of different "stations"
    In the eye of Fame
Here are very quickly
    Coming to the same.

High and lowly people,
  Birds of every feather,
On a common level
  Travelling together.

Gentleman in shorts,
  Looming very tall;
Gentleman at large,
  Talking very small;
Gentleman in tights,
  With a loose-ish mien;
Gentleman in grey,
  Looking rather green;

Gentleman quite old,
  Asking for the news;
Gentleman in black,
  In a fit of blues;
Gentleman in claret,
  Sober as a vicar;
Gentleman in tweed,
  Dreadfully in liquor!

Stranger on the right,
  Looking very sunny,
Obviously reading
  Something very funny.
Now the smiles are thicker,
  Wonder what they mean?
Faith, he's got the KNICKER-
BOCKER Magazine!

Stranger on the left,
  Closing up his peepers;
Now he snores again,
  Like the Seven Sleepers;
At his feet a volume
  Gives the explanation,
How the man grew stupid
  From "Association."

Ancient maiden lady
  Anxiously remarks,
That there must be peril
  'Mong so many sparks;
Roguish-looking fellow,
  Turning to the stranger,
Says it's his opinion
  She is out of danger!

Woman with her baby,
  Sitting *vis-à-vis*,
Baby keeps a-squalling,
  Woman looks at me;
Asks about the distance,
  Says it's tiresome talking,
Noises of the cars
  Are so very shocking!

Market-woman, careful
  Of the precious casket,
Knowing eggs are eggs,
  Tightly holds her basket:
Feeling that a smash,
  If it came, would surely
Send her eggs to pot
  Rather prematurely.

Singing through the forests,
  Rattling over ridges,
Shooting under arches,
  Rumbling over bridges,
Whizzing through the mountains,
  Buzzing o'er the vale;
Bless me! this is pleasant,
  Riding on the Rail!

JOHN G. SAXE

"HAEC OLIM MEMINISSE IUVABIT"

I

Oh, back in the fall of nineteen-two, when I was a freshman
green,
I planned to be one of the cultured few, with a high and
beetling bean.
 So I took on Latin, and German IV,
 French, History V (to the civil war),
 Trig, Algebra I, a ghastly bore
  —and freshman chemistree.
Here, then, are the facts I still retain from nineteen-two
and three:
*We[1] won the "bloody Monday" fight, and made the sophs
retire[2],*
*Dear Lehigh licked the football team[3] by a score that was
something dire;*
 Bill[4] came on from Chicago U.
 With some bar-room stories—and good ones, too[5];
*I got on the glee club, and made Psi U, and sang in the chapel
choir.*

II

As a sophomore, I am proud to state, I was taking the
hurdles clear,
I dreamed of copping the old Phi Bete by the end of my
Junior year.
 I soaked up Logic, and Physics III,
 French Lit. (I was there with the loud *oui oui*),
 Psychology, Shakespeare, Verse—not free—and a couple
  of courses more.
Here's what I recall as I look back on nineteen-three and
four:
*Weary chairmaned the Junior prom (his girl was Harriet
White)[6],*
*I played third quarter on the football scrub, while Loup played
centre and right,*

Joe Bauderman ran a record mile,
The baseball team was perfectly vile[7]*,*
I made the track team after awhile, and fussed[8] *each Saturday*
night.

III

By Junior year I had laid away those hopes of a Phi Bete key,
But I toyed with the thought of a proud M. A., and a
possible Ph. D.;
    So I grabbed off Plato and Kant, and such,
    Church History, Banking (the worldly touch!),
    The German bards—whom we termed "them Dutch"
    —such French as I might contrive;
And the following info. still adheres from nineteen-four and
five.
Tom Reilley's[9] *team smeared R.P.I. to the tune of a large*
amount[10]*:*
I made the gym and the track teams both[11]*; they ducked Young*
Blum[12] *in the fount;*
    The glee club trip was a Lakewood treat,
    The base ball team got badly beat[13]*,*
And I got a third at the Wesleyan meet[14]*—but third place*
didn't count.

IV

A Senior now, I was bald and grey with the studious life
I'd led,
But proud of the knowledge stowed away in my small
but well-formed head.
    I killed International (so called) Law,
    Took Spanish and Chaucer (the latter's raw),
    Wound up with a thesis on Bernard Shaw
    —how much of that stuff still sticks?
Well, here is the dope I recollect from nineteen-five and six:
Bill and I wrote the senior show (his book was a mere detail)

And Loup played "Elsie, the Cannibal Queen,"—and looked
like a half-dressed whale;
  The Senior ball was a dream divine[15],
  The Senior banquet was mostly wine,
And F. P. A. ran a piece of mine[16] in the New York Evening
Mail.

DEEMS TAYLOR

[1] That is, the class of 1906.
[2] Weary won't like this, but it's true.
[3] 46-0, if you must know.
[4] William LeBaron, the talented author of "I Love You"—adv.
[5] And a wonderful song, "Kansas."
[6] And maybe he wasn't stuck on her.
[7] As usual.
[8] Some girl, too. She married shortly after that.
[9] Major T. T. Reilley, D. S. C.
[10] 53—0, no less.
[11] I was pretty good, too, but badly handled. I know I could have done the low hurdles in 26 if Mike Cann had only understood me. Stimmie Draper (Arthur S. Draper, London correspondent of the New York Tribune) did the pole vault that year. He was rotten.
[12] I'm not sure of the name. He was going to sue the college, or something, but didn't.
[13] See note 7.
[14] The track up there is so narrow that only three of us could run.
[15] I took Adele Martin, a queen. She married Bill Wildman almost immediately afterward.
[16] It wasn't very good.

DARIUS GREEN AND HIS FLYING-MACHINE

If ever there lived a Yankee lad,
Wise or otherwise, good or bad,
Who, seeing the birds fly, didn't jump
With flapping arms from stake or stump,
      Or, spreading the tail
      Of his coat for a sail,
Take a soaring leap from post or rail,
      And wonder why
      He couldn't fly,

And flap and flutter and wish and try—
If ever you knew a country dunce
Who didn't try that as often as once,
All I can say is, that's a sign
He never would do for a hero of mine.

An aspiring genius was D. Green:
The son of a farmer, age fourteen;
His body was long and lank and lean—
Just right for flying, as will be seen;
He had two eyes as bright as a bean,
And a freckled nose that grew between,
A little awry—for I must mention
That he had riveted his attention
Upon his wonderful invention,
Twisting his tongue as he twisted the strings,
And working his face as he worked the wings,
And with every turn of gimlet and screw
Turning and screwing his mouth round too,
      Till his nose seemed bent
      To catch the scent,
Around some corner, of new-baked pies,
And his wrinkled cheeks and his squinting eyes
Grew puckered into a queer grimace,
That made him look very droll in the face,
      And also very wise.
And wise he must have been, to do more
Than ever a genius did before,
Excepting Daedalus of yore
And his son Icarus, who wore
      Upon their backs
      Those wings of wax
He had read of in the old almanacs.
Darius was clearly of the opinion
That the air is also man's dominion,
And that, with paddle or fin or pinion,
      We soon or late shall navigate
The azure as now we sail the sea.

The thing looks simple enough to me;
    And if you doubt it,
Hear how Darius reasoned about it.
      "The birds can fly an' why can't I?
      Must we give in," says he with a grin,
      "That the bluebird an' phoebe
      Are smarter'n we be?
Jest fold our hands an' see the swaller
An' blackbird an' catbird beat us holler?
Doos the little chatterin', sassy wren,
No bigger'n my thumb, know more than men?
      Just show me that!
      Ur prove 't the bat
Hez got more brains than's in my hat.
An' I'll back down, an' not till then!"
He argued further: "Nur I can't see
What's th' use o' wings to a bumble-bee,
Fur to git a livin' with, more'n to me;—
      Ain't my business
      Important's his'n is?
      That Icarus
      Made a perty muss—
Him an' his daddy Daedalus
They might 'a' knowed wings made o' wax
Wouldn't stand sun-heat an' hard whacks.
      I'll make mine o' luther,
      Ur suthin' ur other."

And he said to himself, as he tinkered and planned:
"But I ain't goin' to show my hand
To mummies that never can understand
The fust idee that's big an' grand."
So he kept his secret from all the rest,
Safely buttoned within his vest;
And in the loft above the shed
Himself he locks, with thimble and thread
And wax and hammer and buckles and screws

And all such things as geniuses use;—
Two bats for patterns, curious fellows!
A charcoal-pot and a pair of bellows;
Some wire, and several old umbrellas;
A carriage-cover, for tail and wings;
A piece of harness; and straps and strings;
      And a big strong box,
      In which he locks
These and a hundred other things.
His grinning brothers, Reuben and Burke
And Nathan and Jotham and Solomon, lurk
Around the corner to see him work—
Sitting cross-legged, like a Turk,
Drawing the waxed-end through with a jerk,
And boring the holes with a comical quirk
Of his wise old head, and a knowing smirk.
But vainly they mounted each other's backs,
And poked through knot-holes and pried through cracks;
With wood from the pile and straw from the stacks
He plugged the knot-holes and caulked the cracks;
And a dipper of water, which one would think
He had brought up into the loft to drink
      When he chanced to be dry,
      Stood always nigh,
      For Darius was sly!
And whenever at work he happened to spy
At chink or crevice a blinking eye,
He let the dipper of water fly.
"Take that! an' ef ever ye git a peep,
Guess ye'll ketch a weasel asleep!"
      And he sings as he locks
      His big strong box:—
   "The weasel's head is small an' trim,
    An' he is little an' long an' slim,
    An' quick of motion an' nimble of limb
      An' ef you'll be
      Advised by me,
  Keep wide awake when ye're ketchin' him!"

So day after day
He stitched and tinkered and hammered away,
    Till at last 'twas done—
The greatest invention under the sun!
"An' now," says Darius, "hooray fur some fun!"
    'Twas the Fourth of July,
    And the weather was dry,
And not a cloud was on all the sky,
Save a few light fleeces, which here and there,
    Half mist, half air,
Like foam on the ocean went floating by—
Just as lovely a morning as ever was seen
For a nice little trip in a flying-machine.
Thought cunning Darius: "Now I shan't go
Along 'ith the fellers to see the show.
I'll say I've got sich a terrible cough!
An' then, when the folks 'ave all gone off,
I'll hev full swing fur to try the thing,
An' practise a little on the wing."
"Ain't goin' to see the celebration?"
Says brother Nate. "No; botheration!
I've got sich a cold—a toothache—I—
My gracious!—feel's though I should fly!"
    Said Jotham, "Sho!
    Guess ye better go."
    But Darius said, "No!
Shouldn't wonder 'f you might see me, though,
'Long 'bout noon, ef I git red
O' this jumpin', thumpin' pain 'n my head."
For all the while to himself he said:—

    "I tell ye what!
I'll fly a few times around the lot,
To see how 't seems, then soon's I've got
The hang o' the thing, ez likely's not,
    I'll astonish the nation,
    An' all creation,
By flyin' over the celebration!
Over their heads I'll sail like an eagle;

I'll balance myself on my wings like a sea-gull:
I'll dance on the chimbleys; I'll stand on the steeple;
I'll flop up to winders an' scare the people!
I'll light on the liberty-pole, an' crow;
An' I'll say to the gawpin' fools below.
   'What world's this 'ere
    That I've come near?'
Fur I'll make 'em b'lieve I'm a chap f'm the moon;
An' I'll try to race 'ith their ol' balloon!"
   He crept from his bed;
And, seeing the others were gone, he said,
"I'm gittin' over the cold 'n my head."
   And away he sped,
To open the wonderful box in the shed.

His brothers had walked but a little way,
When Jotham to Nathan chanced to say,
"What is the feller up to, hey!"
"Don'o'—the 's suthin' ur other to pay,
Ur he wouldn't 'a' stayed tu hum to-day."
Says Burke, "His toothache's all 'n his eye!
He never 'd missed a Fo'th-o'-July,
Ef he hedn't got some machine to try."
Then Sol, the little one, spoke: "By darn!
Le's hurry back an' hide 'n the barn,
An' pay him fur tellin' us that yarn!"
"Agreed!" Through the orchard they creep back
Along by the fences, behind the stack,
And one by one, through a hole in the wall,
In under the dusty barn they crawl,
Dressed in their Sunday garments all;
And a very astonishing sight was that,
When each in his cobwebbed coat and hat
Came up through the floor like an ancient rat
   And there they hid;
   And Reuben slid
The fastenings back, and the door undid.
   "Keep dark!" said he,
"While I squint an' see what the' is to see."

As knights of old put on their mail—
     From head to foot an iron suit
Iron jacket and iron boot,
Iron breeches, and on the head
No hat, but an iron pot instead,
     And under the chin the bail,
(I believe they called the thing a helm.)
Then sallied forth to overwhelm
The dragons and pagans that plagued the earth
     So this *modern* knight
     Prepared for flight,
Put on his wings and strapped them tight
Jointed and jaunty, strong and light—
Buckled them fast to shoulder and hip;
Ten feet they measured from tip to tip
And a helm had he, but that he wore,
Not on his head, like those of yore,
     But more like the helm of a ship.

     "Hush!" Reuben said,
     "He's up in the shed!
He's opened the winder—I see his head!
He stretches it out, an' pokes it about,
Lookin' to see 'f the coast is clear,
     An' nobody near;—
Guess he don' o' who's hid in here!
He's riggin' a spring-board over the sill!
Stop laffin', Solomon! Burke, keep still!
He's a climbin' out now—Of all the things!
What's he got on? I vum, it's wings!
An' that 'tother thing? I vum, it's a tail!
An' there he sits like a hawk on a rail!
Steppin' careful, he travels the length
Of his spring-board, and teeters to try its strength.
Now he stretches his wings, like a monstrous bat;
Peeks over his shoulder; this way an' that,
Fur to see 'f the' 's any one passin' by;

But the' 's on'y a caf an' goslin nigh.
They turn up at him a wonderin' eye,
To see— The dragon! he's goin' to fly!
Away he goes! Jimminy! what a jump!
       Flop—flop—an' plump
        To the ground with a thump!
Flutt'rin' an' flound'rin' all 'n a lump!"

As a demon is hurled by an angel's spear,
Heels over head, to his proper sphere—
Heels over head, and head over heels,
Dizzily down the abyss he wheels—
So fell Darius. Upon his crown,
In the midst of the barn-yard, he came down,
In a wonderful whirl of tangled strings,
Broken braces and broken springs,
Broken tail and broken wings,
Shooting-stars, and various things;
Barn-yard litter of straw and chaff,
And much that wasn't so sweet by half.
Away with a bellow fled the calf,
And what was that? Did the gosling laugh?
'Tis a merry roar from the old barn-door.
And he hears the voice of Jotham crying,
"Say, D'rius! how do you like flyin'?"
Slowly, ruefully, where he lay,
Darius just turned and looked that way,
As he stanched his sorrowful nose with his cuff.
"Wal, I like flyin' well enough,"
He said; "but the' ain't such a thunderin' sight
O' fun in 't when ye come to light."

I just have room for the MORAL here:
And this is the moral—Stick to your sphere.
Or if you insist, as you have the right,
On spreading your wings for a loftier flight,
The moral is—Take care how you light.
           JOHN TOWNSEND TROWBRIDGE

AN INTERMEZZO FOR THE FOURTH ACT

If my peculiar pulchritude in Paris seemed to please,
Upon the Champs Elysees 'mongst the blooming chestnut
trees,
Or if along the Rivoli in hell's mélange of men
Which bubbled in the war brew, you observed me now and
then;
Or if the picture rising, of my roly-poly form,
A-toddle down the boulevards should make your heart
grow warm—
O Phyllis, wipe that picture from your memory cold and
flat—
You should see me in my new straw hat!

For I'm in London now, my dear, in London old and gray;
And spring is fading in the past, and summer's under way.
But London is a decent town, polite and snug and curt;
It breaks her heart to frivol and one breaks her laws to flirt!
And how she works and how she frets, and yet she's always
sweet;
So I am here in London for to give the town a treat.
And if I'm middle aged and bald and slow and rather fat—
You should see me in my new straw hat!

Perhaps we're not immortal, lass, but O I wish we were;
Though not to save some prudish saint or pale philosopher,
I want to find those lads whom life's sweet, poignant beauty
wracked,
Who had to duck and cut the show, before the second act—
Say Schubert, Keats, or Phidias, those olden, golden boys—
And tell them something of the play, and how it never cloys.
For I have seen three acts, and now I'm fifty—but, at that,
You should see me in my new straw hat!

WILLIAM ALLEN WHITE

TO WILLIAM ALLEN WHITE

If you're in London, Will'um, then I take it you're en route,
And perhaps you'll stop and see me in my new sports suit.
The skirt is satin fan-ta-sie, the coat is silk (Chinese),
The whole is most unusual—and you know we aim to please.
I've missed you something fearful while you've been in
    foreign parts,
Where you've chaperoned the Wilsons and demolished
    Paris hearts.
You've mingled with the rich and great, you've learned to
    parlez-vous,
I suppose you're even chummy with this here, now, Clem-
    ensue.
You'll probably attempt to pull an airy, snappy "ma
    cherie,"
Forgetting that I know your awful taste in haberdashery.
I've seen your Palm Beach suit, and, Bill, I want to tell you
    that
I never want to see you in your new straw hat.

EDNA FERBER

SKIPPER IRESON'S RIDE

Of all the rides since the birth of time,
Told in story or sung in rhyme,—
On Apuleius's Golden Ass,
Or one-eyed Calendar's horse of brass,
Witch astride of a human back,
Islam's prophet on Al-Borak,—
The strangest ride that ever was sped
Was Ireson's, out from Marblehead!
Old Floyd Ireson, for his hard heart,
    Tarred and feathered and carried in a cart
        By the women of Marblehead!

Body of turkey, head of owl,
Wings a-droop like a rained-on fowl,
Feathered and ruffled in every part,

Skipper Ireson stood in the cart.
Scores of women, old and young,
Strong of muscle, and glib of tongue,
Pushed and pulled up the rocky lane,
Shouting and singing the shrill refrain:
　　"Here's Flud Oirson, fur his horrd horrt,
　　Torr'd an' futherr'd an' corr'd in a corrt
　　　By the women o' Morble'ead!"

Wrinkled scolds with hands on hips,
Girls in bloom of cheek and lips,
Wild-eyed, free-limbed, such as chase
Bacchus round some antique vase,
Brief of skirt, with ankles bare,
Loose of kerchief and loose of hair,
With conch-shells blowing and fish-horns' twang,
Over and over the Maenads sang:
　　"Here's Flud Oirson, fur his horrd horrt,
　　Torr'd an' futherr'd an' corr'd in a corrt
　　　By the women o' Morble'ead!"

Small pity for him!—He sailed away
From a leaking ship, in Chaleur Bay,—
Sailed away from a sinking wreck,
With his own town's-people on her deck!
"Lay by! lay by!" they called to him.
Back he answered, "Sink or swim!
Brag of your catch of fish again!"
And off he sailed through the fog and rain!
　　Old Floyd Ireson, for his hard heart,
　　Tarred and feathered and carried in a cart
　　　By the women of Marblehead!

Fathoms deep in dark Chaleur
That wreck shall lie forevermore.
Mother and sister, wife and maid,
Looked from the rocks of Marblehead

Over the moaning and rainy sea,—
Looked for the coming that might not be!
What did the winds and the sea-birds say
Of the cruel captain who sailed away?—
   Old Floyd Ireson, for his hard heart,
    Tarred and feathered and carried in a cart
     By the women of Marblehead!

Through the street, on either side,
Up flew windows, doors swung wide;
Sharp-tongued spinsters, old wives gray,
Treble lent the fish-horn's bray.
Sea-worn grandsires, cripple-bound,
Hulks of old sailors run aground,
Shook head, and fist, and hat, and cane,
And cracked with curses the hoarse refrain:
   "Here's Flud Oirson, fur his horrd horrt,
    Torr'd an' futherr'd an' corr'd in a corrt
     By the women o' Morble'ead!"

Sweetly along the Salem road
Bloom of orchard and lilac showed.
Little the wicked skipper knew
Of the fields so green and the sky so blue.
Riding there in his sorry trim,
Like an Indian idol glum and grim,
Scarcely he seemed the sound to hear
Of voices shouting, far and near:
   "Here's Flud Oirson, fur his horrd horrt,
    Torr'd an' futherr'd an' corr'd in a corrt
     By the women o' Morble'ead!"

"Hear me, neighbors!" at last he cried,—
"What to me is this noisy ride?
What is the shame that clothes the skin
To the nameless horror that lives within?
Waking or sleeping, I see a wreck,
And hear a cry from a reeling deck!

Hate me and curse me,—I only dread
The hand of God and the face of the dead!"
  Said old Floyd Ireson, for his hard heart,
  Tarred and feathered and carried in a cart
    By the women of Marblehead!

Then the wife of the skipper lost at sea
Said, "God has touched him! Why should we?"
Said an old wife, mourning her only son:
"Cut the rogue's tether and let him run!"
So with soft relentings and rude excuse,
Half scorn, half pity, they cut him loose,
And gave him a cloak to hide him in,
And left him alone with his shame and sin.
  Poor Floyd Ireson, for his hard heart,
  Tarred and feathered and carried in a cart
    By the women of Marblehead!
                    JOHN GREENLEAF WHITTIER

Sport

BASEBALL'S SAD LEXICON

These are the saddest of possible words:
  "Tinker to Evers to Chance."
Trio of bear cubs, and fleeter than birds,
  Tinker and Evers and Chance.
Ruthlessly pricking our gonfalon bubble,
Making a Giant hit into a double—
Words that are heavy with nothing but trouble:
"Tinker to Evers to Chance."

FRANKLIN P. ADAMS

COLLEGE SONG

When the Tigers claw the Bulldogs
  Into tiny little chunks
And the Leopards smite the Bearcats
  And the foxes maul the Skunks,
Then it's sure the Fighting Irish
  Would sooner die than fail,
And it's good-night City College
  And hurrah for Eli Yale!

CHORUS

So we'll drink a toast to Harvard,
  And her home at old Nassau
Where the Army greets the Navy
  With a loud and long hee-haw!
Where the Army greets the Navy
  With a loud and long hee-haw-w-w-w-w!

It's the good old fight that conquers
  As the pitcher on the mound
Intercepts a pass and gallops
  Like a racehorse o'er the ground.

So to hell with Minnesota!—
   And a cheer for good old Penn,
For it takes the Texas Aggies
   To produce real fighting men!

ED ANTHONY

AT THE BALL GAME

What gods or heroes, whose brave deeds none can dispute,
Will you record, O Clio, on the harp and flute?
What lofty names shall sportive Echo grant a place
On Pindus' crown or Helicon's cool, shadowy space?

Sing not, my Orpheus, sweeping oft the tuneful strings,
Of gliding streams and nimble winds and such poor things;
But lend your measures to a theme of noble thought,
And crown with laurel these great heroes, as you ought.

Now steps·Ryanus forth at call of furious Mars,
And from his oaken staff the sphere speeds to the stars;
And now he gains the tertiary goal, and turns,
While whiskered balls play round the timid staff of Burns.

Lo! from the tribunes on the bleachers comes a shout,
Beseeching bold Ansonius to line 'em out;
And as Apollo's flying chariot cleaves the sky,
So stanch Ansonius lifts the frightened ball on high.

Like roar of ocean beating on the Cretan cliff,
The strong Komiske gives the panting sphere a biff;
And from the tribunes rise loud murmurs everywhere,
When twice and thrice Mikellius beats the mocking air.

And as Achilles' fleet the Trojan waters sweeps,
So horror sways the throng,—Pfefferius sleeps!
And stalwart Konnor, though by Mercury inspired,
The Equus Carolus defies, and is retired.

So waxes fierce the strife between these godlike men;
And as the hero's fame grows by Virgilian pen,
So let Clarksonius Maximus be raised to heights
As far above the moon as moon o'er lesser lights.

But as for me, the ivy leaf is my reward,
If you a place among the lyric bards accord;
With crest exalted, and O "People," with delight,
I'll proudly strike the stars, and so be out of sight.

ROSWELL MARTIN FIELD

ADVICE FROM AN EXPERT

(Or William Tatum Tilden 2nd's lecture to Little
Ones revised in the style of Q. H. Flaccus, deceased)

Eat but simple food; go for early rising;
Follow out my plan, daily exercising;
Then your tennis game you will find surprising;
      So, too, will others!

Drink but water pure, not the wine that glitters;
Whiskey let alone, for it brings the jitters;
Sip not even one little glass of bitters;
      Shun it, my brothers!

Thus I reached the top, and thus you should follow;
If, across the net, you would beat all hollow
Playboys of the court. Though they call you Rollo,
      Stick to it cheerly.

Then upon the court, with some crafty blending,
Power, skill and speed you will have for spending.
When the wastrels sag, for a happy ending,
      Ace them severely!

Once we were beset, with the French besetting;
Threats from Anzacs, too, we were always getting;
On my upright life did they base the betting
      I would outlast 'em.

Primed with ozone pure (and with speed a trifle);
Strong with simple food (and a service rifle);
Fresh from calm, sweet sleep (what a tennis eyeful!);
  Say, did I blast 'em!

Place me in a land where it may be snowing,
Or 'neath tropic skies, with the warm winds blowing,
Bring your young net star. When the game gets going,
  I'll dust his jacket.

Thank the simple life (and a service stinging)
That at forty-odd, with the loud cheers ringing,
I—King William still—on the court am swinging,
  Boy, what a racquet!

JOHN KIERAN

THE FAMOUS BALLAD OF THE JUBILEE CUP

You may lift me up in your arms, lad, and turn my face to
  the sun,
For a last look back at the dear old track where the Jubilee
  cup was won;
And draw your chair to my side, lad—no, thank ye, I feel
  no pain—
For I'm going out with the tide, lad; but I'll tell you the
  tale again.

I'm seventy-nine or nearly, and my head it has long turned
  gray,
But it all comes back as clearly as though it was yesterday—
The dust, and the bookies shouting around the clerk of the
  scales,
And the clerk of the course, and the nobs in force, and 'Is
  'Ighness the Pr**ce of W*les.

'T was a nine-hole thresh to wind'ard (but none of us cared
  for that),

With a straight run home to the service tee, and a finish
along the flat,
"Stiff?" ah, well you may say it! Spot barred, and at five
stone ten!
But at two and a bisque I'd ha' run the risk; for I was a
greenhorn then.

So we stripped to the B. Race signal, the old red swallow-
tail—
There was young Ben Bolt and the Portland Colt, and
Aston Villa, and Yale;
And W. G., and Steinitz, Leander and The Saint,
And the G*rm*n Emp*r*r's Meteor, a-looking as fresh as
paint;

John Roberts (scratch), and Safety Match, The Lascar,
and Lorna Doone,
Oom Paul (a bye), and Romany Rye, and me upon Wooden
Spoon;
And some of us cut for partners, and some of us strung for
baulk,
And some of us tossed for stations—But there, what use to
talk?

Three-quarter-back on the Kingsclere crack was station
enough for me,
With a fresh jackyarder blowing and the Vicarage goal
a-lee!
And I leaned and patted her centre-bit and eased the quid
in her cheek,
With a "Soh my lass!" and a "Woa you brute!"—for
she could do all but speak.

She was geared a thought too high perhaps; she was trained
a trifle fine;
But she had the grand reach forward! I never saw such a
line!

Smooth-bored, clean run, from her fiddle head with its
  dainty ear half-cock,
Hard-bit, *pur sang*, from her overhang to the heel of her off
  hind sock.

Sir Robert he walked beside me as I worked her down to the
  mark;
"There's money on this, my lad," said he, "and most of
  'em 's running dark;
But ease the sheet if you're bunkered, and pack the scrum-
  mages tight,
And use your slide at the distance, and we'll drink to your
  health to-night!"

But I bent and tightened my stretcher. Said I to myself,
  said I—
"John Jones, this here is the Jubilee Cup, and you have
  to do or die."
And the words were n't hardly spoken when the umpire
  shouted "Play!"
And we all kicked off from the Gasworks End with a
  "Yoicks!" and a "Gone Away!"

And at first I thought of nothing, as the clay flew by in
  lumps,
But stuck to the old Ruy Lopez, and wondered who'd call
  for trumps,
And luffed her close to the cushion, and watched each one
  as it broke,
And in triple file up the Rowley Mile we went like a trail of
  smoke.

The Lascar made the running but he didn't amount to much,
For old Oom Paul was quick on the ball, and headed it
  back to touch;
And the whole first flight led off with the right as The Saint
  took up the pace,
And drove it clean to the putting green and trumped it
  there with an ace.

John Roberts had given a miss in baulk, but Villa cleared
 with a punt;
And keeping her service hard and low the Meteor forged to
 the front;
With Romany Rye to windward at dormy and two to play,
And Yale close up—but a Jubilee Cup isn't run for every
 day.

We laid our course for the Warner—I tell you the pace was
 hot!
And again off Tattenham Corner a blanket covered the lot.
Check side! Check side! now steer her wide! and barely an
 inch of room,
With The Lascar's tail over our lee rail and brushing
 Leander's boom.

We were running as strong as ever—eight knots—but it
 couldn't last;
For the spray and the bails were flying, the whole field
 tailing fast;
And the Portland Colt had shot his bolt, and Yale was
 bumped at the Doves,
And The Lascar resigned to Steinitz, stalemated in fifteen
 moves.

It was bellows to mend with Roberts—starred three for a
 penalty kick:
But he chalked his cue and gave 'em the butt, and Oom
 Paul marked the trick—
"Offside—No Ball—and at fourteen all! Mark Cock! and
 two for his nob!"
When W. G. ran clean through his lee and beat him twice
 with a lob.

He yorked him twice on a crumbling pitch and wiped his
 eye with a brace,
But his guy-rope split with the strain of it and he dropped
 back out of the race;

And I drew a bead on the Meteor's lead, and challenging
    none too soon,
Bent over and patted her garboard strake, and called upon
    Wooden Spoon.

She was all of a shiver forward, the spoondrift thick on her
    flanks,
But I'd brought her an easy gambit, and nursed her over the
    banks;
She answered her helm—the darling! and woke up now with
    a rush,
While the Meteor's jock, he sat like a rock—he knew we
    rode for his brush!

There was no one else left in it. The Saint was using his whip,
And Safety Match, with a lofting catch, was pocketed deep
    at slip;
And young Ben Bolt with his niblick took miss at Leander's
    lunge,
But topped the net with the ricochet, and Steinitz threw up
    the sponge.

But none of the lot could stop the rot—nay, don't ask *me*
    to stop!
The Villa had called for lemons, Oom Paul had taken his
    drop,
And both were kicking the referee. Poor fellow! he done his
    best;
But, being in doubt, he'd ruled them out—which he always
    did when pressed.

So, inch by inch, I tightened the winch, and chucked the
    sandbags out—
I heard the nursery cannons pop, I heard the bookies shout:
"The Meteor wins!" "No, Wooden Spoon!" "Check!"
    "Vantage!" "Leg Before!"
"Last Lap!" "Pass Nap!" At his saddle-flap I put up the
    helm and wore.

You may overlap at the saddle-flap, and yet be loo'd on the
    tape:
And it all depends upon changing ends, how a seven-year-old
    will shape;
It was tack and tack to the Lepe and back—a fair ding-dong
    to the Ridge,
And he led by his forward canvas yet as we shot 'neath
    Hammersmith Bridge.

He led by his forward canvas—he led from his strongest
    suit—
But along we went on a roaring scent, and at Fawley I
    gained a foot.
He fisted off with his jigger, and gave me his wash—too
    late!
Deuce—Vantage—Check! By neck and neck we rounded
    into the straight.

I could hear the "Conquering 'Ero" a-crashing on Godfrey's
    band,
And my hopes fell sudden to zero, just there, with the race
    in hand—
In sight of the Turf's Blue Ribbon, in sight of the umpire's
    tape,
As I felt the tack of her spinnaker c-rack! as I heard the
    steam escape!

Had I lost at that awful juncture my presence of mind? . . .
    but no!
I leaned and felt for the puncture, and plugged it there
    with my toe . . .
Hand over hand by the Members' Stand I lifted and eased
    her up,
Shot—clean and fair—to the crossbar there, and landed the
    Jubilee Cup!

"The odd by a head, and leg before," so the Judge he gave
    the word:

And the umpire shouted "Over!" but I neither spoke nor
stirred.
They crowded round: for there on the ground I lay in a
dead-cold swoon,
Pitched neck and crop on the turf atop of my beautiful
Wooden Spoon.

Her dewlap tire was punctured, her bearings all red hot;
She's a lolling tongue, and her bowsprit sprung, and her
running gear in a knot;
And amid the sobs of her backers, Sir Robert loosened her
girth
And led her away to the knacker's. She had raced her last
on earth!

But I mind me well of the tear that fell from the eye of our
noble Prince,
And the things he said as he tucked me in bed—and I've
lain there ever since;
Tho' it all gets mixed up queerly that happened before my
spill,—
But I draw my thousand yearly: it'll pay for the doctor's
bill.

I'm going out with the tide, lad—you'll dig me a numble
grave,
And whiles you will bring your bride, lad, and your sons,
if sons you have,
And there when the dews are weeping, and the echoes
murmur "Peace!"
And the salt, salt tide comes creeping and covers the popping-
crease;

In the hour when the ducks deposit their eggs with a boasted
force,
They'll look and whisper "How was it?" and you'll take
them over the course,

And your voice will break as you try to speak of the glorious
    first of June,
When the Jubilee Cup, with John Jones up, was won upon
    Wooden Spoon.

ARTHUR T. QUILLER-COUCH

AFTER READING TWENTY YEARS
OF GRANTLAND RICE

Over the rim of glory,
Flame of an ancient need,
Gray ghosts that wail on a phantom trail,
Raw meat for the Bulldog breed.

Dim on a far horizon,
Throb of the drums of fame,
The bluebells cry to a starry sky,
Dead leaves of the grand old game.

Crown of olive and myrtle,
As John L. rides again,
The Bounding Basque in a gory mask,
North winds in a snowy glen.

High on the peak of struggle,
Off where the legions stray,
The stalwart smash as putter meets ash
Where April holds the way.

DON SKENE

CASEY AT THE BAT

It looked extremely rocky for the Mudville nine that day,
The score stood four to six with but an inning left to play.
And so, when Cooney died at first, and Burrows did the
    same,

A pallor wreathed the features of the patrons of the game.
A straggling few got up to go, leaving there the rest,
With that hope which springs eternal within the human
    breast.
For they thought if only Casey could get a whack at that,
They'd put up even money with Casey at the bat.
But Flynn preceded Casey, and likewise so did Blake,
And the former was a pudding and the latter was a fake;
So on that stricken multitude a death-like silence sat,
For there seemed but little chance of Casey's getting to the
    bat.

But Flynn let drive a single to the wonderment of all,
And the much despised Blakey tore the cover off the ball,
And when the dust had lifted and they saw what had
    occurred,
There was Blakey safe on second, and Flynn a-hugging third.
Then from the gladdened multitude went up a joyous yell,
It bounded from the mountain top and rattled in the dell,
It struck upon the hillside, and rebounded on the flat,
For Casey, mighty Casey, was advancing to the bat.
There was ease in Casey's manner as he stepped into his
    place,
There was pride in Casey's bearing and a smile on Casey's
    face,
And when responding to the cheers he lightly doffed his hat,
No stranger in the crowd could doubt, 'twas Casey at the
    bat.

Ten thousand eyes were on him as he rubbed his hands with
    dirt,
Five thousand tongues applauded as he wiped them on his
    shirt;
And while the writhing pitcher ground the ball into his hip—
Defiance gleamed from Casey's eye—a sneer curled Casey's
    lip.
And now the leather-covered sphere came hurtling through
    the air,

And Casey stood a-watching it in haughty grandeur there;
Close by the sturdy batsman the ball unheeded sped—
"That hain't my style," said Casey—"Strike one," the
    Umpire said.
From the bleachers black with people there rose a sullen roar,
Like the beating of the storm waves on a stern and distant
    shore,
"Kill him! kill the Umpire!" shouted some one from the
    stand—
And it's likely they'd have done it had not Casey raised his
    hand.

With a smile of Christian charity great Casey's visage shone,
He stilled the rising tumult and he bade the game go on;
He signalled to the pitcher and again the spheroid flew,
But Casey still ignored it and the Umpire said "Strike two."
"Fraud!" yelled the maddened thousands, and the echo
    answered "Fraud."
But one scornful look from Casey and the audience was
    awed;
They saw his face grow stern and cold; they saw his muscles
    strain,
And they knew that Casey would not let that ball go by
    again.
The sneer is gone from Casey's lip; his teeth are clenched
    with hate,
He pounds with cruel violence his bat upon the plate;
And now the pitcher holds the ball, and now he lets it go,
And now the air is shattered by the force of Casey's blow.
Oh, somewhere in this favored land the sun is shining bright,
The band is playing somewhere, and somewhere hearts are
    light,
And somewhere men are laughing, and somewhere children
    shout;
But there is no joy in Mudville—mighty Casey has "Struck
    Out."

                                    ERNEST LAWRENCE THAYER

CASEY'S DAUGHTER AT THE BAT

Apologies to the Estate of Ernest Lawrence Thayer

The outlook wasn't brilliant for the Mudvillettes, it seems;
The score stood four to two against that best of softball
    teams;
And when Brenda ("Lefty") Cooney and "Babs" Burrows
    both flied out,
A sickly silence filled the air, and the fans began to pout.

A straggling few got up to go—'t was the ninth and two
    were down—
While the rest had little hope at all that the 'Ettes would
    Go To Town;
Still, they thought if only Casey's gal—Patricia—Patsy—
    Pat—
Could get a lick, they still might win with Casey at the bat.

But Myrna Flynn and Hedy Blake had to hit before Miss C.;
And the former was a sissy, and the latter just a she;
So again upon a Mudville throng grim melancholy sat,
For there seemed no chance whatever that Patricia'd get
    to bat.

But Myrna smacked a single, to the wonderment of all,
And Hedy—known as Flatfoot—fairly flattened out the
    ball;
And when the dust had lifted, there on third and second base
Perched a pair of Mudville cuties, each a-powdering her face.

Then from the howling mamas in the stand in back of
    first
Went up a weird, unearthly scream, like a Tarzan crazed
    with thirst,
Like a million screeching monkey-fans, like a yowling giant
    cat;
For Casey, Patsy Casey, was advancing to the bat!

There was ease in Patsy's manner as she stepped up to the
    plate;
There were curves in Patsy's figure, and a bounce in Patsy's
    gait;
And when responding to the screams she lightly doffed her
    cap,
No Casey fan could doubt 't was Mighty's daughter at the
    bat.

Ten thousand eyes were on her shorts, an orchidaceous hue;
Five thousand tongues commented on her blouse of beige-
    and-blue;
And while the ladies chattered "What a shape!" and "What
    a fit!"
Miss Casey gave her shorts a tug and smoothed her blouse
    bit.

And now the underhanded pitch came hurtling through the
    air,
But Patsy, like her famous dad, just stood a-smiling, there;
And when "Strike one!" the umpire yelled as past that
    softball sped,
"That ain't my style!" is what they say Patricia Casey said.

Again, as in the years a-gone, the crowd set up a roar;
Again, they shouted as they had so many years before,
"Kill him! kill the umpire!"; and as once did Patsy's Pop,
Miss Casey raised a staying hand, and mildly said, "Oh,
    stop!"

And smiling like a lady in a teethy toothpaste ad,
Patricia showed that howling mob she wasn't even mad;
She signaled to the pitcher, who again the ball let fly;
And again like Papa Casey's, Patsy's second strike went by.

Anew, the maddened thousands blamed the strike upon the
    ump;
A racketeer, they labeled him, a floogie, and a frump;

But once again the mob was stilled by Patsy's charming
    smile,
As certain every fan became she'd hit the next a mile.

And now they see her daub a bit of powder on her nose;
They watch her put fresh lipstick on—a shade called Fleur
    de Rose;
And now the pitcher holds the ball, and now she lets it go;
And now the air is shattered by *another* Casey's blow.

Oh! somewhere in this favored land the moon is shining
    bright;
And somewhere there are softball honeys winning games
    tonight.
And somewhere there are softball fans who scream and yell
    and shout;
But there's still no joy in Mudville—Casey's *daughter*
    has struck out.

Al Graham

Translation–Paraphrase

FEBRUARY 14, 22 B. C.

Horace: Book III, Ode 9

"Donec eram gratus tibi . . ."

HORACE

In the happier years gone by me,
   In a well-remembered day,
Yours the custom was to eye me
   In a not unflattering way.
When than I none was than-whicher,
   When none other dared to fling
Arms about you, I was richer
   Than the noted Persian king.

LYDIA

Those the days when sweet the savor
   Of mine overbrimming cup,
When no Chloë found your favor,
   When I was not runner-up.
As I scan my memorabilia,
   I observe with girlish glee
That the famous Roman Ilia
   Hadn't anything on me.

HORACE

Now the roomy heart Horatian,
   Beating loudly in this breast,
By the sweetly singing Thracian
   Chloë's utterly possessed.
If I thought that lovely lass'd
   Like to see me dead, I'd take
Half a pint of prussic acid
   Gladly for her shining sake.

LYDIA

What a fascinating game is
  Love! My current cause for joy—
Thurian Calais his name is—
  He is Ornytus's boy.
If I thought he'd like to view me
  Moribund; that he would laugh
At my corpse, I'd pour into me
  All the poison I could quaff.

HORACE

If no longer I should find her
  As I used to find her—fair;
If I casually consigned her
  To the celebrated air;
This affair—if I should quit it;
  If I gazed again on you;
Do you think that we could hit it
  Off the way we used to do?

LYDIA

Yes. Though Calais is brighter
  Than a coruscating star;
Madder than the sea, and lighter
  Than a piece of cork you are,
Horace, you're the only guy for
  Me. The others I resign.
You're the one I'd live for, die for—
  And I'll be your Valentine.

Franklin P. Adams

ANACREON TO THE SOPHIST

I should grieve to desperation
For the higher education;
  Say, you give me melancholia
  When you pull that kind of con.

Tell your philosophic notions
To the widely-known Boeotians—
  Run along and sell your scholia—
    Go and hire the Parthenon!

If you'd beg me to the blending
Of a line of drinks unending,
  If you'd give me my diploma
    As a Bachelor of Song—
Put me James to all the flighty
Ways of golden Aphrodite—
  It would alter the aroma
    Of the dope you pass along.

Nix on droll Pythagorean!
Boy! Another round of Chian!
  Dionysus and the ladies
    Will be school enough for now.
Let's be wholly to the merry
Till it's time to take the ferry—
  Then go rolling home to Hades,
    Roses round each lovely brow!

                                    B. H.

MARTIAL IN LONDON

Exquisite wines and comestibles,
  From Slater, and Fortnum and Mason;
Billiard, écarté, and chess tables;
  Water in vast marble basin;
Luminous books (not voluminous)
To read under beech-tree cacuminous;
One friend, who is fond of a distich,
And doesn't get too syllogistic;
A valet, who knows the complete art
Of service—a maiden, his sweetheart:
Give me these, in some rural pavilion,
And I'll envy no Rothschild his million.

                          MORTIMER COLLINS

THE KISS-FEST

Catullus: Ode 5

"Vivamus, mea Lesbia, atque amemus"

Lesbia, my love, let's be gay and enjoy ourselves,
    Let's have a soda; let's go for a walk;
We have a right to disport and employ ourselves
    Just as we please. *That* for scandal and talk!
Suns, though they set every night, rise diurnally;
    Our little light but endures for a day;
Once we depart we shall vanish eternally;
    Let's make the most of our limited stay.
Give me some kisses to show your affection, dear,
    Give me a thousand at least for a start;
Then add a hundred to drown my dejection, dear,
    Still one more thousand before we depart.
Thousands and thousands; we'll pile up the kisses so
    None of the envious gossips can count;
What do we care for their sneers and their hisses so
    Long as we run up a goodly amount?

IRWIN EDMAN

TO PHYLLIS

Come, Phyllis, I've a cask of wine
    That fairly reeks with precious juices,
And in your tresses you shall twine
    The loveliest flowers this vale produces

My cottage wears a gracious smile;
    The altar, decked in floral glory,
Yearns for the lamb which bleats the while
    As though it pined for honors gory.

Hither our neighbors nimbly fare,
    The boys agog, the maidens snickering;
And savory smells possess the air,
    As skyward kitchen flames are flickering.

You ask what means this grand display,
  This festive throng and goodly diet?
Well, since you're bound to have your way,
  I don't mind telling, on the quiet.

'Tis April 13, as you know,
  A day and month devote to Venus,
Whereon was born, some years ago,
  My very worthy friend, Maecenas.

Nay, pay no heed to Telephus;
  Your friends agree he doesn't love you.
The way he flirts convinces us
  He really is not worthy of you.

Aurora's son, unhappy lad!
  You know the fate that overtook him?
And Pegasus a rider had,—
  I say he *had*, before he shook him!

Hoc docet (as you must agree)
  'Tis meet that Phyllis should discover
A wisdom in preferring me,
  And mittening every other lover.

So come, O Phyllis, last and best
  Of loves with which this heart's been smitten,
Come, sing my jealous fears to rest,
  And let your songs be those *I've* written.

EUGENE FIELD

DAPHNE AND APOLLO

Ovid's *Metamorphoses*: Book I, Fable 12

You who know unrequited love, who know the tear of
  blighted love,
Who'd leap into the lake at once—if it were not so cold—
For you a tale P. Naso tells; this knowing guy—you'll
  say so!—tells
Of Daphne and Apollo, and of love that blooms too bold.

This Daphne was a wholesome wench: her skin showed not
    a mole; some wench,
  To walk out with no clothes on and preserve unblemished
    flesh!
She knew not what a leach is, and her face was cream and
    peaches, and
  The net result was that she found the men got pretty
    fresh.

But it was not the custom then when they got gay to bust
    'em; *then*
  She had to ask her dad, Peneus, please to acquiesce
In guarding her virginity! Her papa thought a minute—he
  Was struck with much astonishment—but finally said Yes.

Yet grief was soon to follow: came a day when Don Apollo
    came
  Along the road, and saw her, sprawled beneath a sprawling
    oak.
Cried he, "My heart's aglow! Miss, I'll escort you to my
    *do*micyle
  To live and love!" And he was shocked when Daphne up
    and spoke:

"Sir, there's a hitch, and this is it: I do not *like* your kisses; it
  Annoys me most extremely to be folded in your arms!
Your hug is too Gargantuan! Quite willingly I'll grant you
    an
  Extended leave of absence from what people call my
    charms."

(She meant for him to go away.) He simply said to stow
    away
  That line of talk. Does she not know Apollo is the Sun?
He'll go when he has made her his . . . No dad, no man
    could aid her. His
  Breath grew so hot upon her, Daphne started in to run.

[A moment draw the curtain here; permit me to insert in here
  A word or two upon the theme I said that I should sing:
If you would love and win your love, respect this token in your love:
  When woman says she will not love, she will not love a King!]

Though women waited woe-begone, and said to suitors, "No; be gone!
  We love Apollo only, though Apollo is not true,"
The object of their high regard that moment sought to buy regard
  Perversely from the only girl who scorned to let him woo.

Too tragic life, to make men's wants be that which will not slake men's wants,
  To pine for that one passion which forever must be pent!
Not that Apollo thought of this! He meditated naught of this;
  He chased the fleeting Daphne, like a hound upon the scent.

The maid, by great endeavor, ran as fast as Wefers ever ran,
  But Paddock's, which is swifter, was the speed Apollo stole,
So that—does it deject you all?—her flight was ineffectual:
  Again his breath was hot upon the skin-without-a-mole.

Her feet began to flag; a knee gave way; she sank in agony
  By Pa Peneus's river, near a clump of laurel trees.
Those days it was no sin to pray, and so she started in to pray
  That, to avoid Apollo's arms, she might be one of these.

Ah, was it not deplorable, to take such soft, adorable
  (And mole-less) flesh, and change it into hard, unfeeling bark!
He lusted after symmetry: the river offered him a tree
  But, when he sought to hold a maid, he held part of a park!

Yet this much must be said for him: though Daphne now
    was dead for him,
He showed his poker training, and he lost her with a grin.
Said he, "She'd years to live; that gal had pluck! So I'll
    forgive that gal
And, since she is a laurel, I'll make *that* the prize to win!

"Though rules of rhyme be stricter, he shall own a greater
    victory
Who will but come to know that chasing ladies is a curse;
I'll crown him with the laurel-bough who, being called a
    bore, 'll bow
And, rather than pursue the frail, will vent his spleen in
    verse!"

* * *

You who know unrequited love, who know the tear of
    blighted love,
Who leave your plate untouched, oh, take this tip from
    Ovid's time:
The more *he* pined, the more he ate; and *he* was poet-
    laureate!
There is no prize for loving, but there's laurel in a rhyme!
                                       GEORGE MACY

Index of Authors

Index of Titles

Index of First Lines